Wake of the Schooners:

From Placentia to Port aux Basques

Robert Parsons

Wake of the Schooners:

From Placentia to Port aux Basques

Robert Parsons

Creative Publishers
St. John's, Newfoundland
1993

Appreciation is expressed to *The Canada Council* for publication assistance.

The publisher acknowledges the financial contribution of the *Department of Tourism and Culture, Government of Newfoundland and Labrador,* which has helped make this publication possible.

∝ Printed on acid-free Sno-Glo offset paper

Published by
CREATIVE PUBLISHERS
A Division of Robinson-Blackmore Printing & Publishing Ltd.
P.O. Box 8660, St. John's, Newfoundland A1B 3T7

Printed in Canada by:
ROBINSON-BLACKMORE PRINTING & PUBLISHING LTD.
P.O. Box 8660, St. John's, Newfoundland A1B 3T7

Canadian Cataloguing in Publication Data

Parsons, Robert Charles, 1944–

Wake of the schooners

Includes bibliographical references.
ISBN 1-895387-24-8

1. Shipwrecks — Newfoundland
2. Schooners — Newfoundland.   I. Title.

FC2170.S5P373   1993   971.8   C93-098591-5
F1123.P373   1993

Table of Contents

Foreword

ALONG THE RUGGED COASTLINE OF NEW-
FOUNDLAND, over 6000 miles long, more than ten
thousand ships have met their ends. Many of these
wrecks happened within the past two or three genera-
tions when the era of sail and schooner came and went,
leaving behind a litany of heroism and tragedy.

For over a hundred years the schooner was an
important and vital transportation link along
Newfoundland's shores. The maritime records are full
of stories in which schooners—the small coasters and
fish collectors, the six to twelve dory bankers and the
larger foreign going terns—and their crews played an
essential role. Self-sacrifice, daring, skill, wrecks and
rescues are all part of the history of the schooner and the
heritage of the towns that knew them.

With such a large number of shipping losses along
the South Coast, it is possible only to relate some of the
stories. Many remain to be told. Two or three stories
which appeared in my earlier books are retold in this
work from a different perspective and with additional
information.

Wake of the Schooners is a collection of sea stories
gathered after *Lost at Sea* was published. Many friends,
just as interested as I in the tales of heroism at sea, gave
me the encouragement to continue and loaned me
scrapbooks, newspaper clippings, or told their stories
on tape or letter. An example of new information coming from my two previous books occurred not long ago.
A correspondent read, in *Lost at Sea Vol. I* of the *Nordica*,
wrecked in the Mediterranean in 1921, and sent me the
crew list: Capt. George "Pluck" Tibbo, mate Ned Hol-

lett, cook Daniel Gregory, seamen Sammy Caines, George Barnes and Edgar Ralph, all of Grand Bank. My enthusiasm for their sea stories continued to grow. So many stirring accounts certainly deserved to be put in print for all to enjoy; this I have attempted to do.

With such an array of marine related material before me, I kept the chronological scope of *Wake of the Schooners* within the past hundred years and confined the geographical area to the South Coast from Placentia (the *Elizabeth Fearn*) to Port aux Basques (the *Mary F. Hyde*).

Where possible personal interviews were cross-referenced with newspaper accounts and vice versa. These interviews and personal anecdotes (slightly edited for clarity) not only provided interesting and valuable information on ships, wrecks and the toll of human lives, but often gave valuable insights into the folkways, cus-

Courtesy PANL

Over the years many Newfoundland schooners dramatically ended their days stranded on offshore underwater ledges or shoreline cliffs and beaches. This is the *Massachusetts*, wrecked March 29, 1913, at Cap Noir, St. Pierre.

In this case Captain Angus Hynes and his twelve crewmen may have been able to jump or get a rope ashore to effect self rescue. More often than not the ship grounded farther from shore with more disastrous results. Her after cabin has already been dislodged by surging breakers.

Not many schooners were left to die, hauled up on a beach or mud flat like a beached whale. This the *Mary Ruth*, built in Shelburne, Nova Scotia, in 1918 and first owned by Belleoram's Ben Keeping. In the 1920's she was a persistent and elusive rum runner. Rebuilt in Fortune by W. T. Lake in 1945, she was eventually sold to the Hiscock business at Clarenville and ended her days a rotten hulk at Southport, Trinity Bay.

toms, working and living conditions of the times. Much of this information was incorporated into the tales of shipwrecks.

Many stories are short—too short to really satisfy our need to know about past shipping disasters. But if the information had been available, especially in shipwrecks when men gave up their lives to save others or where debris-littered shorelines gave the only clue to a tragedy, it would have been presented.

Schooners have been gone from our coast now for almost half a century and the ranks of the men who sailed them are growing thinner with each passing day. Recorded histories like *Wake of the Schooners* will ensure their stories live on.

Author's Acknowledgements

I WISH TO EXPRESS MY THANKS to the following individuals for information, pictures and encouragement: Frank Elford, John M. King, George Ewart Lake, Gord Noseworthy, Clarence Pierce, Mack Piercey, William Snook, Fortune; William Forsey, formerly of Fortune; Curtis Forsey, Michael Harrington, Otto Kelland, Capt. Harry Stone, St. John's; William Welsh, Clarenville; Eric Hillier, Kitchener, Ont.; Christie Oakley, Montreal; Walter Simms, Corner Brook; John Hackett, Terrenceville; Harold Simms, Norwell, Mass.; Dr. Geoffrey Robinson, Tyne Valley, P.E.I.; John Barnes, Femme; Lucy Stoodley, Harbour Breton; Gertrude Pelley and Freeman Francis, Hant's Harbour; George Mayo, Mission, B.C.; John Sibley, Ramea; William J. Baker, Belleoram; James E. Cluett, Frenchman's Cove; Evelyn Grondin, Fred Hickman, Fred Hollett, Gord LeFeuvre, Lester Myles, Vibert Shave, Burin; Jim Carr, Art and Emma Rodway, Capt. Alex Rodway, Toronto; Christie Thomasen, Willowdale, Ont.; Sam Smith, Mount Pearl; Clyde Hollett, Roy S. Banfield, Joanne Wilson, Halifax; Trevor Bebb, Lockeport, N.S.; Capt. John Smith, Florida; Capt. Michael Croke, St. Brendan's; Vera Piercy, Amherst, N.S.; Con Fitzpatrick, Marystown; Christie Bradley, Annie Buffett, William Buffett, Grand Bank Seamen's Museum Curator Gerald Crews, John Douglas, Rosalind Downey, Robert Evans, Alice Forsey, Clyde Forsey, Grand Bank librarian Mildred Watts, Waterfield Green, Clarence Griffin, Alex Hardy, Leo R. Hillier, Ron Noseworthy, George Pardy, Charles Parsons, Leo Pope, Fred Rogers, Garfield Rogers, Stan Savoury, Capt. Robert Smith, George Squires, Allen

Stoodley, Fred Tessier, Capt. Harry Thomasen, Emma Thornhill, Wallace Thornhill, William T. Thornhill, Russ and Mary Walters, Eugene West, Grand Bank.

In particular I would like to especially thank Jack Keeping of Fortune, R.C.A.F. (Ret.) for not only his positive comments and encouragement, but also for access to his extensive collection of statistics and information on Newfoundland vessels, especially South Coast schooners. Time after time he continued to amaze and to provide. Also William Chapman, whose perceptive advice, knowledge of the people and places and of the written and unwritten history of the South Coast, was invaluable.

Where I have cited books, magazines and newspapers, I acknowledged original sources whenever and where ever possible. So many people provided photos, thus enabling others interested in the heritage of the sea to enjoy the pictures of our past. To those people I owe a debt of gratitude. I tried to get proper and original accreditation to the photos. If any errors occur in sources of information cited or in photo credits, corrections will be made in any subsequent editions of *Wake of the Schooners*.

To my proofreaders who checked for grammatical, historical and geographical accuracy, a thank you. Where the text runs smoothly, without flaws, it is entirely to their credit; the rougher edges are mine.

Chapter One

"They'll Never Live to Get In"

Mayhem on the MONASCO—One of Newfoundland's earliest and most tragic recorded shipwreck tales happened near Corbin, a small settlement not far from Burin. A story both mysterious and tragic, its actual facts are debatable, but according to local historians, a sailing vessel, the *Monasco*, carried 600 tons of iron and many well-to-do immigrants from Gothenburg, Sweden, to America. On her journey she strayed far off course and sank at Silver's Cove near Corbin about 3 a.m. on July 21, 1857.

The captain, his wife and the crew, about twenty-two in all, rowed ashore while all passengers drowned—an unusual occurrence, the residents in the area thought. Anyone left on the ship could have easily rescued themselves by climbing the rigging, for the ship lay steady, partly submerged on a calm, clear night. According to Captain Andrew Daly of the *Monasco*, the passengers could not be coaxed to leave. He said they barred the doors from the inside to keep the water out and resorted to prayer to save themselves.

Rumours of foul play, leaked by a careless crewman from the *Monasco*, hinted that murder and money were behind the tragedy. Apparently the captain's female companion was not his wife—she, Mrs. Emily Hannah Daly, thirty years old, had gone down in the wreck. Furthermore stories circulated of quantities of money, some in the pockets of the captain and some still on the sunken bark.

The men of Corbin knew of a man capable of getting to the submerged cabins; David Dobbin, born in St. Mary's Bay. By the time Dobbin reached the age of 40, he had a wide reputation as a sea captain, diver and self-styled wreck investigator. A few years before, Dobbin had explored the site of several sunken ships near St. Shott's, and from one vessel, the *Sarah Saunders*, he sent $15,000 worth of goods to the surface in five days. From another, the *Falcon* he recovered two strong boxes worth $13,000 in gold and silver. These were two of the many wrecks he had reached. Several days after *Monasco*'s survivors had left for America, Dobbin, perhaps on request of suspicious residents, donned his crude diving apparatus to explore the *Monasco*.

His first report was not a good one. Access to the passenger quarters was nailed shut from the outside, not inside as the captain had said. On subsequent dives, Dobbin opened the doors to find fifty victims, all passengers of the *Monasco*.

One of the first victims found was a woman. Another woman with a one year old child clasped in her arms was brought to the surface. She had a crucifix and prayer beads in her pocket. These first three were buried together. Others were placed in temporary shallow graves and later the men of Corbin properly covered the bodies. More bodies, many with blonde hair and wearing fine jewellery, were brought to shore and buried about a quarter mile from Corbin Head in an area later known as 'Swedes Point.' Thousands of dollars in gold and other valuables were salvaged from the submerged *Monasco*.

Residents in the area believed that in the course of the journey most money and jewellery had been handed over to the captain for safekeeping. As the *Monasco* neared North America, Daly decided to sink the vessel close to what he thought was an isolated shore, keep the money, and run away with a beautiful lady passenger. It was later learned the vessel was American, owned in Warren, Maine, and had left Sweden on June 21 headed for New York.

Although there was a Consul and civil authorities at Burin, the villainous captain, his lady, and *Monasco's* crew, were anxious to avoid English law. They asked to be taken to St. Pierre as quickly as possible and George Inkpen's boat was hired to take them there. Residents in Corbin and Burin wished to know more facts of the accident, but few of the *Monasco's* crew could speak English. One of the stewards spoke French, but before he could be questioned in French, Captain Daly warned him to say nothing.

By July 30, 1857, a few days after the shipwrecked group had gone, suspicious citizens of Burin wrote the following letter to the *Public Ledger*, a St. John's newspaper:

> I am sorry to inform you there was a most melancholy affair of shipwreck happened close to this harbour...the weather was as fine as possible when she ran slap up against the cliff about 3 miles to the west of Burin. The forward part sank, but the after part remained above water and all her spars and rigging.
>
> Fifty dead bodies were taken up the two following days and buried without an inquest or any

investigation. If the passengers had had their liberty there could have been no loss of life...

We think it scarcely possible that the Captain could have been guilty of the fiendish conduct ascribed to him. We trust this statement will be seen by him and he will come forward manfully, and contradict it, if untrue.

The captain did not come forward to contradict the rumours and he didn't receive just retribution for his act, for he eventually married his companion in crime and lived to a ripe old age in the United States enjoying his ill-gotten gains. Today the only verification of the unusual story are local folk legends and songs, a letter published in a Newfoundland newspaper and an area on sea charts near Corbin called Monasco Shoal.

Wreck of the SPENCER NORTHCOTT and ALPHA—In late fall 1874 the iron bark *Spencer Northcott* left Miramichi, New Brunswick, bound for London, her decks and holds laden with heavy pine logs from the maritimes. In the Gulf of St. Lawrence heavy weather caused severe leaking, and her crew, mostly Norwegians, was unable to control the 500-ton vessel.

During the severe gale, they managed to direct the *Spencer Northcott* into the mouth of Fortune Bay where several men of Fortune boarded her to lend a hand. These men knew safe anchorages farther in the bay and they hoped to bring the sinking bark to safety. Before anything could be done, an unexpected shift in hurricane wind direction pushed the ship onto the cobblestone beach between Fortune and Grand Bank.

A few minutes before the *Spencer Northcott* struck, the mate and eight men left in one of the ship's boats, rounded the cape and landed in Admiral's Cove, near

The wreck of the *Quebec*—stranded on October, 1961. In the background is the beach where in 1874, the iron bark *Spencer Northcott* was wrecked. Eighteen years later in 1892, the *Alpha* broke up in the same place.

Grand Bank. When the vessel grounded, the gale and waves threw her broadside to the beach with white capped breakers rolling over her.

As the wind and tide fell, all other crew and the Fortune pilots rowed to safety on High Bank Beach, but not without one incident of bravery. One man, as a boat upset in landing, was pulled out by backwash and undertow. His shipmates chained hands, walked out into the waves, and pulled him in.

Northcott's cargo was sold, and the lumber used in building houses. Those homes had boards in them, two feet wide, sawn from her pine logs. It is also said that persons dying at that time had the distinction, enviable or otherwise, of being buried in coffins made of four boards only owing to the extreme width of the planks. Salvage also included the ship's figurehead, a crouching lion, which for many years formed part of the gate entrance of Mrs. Millie Foote's home in Grand Bank.

NAUGHTLESS No Survivors at Coomb's Cove— Characterized by violent and sudden changes in weather, the South Coast of Newfoundland is often buffeted by raging storms and winds. Turbulent turnarounds in tides and heavy wave action inflict tremendous damage to shipping, especially in winter when schooners faced the rugged shoreline in heavy seas to bring supplies to southern communities.

In the winter of 1875, the *Naughtless* left Prince Edward Island carrying vegetables and other products to Newfoundland. It was a pleasant day as the five crewmen set sail from Charlottetown harbour, but howling winds engulfed the *Naughtless* as she drifted into Fortune Bay and then ploughed headlong into the rocky shelves off Coomb's Cove. Throughout the night waves washed the men away from the stranded schooner; only one lashed himself to the masthead away from the fury of the thundering sea.

Roland Sherwood in his book *Island Harbours* writes of the discovery of the wreck:

> The stark Newfoundland dawn came up from the gray and stormy Atlantic, and on the rugged bluffs that look down on the angry sea, the men of the little fishing village of Coomb's Cove saw the battered vessel. Fighting their way out to the wreck they found the lone sailor, self-lashed to the masthead. But Death had crept in from the sea and found him first.

For days on end the men of Coomb's Cove searched the shores, the bodies of the men swept overboard from the *Naughtless* were never found. All records aboard the luckless vessel were missing. Only the name of the schooner and the dead sailor tied to her masthead were ever known by those who salvaged the wreck. The vessel's name was on her bow—the *Naughtless*—the name of the lifeless sailor was sewn on his sweater. His name was Frank Plummer.

By 1875 Coomb's Cove, situated on the eastern side of Bay de L'Eau, already had a population approaching one hundred. Dates of first settlement are not recorded, but according to local tradition a family of Coombs may have lived there around the 1700's giving the picturesque and sheltered harbour its name. By 1900 it was a viable fishing town; four or five local schooners, as well as those from the nearby community of Wreck Cove, would tie up in the harbour. Early family names were Vallis, Drakes, Bungay, Fiander, Bartlett and these pioneer fishermen families probably witnessed the wreck of the *Naughtless*.

The body of Frank Plummer was buried in the Church of England cemetery at Coomb's Cove. Eventually the *Naughtless'* cargo was salvaged, sold at auction at Coomb's Cove and the schooner was refloated. A fishing business at St. Pierre used her for many years until she was lost with crew on the Grand Banks off Newfoundland.

Disappearance of the IDOL—On the evening of October 16, 1876, Captain Sam Tibbo was a worried man. He had only tacked into Grand Bank harbour when a severe fall storm lashed across the South Coast of Newfoundland. He and his men arrived from Prince Edward Island in the little fifty-ton schooner *Esther Tibbo*.

Gospel Compass, produced by the Mission to Deep Sea Fishermen in England, connected Bible truths and moral teachings to the 32 points of the compass. In addition the chart showed international flag codes, navigational knowledge and maritime code of ethics.

For many years the Gospel Compass hung in the captain's sleeping quarters of the *Esther Tibbo*, a schooner built in Grand Bank in 1881 and jointly owned by Samuel Tibbo of Grand Bank and William C. Job of St. John's. Before the turn of the century she had been sold to St. Pierre interests—her eventual fate is obscure.

His vessel and the *Idol*, captained by William Buffett, each laden with produce and supplies had sailed in company for almost the entire journey. At the outset of the storm not far from home both separated; now the *Esther Tibbo*, a much larger vessel, had harboured, but the *Idol* was nowhere to be seen.

Built in Grand Bank that same year, the *Idol*, even before her maiden voyage, had already received the dubious distinction as a jinxed or bad luck schooner. A month after construction began the owner/builder died. Another owner who took over the work died shortly after.

This did not deter William Buffett who, aged thirty-four and the father of four small children, was starting out in the shipping business. An attractive vessel on the stocks—at twenty tons, fifty feet long and sixteen feet wide—the *Idol* seemed to be a good investment, so Buffett, her new owner, finished the construction in time for launching in September, 1876. A trip to the mainland for supplies was her first journey.

Now, as the *Idol*'s maiden voyage should have been ending, others feared the end of the little vessel. Several times throughout the night as the lightning flared and gale force winds shook his home, Captain Tibbo got up and looked out his window. When he realized the *Idol* had not made port, Tibbo remarked to his wife, "He'll never live to get in. We will not see William Buffett alive in this world again."

His dire omen proved correct. Nothing more was known of the *Idol* until several weeks later her derelict hull, turned bottom up, drove in onto Pass Island on the South Coast. None of her crew was ever found.

At this time in the maritime history of the South Coast, 1886, the 460-ton *Clyde Valley* was launched at Belfast, Ireland. Later in her career she became a familiar sight as she plied her routes between St. John's, Fortune and the communities along the coast.

CLYDE VALLEY Gunrunner Still Afloat—First christened *Balniel,* and later renamed *Londoner,* the *Clyde Valley* frequented ports in the United Kingdom and Europe. During the first World War and in the Irish Rebellion against Home Rule 1914-1916, she was allegedly engaged in gun-running—carrying arms and ammunition illegally to Ireland. To avoid detection by the Royal Navy, she sailed under two false names, *Mount Joy* and *Fanny.*

In 1919 she was seized by England and sold to Nova Scotian and New Brunswick interests. She carried pulpwood around these coasts until she ran ashore and sank in Guysborough, Nova Scotia. Refloated and refitted with new engines, she plied the trade between Nova Scotia and the West Indies. Lake's shipping, managed by H. B. Clyde Lake, bought the vessel in 1953, renamed her *Clyde Valley,* and operated her for twelve years until she ran upon a rock in Burin. For years she was commanded by Johnny Rose, son of Captain Joseph Rose of Jersey Harbour.

Because permanent repairs would cost more than her insured value, she was put on sale. A group in Northern Ireland, seeing her historic value, bought her, transported the *Clyde Valley* to Ulster where she rests today as a floating museum.

SARAH JANE A Victim of the August Gales—In the early years of the bank fishery, the small wooden bankers ventured to the offshore grounds. The first offshore fishing schooners were four dory bankers carrying ten men—eight to fish from two-man dories plus the captain and cook. But the great distance from land put the little schooners in jeopardy in the days of limited communication and inaccurate weather predictions.

In late summer, hurricanes originating near the Topic of Cancer lash their way northward devastating parts of southern United States. By the time these violent winds reach the Maritimes much of their fury is spent, but the final flick of the dying hurricane's tail across the fishing grounds came suddenly and with deadly results for schooners. Locally, these wind storms were called the August (or September) Gales.

As reported by St. John's newspapers, the 1886 gale was violent, the heaviest felt in many years; however the lash was shortlived and lasted only a few hours. Damage to structures and shipping along the Burin Peninsula was, at first, not considered extensive. Two days later it was learned the French vessel *L'Etoile* had driven ashore at Allen's Island, on the eastern side of the Burin Peninsula, with the loss of twelve men.

Then shipping news reported another schooner missing: the *Sarah Jane*, a four dory banker—one of the many small schooners launched in Grand Bank in 1866. At 51 feet long, she netted only twenty-four tons.

A two-man dory makes its lonely way toward the anchored mother ship. When the sea and skies darkened and gales howled, schooners like the *Sarah Jane* either had to lie to anchored or leave for a sheltered shore.

Owner and captain William Evans, who had done well that year realizing eighteen hundred quintals for the season, planned to retire from the bank fishery in September. *Sarah Jane* left the fishing grounds in early August 1886, stopped briefly at St. Pierre for supplies, and then proceeded to her home port to discharge.

However, an outbreak of smallpox had been reported in St. Pierre. Rumours claimed that in St. Pierre up to thirty people a day for a week were diagnosed, including the French Governor and his children. People on the South Coast were panic-stricken; they knew how fast smallpox spread with no known cure to hold it in check.

Author's collection

The August Gales, the 'tail end' of tropical hurricanes, was a weather phenomenon much respected by early banking captains. Their thirty to sixty-ton schooners were often caught without warning far from land often with disastrous results.

This gravestone is a mute reminder of the August Gale of 1892.

Since *Sarah Jane* had been to St. Pierre, the local medical authority at Grand Bank immediately prevented the schooner from entering port. *Sarah Jane* was put under quarantine despite the crew's claim that no one aboard had the disease. A vessel under quarantine was required to raise an identifying yellow flag and was not allowed in port until cleared by a doctor.

While the schooner was anchored on the bar outside the harbour, her fish was offloaded and carried into Grand Bank while supplies—water, food, fishing gear—were brought out. Around mid-August the *Sarah Jane* left for the Virgin Rocks, a lucrative fishing ground off Newfoundland.

First official reports of her loss came via *S.S. Curlew*, the coastal mail and passenger vessel. *Curlew* had been to Grand Bank on her usual run from St. John's to Channel and return. When she arrived in St. John's on September 16, Captain Francis reported the schooner had been missing for a month.

It is presumed an unexpected August gale of the 17th claimed the schooner and her crewmen—Captain William Evans, age forty-one; his brother Thomas; the captain's two sons, Joseph and William, all of Grand Bank; two crewmen from Brunette Island and four others. *Sarah Jane* failed to report and her loss was the first major fishing tragedy to ravage the town.

BURIN BANKERS ARRIVED.

How They Fared With the Fish on the Banks.

SEVERAL of the Burin bankers arrived from the Grand Banks the latter part of last week, and with good fares, too, when it is considered that they, for the greater part, only carry four and five dories. Here are their names and catches:—

The *Ocean Plough*, Vigus, master and owner, 300 quintals.

The *Bloodhound*, Benjamin Hollett, master, Bishop & Co., owners, 240 quintals.

The *Nereid*, Morgan Hollett, master, Robert Inkpen, owner, 190 quintals.

The *Hecla*, Kirby, master, George Inkpen, owner, 150 quintals.

The *Sammy Hick*, John Kirby, master, Bishop & Co., owners, 195 quintals.

The *Jessie*, Weir, master and owner, 160 quintals.

The *Antelope*, Bugden, master and owner, 160 quintals.

Lily, Goddard, master and owner, 100 quintals.

Happy-Go-Lucky, Roberts, master, Keech, owner, 100 quintals.

Artist, Vigus, owner, 150 quintals.

May Belle, Smith, master, Goddard, owner, 120 quintals.

And the *Resium*, William Kirby, master, Bishop & Co., owners, 130 quintals.

Twelve Burin bankers active before the turn of the century as indicated from this newspaper clipping taken from *Evening Telegram*, August 1893. The fate of most is obscure, but it is known the *Antelope* was cut down on the Grand Banks by the S.S. *Majestic* with the loss of two men. *Neried*, built in Essex in 1891, was later sold to interests in Fortune, then to Grand Bank. She was later lost on a Nova Scotian shore in 1933.

Chapter Two

Disaster on the Islands

In the 1880s, the Newfoundland government, seeing the unfair advantage the French fishermen had in obtaining and selling cod, attempted to stop the supply of bait by Newfoundland fishermen to the St. Pierre fishery. After the establishment of the Bait Act in 1888, Newfoundland fishermen were not permitted to sell bait to the French. Many South Coast schooner owners could still legally supplement their income by selling bait, mainly herring to the American fishing fleet.

ROSIE Disaster on Green Island—John Bonnell of Lamaline, the owner of a sixty-ton schooner, the *Rosie*, supplied bait to the Americans and had hired two young men—John Walters, age nineteen and John Hepditch, eighteen—to go with him to Harbour Breton, the base for the Fortune Bay herring fishery. On February 27, 1894, the *Rosie* left Fortune Bay to return to Lamaline.

While rounding Dantzic Point on the Burin Peninsula, the wind and weather changed, all signs pointing to a storm. Determined to reach home, the three men sailed on, but a little past the point the wind pitched around northeast, a virtual hurricane. Bonnell decided to run to St. Pierre.

Within an hour, despite keeping a lookout for land through the blinding seas and weather, the *Rosie* ran aground in a small cove on Little Green Island, an uninhabited island between St. Pierre and the Burin Peninsula. As the schooner grated on the rocks and heeled over, a sea swept across her deck washing the three men overboard. Walters and Hepditch, young and strong, struggled ashore, but there was no sign of Captain Bonnell. After a while they gave up looking, for a wet and cold night was coming on.

At the top of the cliff in the low bushes they found an overturned flat and a small cache of basic food with some matches. This apparently had been left there by some fishermen, perhaps for emergencies. They cut a hole in the bottom of the flat and lit a fire.

Kept warm throughout the raging blizzard that night, Walters and Hepditch survived the long cold hours. The next morning they went to the site of the wreck and saw no sign of the vessel, but on the rocks they found the body of their unfortunate captain.

The two men carried the remains up to their shelter, kept it in a canvas shroud and looked for a way to get themselves and the corpse off the island. Next to their small crag was the slightly larger Green Island which at that time, 1894, had no lighthouse. The larger island seemed no better refuge, so plans were made to get to the mainland. After five days, the storm let up and Walters and Hepditch repaired the small flat in preparation to row to the Burin Peninsula.

With the dead seaman aboard, the two young men set out to row their fragile craft the ten miles to Lories. On the first attempt the weather and seas came up again. They manoeuvred the dory into the same small cove where a few days before the *Rosie* had been wrecked. Again the flat was overturned for a night's shelter.

Next morning dawned fair and clear. The row to Lories took four hours, but ice on the shoreline kept them from reaching the beach. Fortunately residents from the small town saw their distress signals and brought them safely to shore. Later both men and the body of Captain Bonnell reached Lamaline where Bonnell was given a Christian burial.

Drama and Death off St. Pierre—The schooner *J.W. Roberts*, owned in St. John's, was under command of Captain Cook of St. John's. On September 16, 1901, she had loaded coal at Sydney intended for Conception Bay ports. Built in 1889 in Burnt Bay, Notre Dame Bay, this schooner, earlier in her career, had been a banker, but during the summer of 1901, had delivered coal around Newfoundland.

Cook had his brother as mate and the rest of the crew, whose first names were not recorded, were Handcock of Goose Bay, Bonavista Bay; J. Barrett and H. Adams of Trinity Bay and T. Ashford of Rose Blanche. Ashford, married with five children, had joined the *J.W. Roberts* as cook when the schooner put into Rose Blanche to wait out a storm.

After leaving Rose Blanche the schooner, again beset by wind, sheltered in Harbour Breton. But for the captain the worst was not over. After he left Harbour Breton on September 21, rough seas near Miquelon tossed the *Roberts* causing enough damage to her rudder, so that while passing through Langlade Reach, she became unmanageable. To add to problems, a southeast wind threatened to push them on the rocks.

Captain Cook sent three men—his brother, Barrett, and Handcock—ashore to the back of St. Pierre telling them to get the St. Pierre tug as quickly as possible. The latter two landed the mate who left to walk to the town of St. Pierre. Barrett and Handcock decided to row back to the vessel perhaps to help out, but the wind was too strong and they had to return to land.

Both men climbed a hill on the western side of St. Pierre and for two hours they watched their beleaguered schooner, now with the red ensign raised halfway up the rigging, indicating distress. Both men also reported another unusual incident.

A second schooner was in the vicinity, although obviously in no danger, which passed quite close to the sinking *J.W. Roberts*. This schooner, as the two men found out later, was the *Chester Harris*, owned by Samuel Harris of Grand Bank with Captain Royal in command. According to Barrett and Handcock the *Chester* paid no attention to the distress signal nor to the other schooner.

From their vantage point on the hill, both of *Robert's* crew could also see their comrades trying to bring the schooner to the wind by letting down the jib and main sail. Barrett and Handcock figured the handling of sail was too much for the three stranded men— the captain, Adams and Ashford. They also had to attend to the pumps in their efforts to save the schooner.

By this time two hours had passed. *J.W. Roberts* had drifted away and was lost from sight. Not long after, the St. Pierre steam tug passed by and the two men rowed out to board her. They steamed outside Langlade Reach to look for the *Roberts*.

Their vessel was nowhere to be seen. The storm still raged and the search tug returned to St. Pierre harbour. The banker *Chester Harris* sailed in the distance and the men assumed their shipmates were safe on this schooner.

It was later learned the *Chester* arrived in Grand Bank safely and three crew had freely discussed the plight of the *J.W. Roberts*. On September 22, off the French Islands, the St. Pierre pilot boat picked up the mainboom of the *Roberts*, chipped in several places with an axe. Some of the ropes were tied on to it as if the mast had been thrown over by the men on board to provide a crude life raft.

According to speculations of veteran seamen, the missing three men of the *J.W. Roberts*, knowing their ship was sinking, had clung to the wreck as long as possible thinking the tug would come. In all likelihood they also saw the *Chester* passing by. However, the mainmast was all that was ever found—the schooner *J.W. Roberts* and her crew, including Ashford of Rose Blanche, were never located.

IVANHOE And Other Early Burgeo Tragedies—A South Coast town with strong ties to the sea and its tragedies is Burgeo, located about 95 kilometres, or 60 miles, east of Port aux Basques. Burgeo—its name probably a corruption of Virgeo, a thousand virgins— was first settled in the 1700s and by the year 1802 had a population of twenty-three. One of its early merchant houses was Nicolle and Company of Lapoile, and in 1859 Newman's of London set up four large stores, a shop and two cookrooms employing 44 people.

In time other Burgeo business interests prospered and declined including those of DeGruchy, Renouf, and Clement and Company. By the 1890s Robert Moulton's firm, which eventually became known as the Burgeo and Lapoile Export Company, dominated the catching, curing and exporting of codfish.

The 1880s were especially disastrous for the small fishing town of Burgeo. In August 1887, the *Grace Hall*, owned by Clement and Company sailed out of Burgeo for the Grand Banks with Captain John Anderson and

courtesy Arts and Culture Centre, St. John's.

Early Burgeo. Tradition has it, there are 365 islands off the coast of Burgeo—one for every day of the year, but actually there are a little over one hundred. Over the years, approximately a dozen vessels from Burgeo were 'lost with crew' and sailed past these islands never to return.

In December, 1928, Robert Moulton's two-masted schooner *Dannie Goodwin* left Burgeo to fish on the western banks, and failed to return; the fate of Captain Lafosse, William Harris of Hermitage and the other crew is unknown.

eleven crewmen: cook James Wilcox, an Englishman; James Porter, married; Philip and Robert Crew; Thomas Strickland; George and Meskech Mead, John Green, James Simms, Charles Clothier and William Anderson, all of Burgeo. On the 26th a sudden and terrible gale blew from the southeast and later veering to west northwest. Other banking schooners believed the gale foundered the *Grace Hall* for neither vessel nor crew was ever seen again.

In April 1890, the *Annie May* with Captain Louis Colley of Burgeo was lost on Codroy Island, near Cape Anguille, Newfoundland. Her crew was Robert Billard and son Lambert; Morgan Buffett (Sr.) and son; Edward Forward; John and James Carroll; and Thomas Billard. Colley was of French descent.

Driven down the coast by Arctic drift ice packed close to the land, the *Annie May* grounded west of

Codroy. A wall of ice, in places perfectly level and easy to jump to from the rigging, pushed the schooner to shore. There was room for the vessel to sail southward between the ice and land.

Robert Billard and his son chose to jump onto the ice; then watched the vessel drive toward a point, apparently to open water and safety. But *Annie May* struck an unseen ledge of rock and stranded permanently. In the distance and in the approaching darkness the two survivors saw the force of the gale and moving ice crush the trapped vessel's timbers.

By this time it was too late for the remaining seven crew. The rough ice ledges were too far up to reach by jumping. Captain Colley and Forward's body were recovered later—the others were never found. And these marine disasters were only the beginnings of tragedy; Burgeo, with its close association with the sea, was to wear the cloak of sorrow many times.

From the turn of the century to the 1930s Moulton's business of Burgeo was very active in the overseas trade—dried fish to Europe and the West Indies and salt for the curing of fish on the return voyage.

Over the years over twenty terns, or three masters as they were termed locally, ranging in size from one hundred tons to over three hundred tons, were registered to either Thomas, Robert or J. T. Moulton. (See Appendix A for listing) The *Ivanhoe*, one of the first terns owned on the South Coast, was purchased in 1904 by Thomas Moulton.

Built in Liverpool, Nova Scotia, the *Ivanhoe* measured 103 feet long and netted 99 tons; however, this schooner didn't last long. She sailed from Halifax to the Bahamas on November 5, 1904, and was never seen again. In 1921 another of Moulton's terns, the *County of Richmond* was lost with crew. (See chapter four) Over the years from 1910 to the 1930s, Moulton's fleet of foreign going terns disappeared—two lost with crew, thirteen abandoned at sea, two sunk by enemy shellfire, two wrecked and one burned.

COLUMBINE, RIGEL, BRILLIANT STAR Derelicts on the Coast—"Heartrending" is how the newspaper *Daily News* described the circumstances surrounding the loss of the schooner *Columbine*, owned in Stone's Cove, Fortune Bay, by her captain James Tibbo and his two brothers, George and William. A 40-ton two masted schooner and newly built, her name refers to a bell-shaped flower.

AWFUL DISASTER

AT STONES COVE, F.B.

Sailor Would Bet They Would Not Reach Destination.

The circumstances surrounding the disaster which overtook the pretty little schooner Columbine, Capt James Tibbo, of Stones Cove, twelve days ago, is heartrending. As already stated by the NEWS the schooner reached Belleoram from Prince Edward Island and dis

Headlines from *Daily News*, November 30, 1905, describing the loss of the *Columbine*.

Columbine's story begins on November 11, 1905, when the schooner, deeply laden with Prince Edward Island potatoes, stopped at Burgeo, the first leg of a voyage eastward to Belleoram and journey's end at Stone's Cove. Most South Coast gardens could grow a limited supply of table vegetables, but potato, a more staple food requirement, could not be grown in sufficient quantities to last through the long winter due to rocky soil and a short growing season. In the early days of the schooner trade, it was profitable for owners, after the fishing season ended, to take their vessels to P.E.I for potatoes and other vegetables.

In Burgeo harbour, the *Columbine* waited out a typical winter storm—strong northwesterly winds, cold temperatures and snow. From the mainland to Newfoundland the *Columbine* had sailed in company with several other Burgeo schooners: *Jimmy Armstrong*, owned by Clement and Company, Captain J. Ford; Moulton's vessel *Albert M.* coal laden; Webb's schooner *Virgin Bell*, and the *Notice*, commanded by Joe Vatcher. Weather had not been good, so the first refuge for Captain Tibbo was Burgeo where he had two sisters living. His stay with friends he knew well would be a pleasant one.

But the latter four vessels were in home port—the *Columbine* had many more miles to go. Along the South Coast Tibbo was known to be a skilful and experienced navigator. His two brothers, William and George, could attest to that; they had sailed with him on many successful banking voyages.

Columbine's five seamen: Tibbo, his nine-year-old son, the captain's brother, James Bond and William Pope of Stone's Cove had to face winter's raging northwesterlies and strong insets of tide roiled by the rugged southern coastline. Tibbo's young son had gone with his father for a pleasure trip to see mainland Canada.

On November 11, Tibbo sailed down the coast to Belleoram where he discharged all his cargo except seventy-five barrels of potatoes, destined for Stone's Cove.

By this time the storm had intensified, but Stone's Cove was only 15 miles away and all the crew belonged there. Tibbo decided, despite the increasing storm, to make the run. After all he had weathered other storms, some more vicious than this one. As she slipped her lines and moved away into the gathering winter tempest, wizened seadogs peering out into the dark Belleoram night from the snug safety of their homes could only shake their heads and think unspeakable thoughts.

Another vessel in Belleoram due to sail east would not leave in the face of the weather. A few days later when the howling storm had abated, this same schooner arrived at Stone's Cove, and not seeing the *Columbine* there knew what had happened. An immediate search for the missing schooner began.

Shortly after parts of the *Columbine* were found between Long Point and Hare Harbour Rocks near Stone's Cove: planking smashed, mast and spars in fallen disarray. Debris littered the nearby coastline; ship's gear, barrels of potatoes and cases of oranges drifted on the Stone's Cove beach, some immediately below the home of the schooner's owner, James Tibbo.

According to folk history of the town, the captain's wife, hearing the shouts and seeing people run along the shoreline early that Sunday morning, inquired what the commotion was about. When told schooner wreckage had been found, she intuitively knew which ship it was.

Examination of her *Columbine's* hull showed the paint on her bottom intact which led relatives to think that the schooner, being light, had turned over and then drove ashore. No sign of life was to be found; not one had escaped to climb the jagged rocks in self-rescue.

Residents of Stone's Cove searched for bodies without success. One submerged body, believed to be the captain's son, could be seen on the bottom with the aid of a fish glass, but the victim could not be brought to the surface.

The Belleoram people recalled events leading up to her final departure and told a touching story of the teenaged crewman, William Pope, who didn't want to make the stormy trip. Previous to the *Columbine's* leaving, Pope went into one of the stores in Belleoram. Tibbo sent for him, but the young man at first refused to board the *Columbine*.

Then, being accused of fear, he made up his mind to join his shipmates, but made a side bet with a Belleoram companion saying, "I will not give it to anyone to say that I am afraid to go, but I will bet $5.00 we will never see Stone's Cove." With these words he ran down to the wharf and jumped aboard the *Columbine* to his death.

Financial hardships faced the stricken families. Fifteen hundred dollars, a sizable sum of money for those times, disappeared with the missing crew. Tibbo's creditor who outfitted the *Columbine* with food and supplies for the summer fishing voyage, was a Belleoram merchant and he had settled up their season's fishing voyages.

Tibbo owed the merchant $800, but the captain wished to sail as soon as possible in view of the impending weather. Before the *Columbine* cast off her lines he said to his creditor, "I have the money here but I'll be back in a day or two and settle up then." But in the end, the sea had wiped the slate clean.

The economy of the South Coast depended almost entirely on the bountiful sea, but the treacherous ocean highway exacted its wages. For years to come shipwrecks, loss of life and grief became the heritage of towns which once knew the tall sails of ships like the ill-fated *Columbine*.

Violent winter storms claimed two other South Coast schooners. The 83-ton *Rigel*, owned by Philip E. Lake of Fortune and built in 1889 at Essex, Massachusetts, was lost on her way from North Sydney to Fortune laden with coal. On November 18, a few miles from home port, a wind storm drove the former banking schooner onto Langlade Island, St. Pierre. When the gale was at its height, the *Rigel* stranded; Captain Sam Mayo of Fortune and his crew barely escaped, but lost all personal belongings.

Channel schooner *Brilliant Star* was stranded on November 29, 1905, at Ingonish, Nova Scotia. Like the *Columbine*, the *Brilliant Star* left Souris, P.E.I., with a winter's supply of produce. Some cargo was salvaged, but the schooner, built in Jeddore in 1886 and owned by Clement and Company, was lost. Captain Joshua Mead and his crew escaped.

ORPHEUS   Wrecked on Prince Edward Island—Captain William Courtney of Grand Bank had purchased the two masted *Orpheus* from Waller and Sons at Gloucester in the spring of 1906 and used her in the summer bank fishery. Netting 78 tons and built in 1891 at Essex, Massachusetts, she bore the name of a mythical Greek deity. On fishing voyages the schooner carried twenty or more men for her ten dories, but on the coastal trade run five crew would be her complement.

That fall, Courtney loaded dry fish at Port Daniels, Quebec, intending to discharge at N & M Smith's premises at Halifax. However Courtney and the *Orpheus* never reached their destination, but ended up wrecked on what was termed 'the treacherous horns of the crescent' on the northern coast of Prince Edward Island.

After the *Orpheus* left Port Daniels on October 30, 1906, a succession of strong northeast gales pushed the schooner into the grip of a powerful westerly current. For two days the storms increased; there was nothing the men could do to bring her around and out of the vice of wind and tide.

Unable to save his vessel, the best Captain Courtney could hope for himself and the lives of the men under him was to beach near some inhabited spot on the shores of Prince Edward Island. Courtney drove ashore about five o'clock in the morning of November 6 on Priest's Point about one mile west of the Campbell's Cove breakwater and near the point named Cable Head on the map.

Exhausted by their week-long struggle against nature's elements, the five men were unable to reach shore. In the course of the storm, the schooner's dory was smashed in or broken up on the side of the schooner as the men tried to launch them. Huge combers soon broke the back of the schooner and it became obvious to

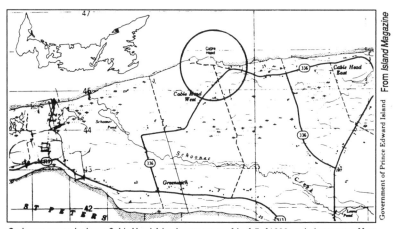

Orpheus was wrecked near Cable Head. Island newspapers of the fall of 1906 carried accounts of four shipwrecks near Cable Head: steamer *Turret Bell* on November 2; the Grand Bank schooner *Orpheus*, November 3; barques *Olga* and *Sovinto*, the latter with the loss of 10 men on 4th of November.

The Shelburne-built *Cardenia* was wrecked in August, 1911, as she brought coal from North Sydney to Newfoundland. In the thick fog that often surrounds the tip of the Burin Peninsula, the the schooner grounded on a sharp underwater reef off Peninsula Rock. Her captain, knowing the *Cardenia* had broken in two and was doomed, had all sails, booms and gaffs removed.

the Newfoundlanders that in a matter of hours the *Orpheus* would be reduced to debris beneath them.

Fortunately, the hopeless plight of the schooner had been seen by residents of Campbell's Cove. Soon a volunteer rescue party of men from Campbell's Cove, Priest Pond and Bayfield came to their aid. Two men of that team, determined in the daylight hours of a Sunday morning to assist five shipwrecked sailors, were John Ryan and James Campbell.

What these rescuers endured and by what ingenuous means they reached the wreck is not recorded, but courage was at the very fibre of their motive. This is evidenced in one brief article in the Prince Edward Island newspaper *Daily Patriot* stating that "the crew

were saved after considerable difficulty" and the rescuers "deserve great credit for taking off the crew."

William Courtney and four other Newfoundland
sailors stood in their wet clothes; that was, in effect, all
they had saved from the shipwreck. Ryan, Campbell
and the others were not finished yet. Without money,
extra clothes, food or personal effects, the stranded
mariners were afforded the best of care, presumably in
local homes until arrangements were made for their
transport to Newfoundland. Only the fish cargo had
been insured by the shipping company at $15,000. But
through the undaunted courage of the island men, five
Newfoundlanders lived to sail again.

RUBY, T.A. MAHONE The Hazards of Fishing—
One of the early wrecks of the decade happened on May
5, 1910, when Samuel Harris' sixty-ton banker *Ruby*,
captained by Joe Hiscock of Grand Bank, was lost at
Louisbourg harbour, Nova Scotia, while going in for
bait.

She had been on her spring fishing trip and was
laden with 99 quintals of fish, her entire catch. Although
the schooner was insured for $4,000, her cargo worth
about the same amount, was not insured. She carried 8
dories and eighteen men. Hiscock survived this wreck,
but in February 1917, he disappeared with his crew and
schooner *John McRea* off the southern Avalon.

The schooner *T.A. Mahone*, owned by John Rose of
Jersey Harbour and captained by Owen Fiander of
Coomb's Cove, carried seven dories and 16 men. On the
same day of the *Titanic* disaster, April 15, 1912, while
fishing on Banquero (Quero) Bank, two dorymen,
George Barnes and Arch Bungay of Coomb's Cove,
went astray from the *T.A. Mahone* in dense fog. For

Bungay, at age 16, it was his first trip to the banks and one never to be forgotten.

It had been a miserable day for Bungay who was seasick and not feeling well. He had no breakfast and took no food into the dory, neither did his dorymate. After an hour or so, their trawls were set and they made their way back to the schooner, but in the thick fog and rough seas, could not locate her. About 3 p.m. they gave up hope of finding the *Mahone*, put up the dory's small sail and attempted to sail for land.

Both men were adrift and lost without sufficient food or water. Their only food was a piece of cake, but a ten pound butter tub filled with ice as it accumulated on the dory helped slake thirst. On April 17 their dory was caught in a field of Arctic pack ice and drifted nine days with the floes.

During one night while they were on a pan of ice, they put two trawl tubs together to make a crude shelter which they used one at a time. Their dory was badly broken in the crush of ice. To repair her, Barnes and Bungay nailed bulkhead boards to the outside, chinked the seams with rag and parts of their mitts and somehow made the dory more watertight.

On April 26 the men left the ice pans and drifted aimlessly for three more days. By this time both men were half-conscious and partly frozen in the bottom of the dory. They might well have succumbed to the cold but for the fact that their damaged dory had to be bailed constantly. The extra work may have kept them from freezing to death.

Nine thirty in the morning on April 29, Bungay saw the sail of a schooner in the distance. He dropped the bailing scoop and rowed, although it was agony to do so after fourteen days without food and rest, toward the vessel which proved to be the 90-ton schooner *Francis*

M, captained and owned by William Spencer of Fortune. Both men, barely alive were carried to hospital in Sydney, Nova Scotia.

Barnes died in hospital on May 9, 1912; Bungay, severely frostbitten, had both feet and one hand amputated in the same hospital on May 10. In December he came back home to Coomb's Cove. When he recovered from his debilitating injuries, he learned telegraphy and for several years operated the telegraph service in Ramea and other Fortune Bay communities.

MARY SMITH Dune Sands Casualty—The captain of the Harbour Breton schooner *Mary Smith* went through a terrible experience when his vessel stranded on the Dune Sands.

When Jack Lewis of Holyrood, Conception Bay, reached home on January 13, 1913, he told reporters from a St. John's newspaper how he and his crew spent thirteen hours in the rigging on a bitterly cold night with sea and spray lashing over them. *Mary Smith*, owned by John Smith of Harbour Breton, was bound from Halifax to Smith's premises in late December 1912 with a load of hard coal and general cargo when a blinding storm pushed the schooner onto the west side of the Dune Sands of Langlade, near St. Pierre.

All through the night five men sought refuge from the cold water by climbing to the mast heads and lashing themselves on. Occasionally the men called to each other for encouragement. In the early hours of the morning, mate Vincent Cox, age 23, died of exposure. Lewis and the other three attempted to make shore, but seaman Thomas Saunders died on the shoreline. The others, including William Johnson of Harbour Breton, stumbled on. Captain Lewis reached safety first and directed help to his remaining two men, who were barely alive.

To John Smith of Harbour Breton the loss was a severe one. No insurance was carried on vessel nor cargo, and although the *Mary Smith* was pulled from her precarious position on the Dune Sands by the St. Pierre tug, repairs cost $5,000. This was more than the owner could afford. Then to add to Smith's shipping woes, in 1917, his schooner *Lucy House* was sent to the bottom by German submarines. Smith eventually sold two other schooners, the *Cecil Smith* and *Stanley Smith*, and closed out his Harbour Breton shipping business.

ANNIE ROBERTS One Survivor—Only one of her crew lived to tell the tale when the schooner *Annie Roberts* was hit by the steamer *Wabana*. *Annie Roberts* left Sydney on the 22nd of October 1913, laden with coal for Lamaline. Storm conditions, a southwest gale, lashed the craft and Captain Buffett had the fore and mainsail reefed.

Owned in Lamaline, the *Roberts* had only left port when the iron ship struck her amidships, practically breaking her in half. *Wabana* swung around to look for survivors. Four drowned—the captain, John Francis, Arthur Coffin and John McDonald—but John Bennett, a seaman, survived by grabbing an oar to stay afloat. Bennett afterward claimed the *Annie Roberts* sank within three minutes after collision.

When the body of Francis, the cook, drifted ashore at Morien, Nova Scotia, it was identified by John Bennett, the only survivor of the wreck.

GRAND FALLS Posted 'Missing without a Trace'—Launched in April 1910, at Shelburne, Nova Scotia, and classed as a semi-knockabout, the tern *Grand Falls* was one of the fastest sailers in the foreign trade. She measured 121 feet long and 26 feet beam, and registered 145 tons.

Owned by Albert Dyett of St. Jacques, Fortune Bay, and Rendells of St. John's, in early January 1914, she became overdue, bound from Harbour Breton to Oporto laden with salt fish. A series of storms had swept the Atlantic which might have foundered the schooner.

Before the winter of 1914 ended, Atlantic storms claimed two other South Coast schooners, both without loss of life: on January 22, H.E. Petite of Mose Ambrose lost the *Tobeatic*; and a month later the *Elinor* of Pushthrough was wrecked.

Tobeatic left St. John's for Burin on October 11, 1913, discharged salt and left for Europe laden with fish from Hollett's business. The tern had a fine run over making the trip in 18 days, discharged fish at Alicante, Spain, then loaded salt at Santa Pola. Captain John White, mate

Courtesy *Those Bright Days* souvenir booklet of St. Jacques/Coomb's Cove, 1992

Built in Liverpool, Nova Scotia, in 1908; within a year the 102-foot long *Tobeatic* was sold to Henry Petite. He, in turn, sold majority shares to A.E. Hickman's and Rendell's businesses at St. John's although Petite still managed the vessel.

Banfield, cook A. Reid, seamen John Collins, Joseph Mitchell and D. Reid went through very rough seas until they reached the northern edge of the Gulf Stream on January 17, 1914.

By this time all sails, as well as her booms and gaffs, were blown away. Most schooners carried a second set of sails when on transatlantic voyages and the crew bent on a spare mainsail, but this was also torn to shreds. During the height of the storm a large square-rigged vessel passed the *Tobeatic* but paid no attention to distress signals that were flying from the wallowing tern.

On January 18, a steamer stopped and stood by the schooner for an hour, but Captain White could not hold *Tobeatic* into the wind and she drifted past. Four days later and about 190 miles off the Azores at latitude 41.16, longitude 30.04, the oil tanker *Leda* saw the sinking schooner, came close enough to send a lifeboat over and the *Tobeatic*'s crew was taken off. Fifteen days later the *Leda* landed them at New Orleans. They later reached New York and came to St. John's on the *Stephano*.

For Captain Evans and his 8 men on the *Elinor*, rescue came about in a different way. *Elinor* left St. Pierre, where she had been under repair, for Rose Blanche to prosecute the winter fishery. From the beginning of her journey, February 19, high northeast winds, snow and intense frost plagued the schooner. Sails and frozen rigging could not worked and Evans gave orders to lie to in the wind. One high sea swept over the vessel inflicting severe damage: everything moveable was washed overboard including the dories, part of the bulwarks were torn off, sails were ripped and a subsequent sea carried the wheel away. *Elinor* began to leak at an alarming rate forcing the men to pump constantly.

The wind storm had pushed the schooner near the Cape Shore, at the southwestern end of the Avalon

Peninsula. Slob ice covered the sea, but it was not heavy enough to prevent the *Elinor* from being pushed nearer and nearer to the land. The men climbed down to the slob, but sank to their armpits. Determined to save himself and his men, Captain Evans took a line and some planks with him and crawled over the ice using the planks as support to the shore, not far from Patrick's Cove. Evans had fallen into the ice several times, but had strength enough to fasten the lifeline to a rock.

Each man in turn left the *Elinor* with planks in case they fell through the ice and, guided by the line, reached shore. Before the vessel went to pieces the next day, most of the crew's belongings were salvaged. The men, some of whom had suffered frostbite on the hands and face, were cared for by the people of Patrick's Cove.

MARION Seventeen Lives Cut Down—In June 1915, the schooner *Marion* mysteriously disappeared while on a voyage from St. Pierre to the Grand Banks. According to an interview done with three residents of Fortune Bay by the CBC television program *Land and Sea* in 1987, there is reason to believe she was deliberately rammed at sea.

Registered to Denis Burke at St. Jacques, the 63-ton *Marion* had an overall length of 73 feet and was built in LaHave, Nova Scotia, in 1903. In January, five months before her fatal rendezvous with death, the *Marion*, while in charge of Skipper Dick Nurse, harboured in Cape La Hune. During a gale she was driven ashore. In St. Pierre the *Marion*'s damaged keel was repaired, giving the owner added expenses.

For the fishing season she was captained by Isaac (Ike) Jones, who was also known as Ike Skinner, and manned by sixteen fishermen for her banking dories. The *Marion* left St. Jacques, Fortune Bay, in the second week of June on a voyage, called by the bank fishermen, the 'caplin trip,' when hook and line trawls were baited with caplin. Fresh caplin could be had in Miquelon and Jones went to Spyglass Point on Miquelon for a supply.

From Miquelon the *Marion* docked at the slip in St. Pierre harbour for minor repairs or recaulking. For a schooner needing examination of her bottom, docking at St. Pierre was a necessity at the turn of the century, for the dry dock in Burin had not yet been built.

At St. Pierre one of her regular crew members, the captain's brother Reg, left the *Marion* and his place was taken by Morgan Miles. It was Miles' first trip to the banks.

Repairs completed, the *Marion* left St. Pierre on the 15 of June, around 10 a.m. Several hours later, a French beam trawler slipped her ropes from the wharf and followed the wake of the *Marion*. By evening the French trawler was back. This unusually short voyage was

Author's collection

South Coast schooners like the *Marion* often used the dry dock slip at St. Pierre. In this photo taken in the 1950s, Grand Bank's *L.A. Dunton* is hauled up for repairs to her bottom.

witnessed by other Newfoundland sailors who eyed the French trawler suspiciously.

According to other stories concerning the *Marion* told in Boxey, the French vessel left St. Pierre that night, waited outside in the 'roads,' and watched schooners leave port. It turned its searchlights on each until she apparently found the *Marion* and followed her. Other schooners had been spotted by the trawler, but at the time thought nothing of it.

On June 15th the *Marion* and her seventeen crew members vanished without a trace. Within the next two or three weeks, as other South Coast schooners came back from their fishing trip to the banks, each was asked the whereabouts of the *Marion*. No vessel had any report of her. By August grieving relatives of Boxey, St. Jacques and Coomb's Cove—Childs, Vallis, Skinner and Miles—gave up hopes of ever seeing the Fortune Bay schooner again.

According to the belief of those left behind, the *Marion* must have been rammed or cut down by the French trawler and there were no survivors to tell the tale. But why? Seamen from Boxey knew that on a previous occasion, the *Marion*'s skipper, Ike Jones had a dispute with a Frenchman—the same captain of the French trawler that had later apparently pursued the *Marion*. Jones had bested him in a fight.

But the beaten man had uttered a vile threat, "Never mind," the French captain said, "there's more room on the sea than on the land." If these stories of violence and threats are true, then the man wanted revenge.

Both in terms of lives and financial loss the disappearance of the *Marion* devastated the people of Boxey who had so many of their relatives and friends on board. The tiny community on the western side of

Fortune Bay never fully recovered from the loss of its young men.

HIAWATHA Explodes in Halifax Harbour—The ninety-eight ton *Hiawatha*, owned in Burin and commanded by Captain Hubert Clarke, was moored in Bedford Basin, a section of Halifax harbour, on the morning of September 10, 1915. Clarke had four Burin crew with him: cook Tom Farrell, Tom Hussey, James Saunders, Fred Kirby, plus William Hooper of Lamaline.

Built in Lunenberg as a two masted schooner to be used in the foreign trade, *Hiawatha* had made many voyages overseas, but on this trip she was scheduled to deliver gas to Burin—four hundred barrels of gasoline and one hundred barrels of oil. Captain Clarke, who for years had handled and carried cargoes of this sort, was considered a careful and reliable man in the matter of fire and matches.

After the gasoline was loaded, Clarke awaited suitable sailing conditions. On the morning of departure, cook Tom Farrell lit the galley stove using gasoline. Flames shot up, partially burned Farrell's beard and face, caught flammable materials nearby and set schooner's galley afire.

Clarke's clothes caught and he jumped overboard to extinguish the flames, but later died from his burns. Hooper and Saunders lost their lives. Farrell and Kirby, who broke his leg, were taken to Victoria General Hospital; only Hussey escaped uninjured.

Cook Farrell later told this story about the loss of the *Hiawatha*:

> We were going to sail this morning for Newfoundland and I had gone forward in the galley to get breakfast for the boys. We had not been able to

sleep in the fo'scle the night before because of the fumes from gasoline which had settled there.

I went to light the fire in the stove, when suddenly there was a sharp explosion and the forecastle was a mass of flames. I leaped for the companionway, and got through safely but just in the nick of time. I jumped overboard and escaped with minor injuries.

Kirby who was leaning on the starboard rail, was thrown to the deck by the explosion and he, too, jumped into the water. In doing so he fractured his leg. I think Captain Clarke also jumped from the ship. It all happened so quickly, it is hard to say what each man did. Saunders, Clarke and Hooper perished in the flames.

Hiawatha burned to the water's edge and stranded on a reef near the Bedford Basin pier of the Imperial Oil Company. Her deck caved in; her ribs protruded from what was left of the hull. The fire was also witnessed by men on a warship anchored close to the schooner. In a report written for the Halifax papers it stated:

At 6:30 a.m. they heard an explosion and looking toward the schooner, saw a sheet of flames sweep along the deck and up the masts and rigging. Flames took full possession of the ship and it was impossible to board her.

The cries of the men who had jumped overboard were heard and they were quickly brought to shore. The mate made his way to land. Thanks to the work of the oil company's tug *Togo*, the blaze did not spread to the oil storage tanks. The schooner, however, was totally destroyed.

Hiawatha's value was $5,000 and the cargo, not insured, was worth about the same.

ALBATROSS Dr. Fitz-gerald's Schooner Rammed—
In 1873, when Dr. Con Fitz-gerald first arrived on the
South Coast from England to set up his medical practice, he found transportation around the coast very
difficult. His practice was a large one, and calls to all
parts of Fortune Bay were numerous. To get around the
coast more comfortably, he ordered his own schooner
built—the 30-foot *Albatross*, constructed at Belleoram
by John Cluett in the winter of 1875. Although the
schooner was built and used in the Atlantic, the doctor
ironically named her for a large Pacific seabird.

For the next forty years Dr. Fitz-gerald and his
Albatross became a household word in every harbour
along that coast. In the beginning the doctor used Harbour Breton as home base, but later, near the twilight of
his medical career he moved to St. Jacques, a more
central location for his work.

The end of the *Albatross* came on the night of July
30, 1916. That evening at dusk the lighthouse keeper on
St. Jacques Island, Isaac Burke, watched a small yacht,
the *Caribou*, beating its way out of the bay against a stiff
breeze.

He recognized the vessel and knew its two occupants, Mr. Ryan the telegraph operator at Long Harbour and Harry Clinton, the custom's officer stationed
at St. Jacques. A few minutes later, about a mile from the
lighthouse, the *Caribou* capsized throwing Ryan and
Clinton into the water.

The lightkeeper rowed to Dr. Fitz-gerald's home at
St. Jacques to engage the doctor and the *Albatross* for a
possible rescue. Fitz-gerald, George and Alexander
Tibbo of St. Jacques and the keeper set out, using the
schooner's small motor and foresail, into the dark
waters of the bay with the wind whistling ominously in
the rigging.

A lantern was lit and hung on the jibstay as a guide to the two men of the *Caribou* in case they clung to their overturned yacht. Burke, the lighthouse keeper, had no oilclothes and stood in the warm cabin while the other three took a position on the bow or in the rigging scanning the water for a wreck.

After searching for hours, Fitz-gerald saw a ship's light in the direction of Belleoram Barachois and supposed it to be the local mail steamer *Hump* which the doctor thought had now joined the search. *Hump*, a former whaling vessel replacing the regular mail steamer, was fast approaching the *Albatross* and at first it appeared she would cross behind her.

But apparently the helmsman of the *Hump* did not see the little schooner. The four men on the doctor's schooner felt no uneasiness for they guessed her speed of five knots would take her away from the onrushing steamer. Dr. Fitz-gerald describes what happened next in the book *The Albatross*, written by his grandson in 1930.

> Through the blackness of the night emerged her stem rushing straight for the middle of the *Albatross*. I jumped from the standing-room...and as the corner of her stem came in reach, I put both hands out to lessen the impending blow and was struck in the chest as the *Hump* crashed into the poor old *Albatross* just forward of the main rigging on the starboard side.
>
> White splinters of wood gleamed through the blackness of the night, the deck seemed to melt away under me, and I fell into the water about two feet clear of her stem and was rolled over and over in the rushing water. I felt uneasy about the ship's propeller as she slid by me.

When Dr. Fitz-gerald came to the surface, he swam away and then heard a voice on the *Hump* shout out, "Stop that propeller!" The doctor felt the *Albatross'* small boat strike his shoulder, grabbed it and climbed aboard. Another of the doctor's crew found the small boat and tumbled in.

By this time the *Hump* had stopped and its lifeboat had been put off to look for survivors of the *Albatross*. Dr. Fitz-gerald asked the searchers if they had found anyone. They had not, so the doctor rowed to his schooner's wreckage which he thus described:

> I started off again and came across more wreckage, my cabin-house with the funnel sticking up, hatches, etc. but no man; so back to the *Hump*, to hear that another of my men had been hauled over the bows half-dead. No sign of the lighthouse-keeper. I firmly believe the keeper was standing in the cabin when the *Hump* struck us and was instantly killed.

Fitz-gerald, with chest injuries and a broken rib, rowed into Belleoram. He later learned the *Hump* had left Belleoram to look for Ryan and Clinton and the mailboat lookouts saw a light, which they believed to be on the overturned *Caribou*. The captain of the *Hump* wished to get near what he thought was a stationary light of Ryan's semi-submerged *Caribou* and ran over the unsuspecting *Albatross*.

Both men in the capsized yacht drowned, making two wrecks that night with three deaths. The doctor was never offered any compensation for the loss of his ship, the *Albatross*, nor was there any official inquiry into the accident.

According to Fitz-gerald, no one ever knew how or why a steamer sent to rescue two men supposedly clinging to an overturned boat, could ram and sink another craft on the same errand of mercy, endangering the lives of three other men and actually killing a fourth, the St. Jacques lighthouse keeper.

A few days later Reverend Templeton, the Church of England clergyman at Belleoram, lost his boat the *Saint Augustine* on rocks off St. Pierre in the fog. Three vessels had gone down, all within a week; each one had been extensively used in serving the people of Belleoram and vicinity.

Although the doctor was seventy years old at the time of these terrible events, he ordered another schooner built, the *Albatross II*, but rarely sailed her; eventually she was sold to Chesley Yarn in Mose Ambrose.

Mail Steamer HUMP, A Wreck at St. Lawrence—Less than a month after ramming Fitz-gerald's schooner, the *Hump* herself was involved in a collision that sent her to the bottom. *Hump*, a steam-sail vessel at 95 tons, was built in Norway in 1904 and had been purchased by the Newfoundland Whaling Company based in St. John's.

As she entered St. Lawrence at 3 a.m. on August 24 in dense fog, Captain Horwood failed to see the *S.S. Argyle* slowly steaming out of St. Lawrence. *Argyle* nudged the smaller steamer, hitting her below water line about amidships, but with enough impact the *Hump* quickly filled with water.

Orders were given to launch *Hump's* lifeboat; then, her crew rowed away from their sinking vessel. The mail steamer went down in ten minutes although there were no heavy seas running. Horwood and his crew barely escaped saving no clothes or belongings. *S.S. Argyle*, undamaged in the incident, landed the shipwrecked crew back in St. Lawrence.

The offshore bank fishing industry of St. Lawrence was not as great as that of other South Coast communities, but nonetheless, the history of the town includes a number of missing schooners: the *Contest*, 1898, and the *Creusa G.*, 1917, both lost with crew while delivering coal. Another unsolved mystery centres around the *P.K. Jacobs*, a thirty-ton schooner built at St. Lawrence in 1900 and owned by Robert Reeves.

This vessel fished the summer of 1900; then, on September 12 she went to St. Pierre to obtain a supply of squid for bait and left again for the banks. From that point nothing was ever known of the 58-foot schooner nor her nine crew, all of St. Lawrence: Captain Joseph Jacobs, James Reeves, George Poole, William Turpin, Patty Murphy and four Pikes—Louis, Archibald, Samuel and Robert.

To seafaring communities no shipping notice was so dreaded as 'Posted as Missing' as announced by Lloyd's, an insurance and shipping company which kept registers of most North American vessels. Overdue ships must eventually be withdrawn or stricken from their records and owners notified to collect insurance, if any had been carried on the missing ship.

To towns dependent on the sea, that single sentence, albeit brief, carried a significant message: a marine tragedy with a mere handful of men in a frail ship pitting their human strength against the might of the ocean.

'Posted as Missing' became an all too familiar phrase to Newfoundlanders especially in the period 1900 to 1930; most South Coast people have experienced the anxious time of waiting, hoping and despairing for the message of salvation which often never came.

SUSAN INKPEN   An Early Burin Tragedy—One of the first shipping tragedies to ravage the Burin fleet of schooners during the Great War was the disappearance of the Burin schooner *Susan Inkpen*. This 113-foot long two master was built in Shelburne and netted 101 tons. Owned by Leonard Inkpen, she left Burin on October 16, 1916, and neither the ship nor crew was ever seen again.

Today on the Lloyd's registry of shipping and in the town's roster of schooners, she is listed as 'missing without a trace,' her loss attributed either to German raiders operating in the North Atlantic or to severe storms. Yet South Coast towns, as long as there was a ship left to navigate and men to sail it, continued to send their fleets to the fishing grounds and overseas. Appendix B lists other Burin schooners lost with full or partial crew.

On December 27, news arrived in Newfoundland that the *Hasperia*, a schooner owned and captained by Abraham J. Skinner of St. Jacques, had been shipwrecked two days previously with all five crew not far from Pointe Platte near the western Dune Sands between Langlade and Miquelon. Built at Copper Island, Trinity Bay, in 1901, she had been to Sydney for coal and was delivering her cargo to St. Jacques when a storm pushed the 56-ton *Hasperia* onto the treacherous shore.

Stretching for over twelve kilometres of sandy beach, the isthmus of Dune Sands connects Langlade and Miquelon islands. Since 1790, when official records of vessel losses were first kept, there have been hundreds of shipwrecks along its shores, caused either by navigational error, dense fog, or unpredictable winds and currents. The Dune Sands first began to show above the surface of the sea some two hundred years ago and, as more and more wrecks piled up, the beach building process speeded up.

Local residents on Langlade witnessed the *Hasperia*'s breakup and, seeing the crew men alive and clinging to the masts, immediately sent for the St. Pierre tug to assist the stranded men. There was no way a small dory or lifeboat could broach the breakers. But by the time help arrived it was too late—all were swept into the frigid December seas.

For residents of Boxey and St. Jacques, home of the victims, Christmas celebrations ceased as families were notified of the deaths. By early January, three bodies had been recovered and buried at Langlade.

On a map of St. Pierre shipwrecks—situated between the 1912 wreck of the Harbour Breton vessel *Mary Smith*, and the *Kathleen Creaser*, owned by Fudge in Belleoram and wrecked in 1943—lies the St. Jacques schooner *Hasperia*, lost with crew in 1916.

Chapter Three

An Added Danger—
German U-Boats

SEVERAL MONTHS after the outbreak of World War One, the German war machine resorted to its submarine fleet to bring Britain to her knees. By January 1917 the Germans, convinced they could starve Britain in five months, entered into unrestricted submarine warfare.

To the enemy this policy, at least in its initial stages, was spectacularly effective. Allied shipping losses in-

A German World War One submarine in the Kiel Canal, in North West Germany. In the years leading up to the Great War, German technology put their subs, often called U-Boats, at the forefront.

In 1906, the German navy was one of the first to adapt the diesel engine to the submarine, providing an underwater craft with a means of strong propulsion. With the development of the periscope and the self-propelling torpedo, the submarine became a formidable factor in naval warfare.

creased throughout the war reaching a peak of 869,000 tons sent to the bottom in April 1917.

During the last two years of the Great War, American, Canadian and Newfoundland sailors knew their vessels had little chance of making a voyage across the North Atlantic without being intercepted by a German submarine. German U-boats preyed on enemy ships sinking unarmed merchantmen on sight. Those merchantmen were wooden, sail-driven schooners, unarmed and carrying only salt fish for Greece, Portugal or Spain or fishery salt from Cadiz or Setubal on the east to west voyage.

Strangely, German submarine commanders showed a special humanity toward the crews of these lonely sailing vessels they were forced to sink. Time was often allowed to let the crews get away in their lifeboat; then, the schooners were destroyed usually by planted bombs—the more expensive torpedoes and shells were reserved for larger and more important targets.

One Burin Peninsula man, Captain B.C. Hooper, a Lamaline resident born in 1892, spent the war years in an unusual way. He had gone to Halifax in 1916 to look for work and signed on the Nova Scotian tern schooner *Perce* with Captain Kohler readying to sail south. *Perce* had a fine voyage to Brazil, but on the return trip she was apprehended by the *Seeadler*, a full-rigged German warship. *Seeadler*, was commanded by the notorious German Count von Luckner, known as the Sea Devil. Hooper's vessel was sunk and he, along with the rest of the *Perce's* crew, was taken prisoner.

As a German prisoner, according to Hooper's story told later, he was required to work, but he was also educated and trained. Hooper learned a great deal from his captors. Eventually Hooper was repatriated; ultimately he joined the Dominion Steel and Coal Corporation at Sydney, Nova Scotia, where he rose in the ranks to marine superintendent.

PERCY ROY, THOMAS Victims of the War—
Throughout the course of war several Newfoundland schooners were intercepted, their crews questioned and the vessels sent to the bottom by enemy marauders. On March 26, 1917, the *New York Times* reported that six Newfoundland sailors, victims of a German submarine, had arrived in New York. Their schooner, now on the bottom of the Mediterranean, was the 110-ton *Percy Roy*, registered in St. John's to Smith Company, and once owned by John B. Foote of Grand Bank.

Percy Roy, bound from Santa Pola, Spain, to Italy was stopped by an enemy U-boat on February 13 in the Gulf of Lyons. After the *Percy Roy* was bombed and sunk, the crew made their way in a small boat to the French coast. After several weeks a British freighter brought them to the United States.

From the turn of the century to the 1930's Harvey and Company, a business based in St. John's, owned and operated several schooners out of Belleoram on the South Coast. One schooner was the *Thomas*, a 115-ton tern schooner, with two square rigged sails on her foretop. She had been purchased in Norway some years before. *Thomas'* chief work was to carry fish from Belleoram to food-starved European ports, mainly in Portugal.

In April of 1917, she met her end. After leaving Cadiz, Spain, laden with salt, she encountered a lurking German U-boat off the coast of Portugal. On that voyage the *Thomas* was in command of Captain Reginald Keeping with his navigator Harold Baker and three other Belleoram crewmen: William Foote, Gabriel Fudge and William Cluett.

On April 23, an enemy sub surfaced near the *Thomas* and asked the navigating officers of the schooner to go aboard the U-Boat. Baker and Captain Keeping rowed over carrying the British flag, their vessel's registration papers and destination orders.

The old German sub commander knew no English, but had a young first officer speak for him. After several questions regarding the *Thomas'* destination, port of departure and cargo, the first officer said, "Sorry to sink your ship. Pick off your crew men and row for the nearest land."

Before the two Belleoram men left the submarine, they were given several packs of German cigarettes. The enemy, showing no sign of inhumanity or hostility, asked if the lifeboat was fully provisioned and when Keeping assured them it was, the *Thomas* was sunk by gunfire. In three days the South Coast seamen rowed to the coast of Portugal.

Eventually the men were transported by various transatlantic steamers back to their Belleoram homes. Baker and Keeping, who both lived well into their eighties, always claimed that the first officer on the German submarine who had interrogated them so thoroughly was an Englishman.

Undaunted by these and other setbacks on the sea, seafaring men like Captain Keeping acquired other ships, continued in the foreign trade and kept the vital food and supply lines flowing between Europe and North America.

Loss of the WILLIAM MORTON—Later in the year Keeping was given command of the schooner *William Morton*, a tern schooner built in 1905 at Portmadoc, Wales, to make a trip overseas with fish to Alicante, Spain. From there she loaded salt at Cadiz, headed for

Belleoram, but ran into typical winter storms on January 5, 1918.

The story of the *William Morton* illustrates what happened to men forced to abandon ship in midatlantic. Their schooner, despite vigourous pumping and every effort to keep it afloat, was gradually pulled down into the cold Atlantic.

Often, despite a diligent lookout on the sinking schooners, no ocean liners came in sight to pick off the weary men. The only recourse was to prepare the lifeboat, or the ship's dory, and wait until the last possible moment before stepping off the sinking schooner. Such was the case of five Belleoram men when their leaking vessel settled lower and lower into the raging ocean.

In the January gale Keeping was forced to heave to, then to lower all sails, but the damage had been done to the *William Morton*—seams were open and water poured in. Constant pumping and bailing with buckets from forecastle and cabin failed to keep the *Morton* afloat.

At 5:00 p.m., with some moderation in wind and sea, seven men stepped into a lifeboat hundreds of miles off the coast of Portugal. Knowing an indefinite time on the raging Atlantic faced them, the crew provisioned the tiny craft with water, food and extra clothes.

About five minutes after being abandoned, the *Morton* went down. Seas and wind, lashed with cold rain, increased. Around midnight the lifeboat capsized and four of the seven men grabbed it and hung onto its bottom. The other three, one of whom was the captain's seventeen-year-old brother and another, his cousin, were not seen nor heard of again. The four survivors turned over the boat, bailed her out and discovered that all water and food, which had not been lashed down, had disappeared.

At daylight the little craft turned over again, and once more the weary, cold men were forced to upright the boat, climb aboard and bail her out. Before the afternoon ended, the lifeboat turned over again and was uprighted a third time. By now the men had reached the limits of their endurance, but two circumstances intervened to save their lives—the wind and seas abated, the day turned warm, and later a Spanish steamer, the *Durango*, bound for Seville, came by.

Exhausted, suffering from hunger and dehydration for they had been without food and water for over two days, the *William Morton*'s surviving crew were taken aboard the *Durango*. The mate, John Cluett of Belleoram, was semi-conscious and raving for a day after rescue, while Captain Keeping gradually became weaker probably suffering from pneumonia.

On February 19, 1919, the British freighter *Freshwater* arrived in New York from Spain and when the men reached Saint John, New Brunswick, Keeping remained in a Saint John hospital for several days.

GEORGE EWART Cut Down by an Unknown Ship— According to first reports coming back to Newfoundland, it was first thought the tern *George Ewart* had been intercepted and destroyed by a German U-boat. Built in 1913 in Fortune, the 148-ton *George Ewart* was owned by Lakes and captained by Edward Hillier of Fortune.

Early in September 1917, she left St. John's bound for Gibraltar. Off the European coast a severe storm forced Hillier to lie to and wait for better weather. On September 19 at eleven o'clock in the evening off Gibraltar the schooner was run into by an iron ship.

According to the shipwrecked crew, the vessel which struck the Fortune tern did not stop to assess damage nor to provide assistance, but steamed off into the night, unidentified. For three hours the men tried to repair the damage while battling the storm which was still raging. Leaks could not be stopped and their only recourse was to abandon the schooner.

A few minutes after the men left the *George Ewart*, a German submarine surfaced nearby, looked over the sinking tern and, seeing that the schooner was about to go down, submerged again.

After eleven hours in an open boat, battered with high winds, the *Ewart's* crew reached the Spanish coast. There they learned the submarine that had viewed their sinking schooner was the same one known to be prowling the waters off Gibraltar and sinking ships for months. The day before it had sunk a British steamer. *George Ewart's* shipwrecked crew reached Gibraltar from Spain and waited 13 days for transportation west.

On October 8, two of the crew arrived in Boston and described how their schooner was wrecked. They claimed that while in Gibraltar they knew of 14 ship crews whose vessels had been sunk by the enemy. These stranded crewmen were waiting in Gibraltar for transportation west.

On December 6, 1917, the schooner *Lizzie M. Stanley*, owned in Burgeo, left St. Pierre for Catalina with a crew of six—Joseph Ingraham; Thomas Buffett; Harold Knott; Simeon Billard; all married, Captain John Collier and Morgan Buffett; both single. She was last seen east of Cape Race by another schooner, both vessels bound north, but a gale came on later that night. Probably her cargo shifted in the storm; however the *Lizzie M. Stanley* never reported and was posted as 'missing with crew.'

HILDA R and Others Sent to the Bottom by German Subs—In November 1917, the *Hilda R* was shelled by a German submarine about 40 miles from Gibraltar. When the U-boat surfaced and began firing on the schooner, five of the seven man crew had enough time to escape in the schooner lifeboat. But Captain Yetman of Harbour Grace and another sailor took refuge in the cabin.

After a number of shots had been fired at the *Hilda R*, both men came on deck and signalled to the sub that they were still aboard. The sub commander ordered the guns to cease. A small boat was then sent to the schooner. The captain and sailor were taken off and landed aboard the submarine where the sub commander explained he did not know anyone remained aboard the schooner.

For five hours the two remained aboard the sub. Yetman described the U-boat as one of the largest in the German fleet, 280 feet long with seventy-five crew, all Turkish except the German commander. Yetman and his companion were later transferred to a Spanish steamer laden with nitroglycerine and other war materials destined for Germany. Before the steamer continued to Germany, the two Newfoundlanders were landed at a Spanish port.

Up to that time Yetman had not learned of the fate of his other five crew, but he presumed they had been picked up safely.

On August 25, the Newfoundland steamship *Eric*, an old sealing ship turned coaster, was sunk by enemy submarine. All 18 men survived the shelling by the sub. Seeing that the *Eric* did not sink, the German U-boat approached the ship, ordered her crew to the sub and placed bombs aboard to finish her off. *Eric's* crew were later transferred to a Newfoundland ship headed west.

In early August 1918, as enemy efforts to impose the food blockade to England increased, a German U-boat surfaced in the middle of the American fishing fleet—about thirty schooners anchored on George's Bank—and opened fire. Thirteen schooners went down: crews from nine of the thirteen escaped, while four vessels and their crews disappeared without a trace. Other ships made their escape while U-boat gunners were reloading and preparing to sink them.

With four of the *Kate Palmer's* survivors aboard, the fishing schooner *Helen Murley* arrived in port on August 12 reporting that a sub was seen sinking the *Kate Palmer, Anita May, Reliance, Star Buck, Progress* and four others, unidentified. *Helen Murley* managed to rescue four of *Palmer's* men. They had been taken aboard the U-boat, interrogated, held prisoner for an hour and then set adrift in their dory. Later the *Helen Murley* found them, but did not report what had happened to the rest of *Palmer's* crew.

Another fishing vessel, the *Gleaner*, saw a shot fired across the bow of a larger schooner. There was a brisk sailing breeze and Captain Proctor of the *Gleaner* decided

SUBMARINE SINKS NINE SCHOONERS

Fleet of Thirty Fishing Vessels, Attacked 60 Miles Off Nantucket Island.

FOUR SURVIVORS RESCUED

Sixty Others Are Known to Be Afloat in Dories on the Atlantic.

AN ATLANTIC PORT, (Monday,) Aug 12 Sixty fishermen, including the crews of nine fishing schooners sunk by a German submarine late Saturday night off George's Bank, are afloat in dories on the Atlantic Ocean, according

Taken from the *New York Times*, August 12, 1918, edition, this clipping shows the extent of sub warfare on the fishing grounds frequented by American, Canadian and Newfoundland schooners.

to take a chance on escaping. He put on all sail and used the power of an auxiliary engine. At the same time he had his dories provisioned and made ready to launch in case the enemy turned their guns his way.

A Wartime Casualty MARION SILVER—Many unarmed schooners transporting fish east or carrying salt on the return journey fell prey to the marauders; several of these vessels were from Newfoundland. However it was not the enemy that sank the *Marion Silver*, but the old nemesis, northwest Atlantic gales.

Marion Silver, Lunenberg-built in 1912, left Barr's premises in St. John's for Oporto, Portugal, on January 21, 1918, with a cargo of dried cod. Originally, Harris interests at Grand Bank owned the *Silver*, but operated her out of his Change Islands branch business. At the time of her loss she was captained by J. Rogers, mate H. Murray, bosun P. Welsh of Witless Bay, cook H. Pike, seamen R. Whiteway and J. Meade of Ferryland.

On the voyage eastward, the *Marion Silver* met with a succession of gales lasting for six days. On the 27th, she was 'hove to' with only the jumbo and jib out. At 3:00 p.m. a huge wave swept the vessel and carried away the jib. As seaman Whiteway stood on the cabin lashing down the main boom, he was washed off the cabin roof. All the crew thought he had gone overboard in a swirl of white water, but somehow he had caught the lee rail and clung on. Dazed and injured from striking the rail, he was confined to bunk for several days.

Then to save his wind ravaged schooner, Rogers put his skill as a sea captain into practice. The jumbo was taken down, but before the *Marion Silver* could run off before the wind, another sea struck the schooner throwing her on beam ends. Water flooded both cabin and forecastle, but the staunch vessel righted herself enough for the crew to get around the deck.

Someone found a crowbar and pried up the cabin floor, allowing water to get to the pumps. From that time on, the pumps were manned constantly. Captain Rogers ordered the masts cut away. After a few chops, the heavy wind did the rest and the mainmast broke off about five feet above the deck. The foremast went from the keelson—the top section of the keel seen in the hold—and broke in two across the rail.

All throughout this ordeal, the wind blew a hurricane from the northwest; dismasted and uncontrolled, the *Marion Silver* drifted before the wind, waves sweeping her decks fore and aft. Captain Rogers was twice washed from the wheel within a thirty minute span, but escaped injury each time.

By this time, all cabin stores; that is food, supplies and bedding, were ruined by the inrush of water. Charts and ships' papers destroyed. Cooking in the flooded forecastle and cabin was impossible and for two days the crew lived on hard bread and raw bacon.

Early on the morning of January 28, a steamer's masthead light was sighted about two miles off. Captain Rogers ordered a flare put up, but the steamer continued her course without apparently seeing the sinking schooner or her distress signal.

Throughout that day, the wind moderated a little. But by the 29th, gales renewed stronger than before. At eleven o'clock that day the westbound American armed transport *San Jacinto* of the Mallory Line came in sight and approached the sinking hulk. *San Jacinto* nearly collided with the *Marion Silver* before she came alongside, lowered ropes over her side and took off the crew.

The 85-ton *Vanessa*, abandoned at sea November 1918, by the plague of salt laden sailing ships—brine-clogged pumps. Her lifeboat is lashed bottom up on the forward hatch.

Vanessa's crew spent several days in the lifeboat before they were rescued by the Norwegian tramp steamer *Severne*. Her crew were all from Burin: Captain Harry Brushett, the youngest at age 19, Alton Brenton, Robert Dear, John Isaac, Thomas Burfitt and Ernest Kirby.

Captain Avery of the *San Jacinto* ordered four shots put into the side of the schooner to ensure a swift sinking and the *Marion Silver* went down soon after. The crew was landed at New York on February 6 where the British Vice Consul supplied them with boots, socks, underwear and other clothing. From New York the crew came to Newfoundland on the *S.S Florizel*. Ironically this was the last voyage the *Florizel* made before she was wrecked at Cappahayden, Newfoundland, on February 24.

Loss of the BELLE OF BURGEO—That fall, off Halifax harbour on the rocks of Inner Sambro, mute evidence of a shipwreck was found. Fishermen picked up pieces of wreckage: one part of a nameplate had *Belle* on it, another with *Burgeo*. Parts of a derelict hull was located floating bottom up while the surface of the sea around Sambro was covered with oil.

On September 8, a few days after the initial sightings, the wreckage was identified as that of a schooner once owned by Moulton of Burgeo, the 70-ton *Belle of Burgeo*. The schooner had left Halifax with a cargo of oil and gasoline—350 barrels shipped by Imperial Oil to St. John's. She had been towed out of Halifax by the harbour tug, and when the tug left, the *Belle* proceeded to sail on.

The tail end of a tropical hurricane swept the Atlantic coast and had apparently pushed her onto the dangerous Sambro ledges—rocks that had claimed many ships in the past. Farquahar and Company, the schooner's agents, valued the cargo at $5,000 and the vessel at $10,000, both insured.

There was no sign of her five crew. At the time of her loss she was registered to James Dunne of North Sydney, captained by John Haldane, with mate George Martin both of Halifax. Her cook was Peter Bennett of Port aux Port, Newfoundland. Two other crew that perished in the shipwreck were Scandinavians who had signed on the *Belle of Burgeo* after their own schooner, the *N.T. Connelly*, was wrecked at Sable Island some weeks before.

MARY D. YOUNG A Failed Breeches Buoy Rescue— World War One was over. The Armistice of November 11, 1918, ended the threat of German U-Boats in the North Atlantic. Hundreds of ships had been destroyed with the loss of thousands of lives. While attempting to bring salt fish to hungry European ports, many Newfoundland schooners had been stopped, bombed or shelled and sent to the bottom—Appendix C lists several of these South Coast vessels. *Mary D. Young* narrowly escaped destruction from the Germans but met her end on the St. Pierre rocks on November 14, a few days after the war ended.

Built in Lunenberg in 1912, the *Mary D. Young* was one of the few terns used as a banker during the fishing season, although at the time of her wreck she was in the foreign-going trade. Originally purchased by Samuel Harris Limited, she was later sold to Samuel Piercy of Grand Bank. Her net weight was 99 tons and she measured 114-foot long. In 1918 she was commanded by Thomas Belbin, cook Charles Parsons, seaman Charlie Thomas and three other seamen, all of Grand Bank.

The story of her end is told by cook Parsons. According to him, the *Mary D. Young* left Newfoundland for Europe on the morning of August 25, 1918, with a cargo of salt fish. After discharge, the *Mary D. Young* took on salt at Cadiz and sailed west on October 21 in company with the *Hawanee*, a schooner owned by Tessier and Company, St. John's.

In the Atlantic both ships parted company, the *Mary D. Young* sailed a compass point further north than the *Hawanee*. And a compass point or the variance in route travelled proved to be the undoing of the latter schooner. It was later learned that the *Hawanee*, built at Lunenberg in 1909, met an enemy U-boat and was sent to the bottom. *Mary D. Young*, travelling on a slightly different course, avoided the sub and reached Grand Bank, Newfoundland, on the first day of November.

At Grand Bank some of her salt was discharged, then her owners sent the *Young* for Change Islands with a partial load of salt for Harris' fish collecting station there. Late in the evening of November 13, two days after the Great War ended, she sailed her final journey. Charles Parsons picks up the story:

On the way to Change Islands we stopped in St.
Pierre. There was wind, a nice breeze and we
struck on the rock going into Gun Point (Pointe aux
Canons) at the entrance to St. Pierre harbour. This
was about two o'clock in the morning on November 14. (Although the war had ended a few days
before, St. Pierre harbour lights were still extinguished because of the wartime regulations; this
reduced visibility, and the southeast wind con-
tributed to the accident).

With the ship firmly grounded and unable to be
freed from the rocks under her own power, Captain
Belbin put a plan into effect which he hoped would save
his stranded schooner. Cook Charles Parsons and
seaman Charles Thomas stayed aboard.

Captain Belbin, with three other men, took the
ship's boat and rowed into St. Pierre harbour to engage
the harbour tug operated by a man known around the
South Coast as Captain Frank. By the time the
schooner's crew called Captain Frank out of bed, and he
got the engineers and the rest of the tug's crew ready, it
was six o'clock and daylight.

In the delay the wind had swung around to a more
intense south southeasterly. It was too stormy for the
tug to reach the *Mary D. Young,* and the two men were
stranded on the tern schooner, now taking a terrific
pounding from white capped waves breaking over her
side.

Mary D. Young, like most terns, had two lifeboats—
one strapped on or over the stern and a dory or another
lifeboat usually lashed over one of the hatches. Before
Belbin left in the dory, he had his men put the ship's
lifeboat put over the stern and tied it on. This was a
safety measure for the two men left aboard. In case they

had to leave ship it would be next to impossible for them to heave off the lifeboat in a storm. Parsons recalled:

> When Charlie Thomas and I went back to get the lifeboat, it was gone, broken up or swept away in the storm. We were aboard the whole day in a storm of wind with the sea going over the schooner all the while. She was now broad side to Gun Point and that's where she stayed.
>
> About 2 o'clock I went down below. Charlie Thomas was up in the rigging then with the flag to try to signal for a dory. By that time there was a

Artist Andrea Hatch

Illustration of a breeches buoy. Although such rescue devices helped save the lives of many sailors, they had their limitations: often the wreck was too far from the shore; some strandings occurred in remote, inaccessible areas; cold and weakened survivors on the wrecked ship sometimes lacked the strength to fasten, get into or hold onto the bosun's chair while being pulled to shore.

huge crowd on the St. Pierre waterfront watching. Then I went down and put on the kettle, had a cup of tea and called Charlie down.

By now Captain Belbin realized the dangerous position his two remaining crewmen were in. With seas pounding over the schooner, she was in danger of breaking up and there was no possible way to send out a dory although the stranded schooner was only a few yards from land. St. Pierre harbour authorities, used to similar accidents happening around the shores of the French Islands, had a breeches gun and buoy ready for such emergencies.

By now the two weary men trapped on the schooner were anxious to get off, but as it turned out the breeches buoy was not the solution. Problems with St. Pierre's equipment were verified by Parsons:

> They sent off a breeches buoy to us—about 4 o'clock in the evening, I suppose. The first shot they fired from the breeches buoy gun went about 20 feet astern of the main boom. The next shot just touched the main boom and slipped off. But the third hung up amidships.
>
> Now all they had there for us to get into was an old square piece of wood with spikes in through it—nothing to hold onto. We couldn't get into that. We tied the tackle onto the mainmast and hauled the thing aboard.

By now, over fourteen hours after the *Mary D. Young* first went aground, the wind had died out. Broadside to the wind, the schooner provided enough lee to get a dory out to the two stranded men and rescue was completed. The cook summed up his experience on the wreck modestly:

Above, *Mary D. Young*, a wreck on the slip. The St. Pierre dock was a slip where schooners, large and small, could be hauled up for examination or repair. *Mary D. Young*, after extensive work on her planking, slipped off the cradle, probably causing the schooner to be hogged, or bent.

By the next morning, the *Mary D. Young* was high and dry on the beach near Gun Point and that was all I ever knew about that schooner. But we had kind of a tough time that day getting off her.

Sheltered in private homes, fed and cared for, the crew of the *Mary D. Young* never forgot the hospitality of the St. Pierrais who took them in after the loss of their ship. In time, the *Young* was pulled off the rocks by the tug and taken to the St. Pierre dry dock for repairs.

Weeks later, repairs almost completed, she slipped off the dry dock cradle and fell over on one side. Her life after these trials is obscure; the *Mary D. Young* may have sailed for a short while, but was eventually wrecked on St. Pierre—her registry closed less than a year later.

HAWANEE's Crew Rowed 500 Miles to Safety— *Hawanee*, after parting company with the *Mary D. Young*, had clear sailing until October 28 when she was about 360 miles west of Cape Finisterre, Spain. Captain King, a native of Bell Island, was in command.

About 5:00 p.m. a German U-boat spotted the *Hawanee*. Minutes later, a shell exploded about four feet away from the schooner and pieces of shrapnel broke up the deck engine box, smashed off the boom and did other minor damage. *Hawanee* then hove to by lowering her mainsail. Captain King ordered out the lifeboat and the crew got off.

By this time the submarine had come near enough to hold conversation with *Hawanee*'s crew and the German commander ordered them onto the sub. German sailors then boarded the schooner's boat and rowed to the schooner where they collected all the supplies and provisions they could.

To sink the schooner, several bombs were placed aboard; then, the Germans rowed back to the sub. When the bombs exploded, the Newfoundland ship went to the bottom.

Hawanee's crew was treated well, given food and refreshments and King was given back his chronometer and other instruments. German crewmen acted kindly—several talked to the Newfoundlanders in very good English.

In the course of the conversation Captain King was told the reason his ship was sunk was that, from a distance, the *Hawanee* was mistaken for an armed yacht. The keel of the overturned lifeboat on her deck looked like a gun and the *Hawanee*, being newly painted, looked very trim.

At seven o'clock that evening, after two hours aboard the U-boat, the Newfoundlanders were ordered into their boat which the Germans had held. There was a large amount of food aboard as King had ordered the lifeboat provisioned when the sub alarm first sounded. Extra food was supplied by the submarine. A sail on the lifeboat facilitated their progress for the stranded men knew they had to travel 500 miles to reach nearest land.

This they did in five days despite some rough weather often accompanied by heavy seas. King was an excellent navigator and had his navigating instruments aboard. Finally they reached Figuiera, Portugal, were taken to the British Consul and after a few days boarded a train for Oporto. They waited there until the Newfoundland schooner *Little Stephano* was loaded with salt; then, Captain King and the cook came home on her. The rest of the crew arrived later on other schooners.

A few days after the war ended the Fortune vessel *P.F.* was reported missing. *P.F.* was a ketch which, unlike a schooner, has a short mainmast situated in front of the rudder post and carries a smaller mainsail. Several vessels named *P.F.* had been brought from

France to St. Pierre to be sold. Built in France in 1879, each averaged about fifty ton. Two were bought in Fortune and one purchased by John Riggs in Grand Bank—all had the unusual names *P.F. 39*, *P.F. 47* and *P.F. 49*.

Usually *P.F.* carried a crew of three, but since the lumber laden voyage from Bay D'Espoir to Fortune was to be the last for the season, Bobbie Roberts was landed at his home in Pushthrough. Despite an intensive search conducted mainly by the Newfoundland steamship *Cabot*, no trace of the Fortune ketch nor her remaining two crew, Captain George Mayo and Edward Thornhill, was ever found.

After the war, examination of German war records revealed the fate of the missing schooner *Douglas Haig*. She left St. John's in late January 1917 for Alicante, Spain, but had disappeared. *Douglas Haig* had been intercepted and sunk by an enemy sub on the first of February. All her South Coast crew were lost: Morgan and Thomas Eavis, Ramea; Alfred Eavis and his brother-in-law Ches Hickman of Grand Bank, and James Green, residence unknown.

Chapter Four

Era of the Tern Schooners

C ESSATION OF HOSTILITIES in war-torn, hungry Europe brought on a post war boom for the fish merchants of Newfoundland. Food, especially salt cured cod, was in short supply in Portugal, Spain and Greece.

On November 14, 1919, the tern schooner *Faustina*, launched that spring at Liverpool, Nova Scotia, for Penny's business of Ramea, was found floating bottom up near Bay Bulls. Captain Jesse Sibley and his five crew members—Ike Payne, John Joe Chambers, James Porter, Harry Warren, Ambrose Morris, all of Ramea—were missing and never seen again.

In this photo, salvagers, chains and straps straddle the overturned wreck in Bay Bulls harbour while divers prepare hoses and pumps to get water out.

To transport their product in greater quantities and in less time, tern schooners with three masts and a greater spread of sails seemed to be the answer. Most South Coast firms had these larger sailing vessels constructed either on the Burin Peninsula or in Nova Scotia.

FAUSTINA Twice a Derelict—Mystery and speculation surrounded the identity of an overturned derelict discovered on November 12, 1919, until it was eventually uprighted eight days later.

When the S.S. *Sable Island*, a Newfoundland passenger ship, arrived in St. John's on November 12, 1919, her captain reported a vessel bottom up about six miles due south of Cape Spear. In an attempt to determine the circumstances of the wreck or if anyone remained alive, *Sable Island*'s lifeboats were sent out, but high seas prevented anyone from boarding the hulk.

According to *Sable Island*'s Captain Murley, the wreck appeared to be new, about 200 tons and painted white with two spars floating nearby. A boom, broken in two places and entangled in the wreckage, was sticking up alongside, but no sign of life or bodies was seen. The hulk was down by the head and showed sixty feet of keel. Breaking seas prevented anyone from determining her name.

At first the derelict was thought to be the *Arnish*, a vessel owned by Flett and Company, abandoned off Newfoundland a few days before. Her crew had rowed into Fogo while the wreck drifted away.

On November 19 and 20, St. John's tug *John Green*, later joined by the *D.P. Ingraham*, attached lines to the wreck and towed it to Bay Bulls. By that time seas had abated and the vessel's name could be read—it was not the *Arnish* but the *Faustina*. Diver John Taylor, who entered the ship shortly after she was uprighted and partially pumped out, found no bodies.

When the uprighted *Faustina* was examined, it was discovered her three masts had been chopped off, probably with an axe. Contact with her owners, Penny's firm at Ramea, confirmed her identity and destination.

In late October she left Ramea via the route around the Avalon for St. Anthony where she was to take on a cargo of fish for Greece. At the time she may have been off the eastern Avalon there had been a severe storm. These two pieces of information—her location and recent weather conditions—led to the conclusion that *Faustina*'s salt cargo had shifted during the storm, she hove out on her beam ends and her masts were cut in hope that she could be brought on an even keel.

Later the *Faustina* was refitted and returned to Ramea. For many years, she sailed across the Atlantic without incident, until October 15, 1930, while on a voyage to Europe for Penny's business she had to be abandoned. Unlike the schooner's first abandonment in which no one lived to tell the tale, all the crew survived: Captain Steve White, a resident of Ramea, but born in Jersey Harbour, George Kendall, Joe Eavis of Ramea; Tom Coley, Fox Island; George Coombs, Fortune Bay and Julio Augustus, a resident of Ramea but originally from Portugal.

Faustina's final hours can best be told by Captain David B. Storey, who as a young sailor on the Red Star liner *S.S. Westernland*, helped deliver the weary crew from imminent death in the unfriendly Atlantic.

In October 1930, the S.S. *Westernland* was en route from Montreal to the Mediterranean. Storey, an apprentice sailor at age 19, was on his first trip to sea. As he tells it, "By mid-October cold, blustery winds, storms and high seas were beginning to make their debut." His ship had run into three successive days of gale force winds and mountainous seas.

About 9 a.m. on the morning of October 15, the third officer on watch sighted a dismasted vessel and notified the captain. He altered course to swing toward the troubled ship which proved to be a tern schooner practically sinking and ready to founder at any moment. She flew her ensign upside down, indicating distress.

According to seaman Storey, the schooner's several men stood on the poop deck of the schooner, the only dry space available as the decks were awash. *Westernland*'s captain called for volunteers to row the steamer's lifeboat to the rescue. Storey remembers:

> There were plenty of volunteers, including myself, with the chief officer going along in charge of operations. Due to the heavy swell it took us a long time to row the several hundred feet to the disabled schooner.
>
> Some difficulty was experienced in taking the luckless sailors off the schooner, as they were suffering from shock and exposure and were not in very fit condition to help themselves. However, in the operation we incurred no injury or loss of life.

Storey and the crew of the steamer *Westernland* soon learned the schooner was the *Faustina*, bound from Cadiz, Spain, to Newfoundland. She had been eighteen days out from Cadiz, about 800 miles west, but made little progress because of unfavourable weather. After shipping seas for many hours, the leaky *Faustina* began to settle in the water.

It was then the *Westernland* appeared on the horizon and the steamer steered a course almost directly in the path of the hapless Ramea schooner. Shortly

Crew of abandoned *Faustina* and some of their rescuers on the deck of the *Westerland*. Back row sitting,(l-r) Augustus, Eavis with cap in hand; Captain White with book; Coombs and Cole. Front row left is George Kandall.

after her crew was taken aboard, the *Faustina*, relentlessly pounded by the Atlantic, gave up its fight and slipped beneath the surface.

As a result of his bravery seaman Storey and the other members of the rescue team were awarded the Emile Robin Award as well as a silver medal and clasp from the Shipwrecked Mariners Society of Britain. In time David Storey became a captain, commanding such steamers as the S.S. *Cheticamp*, a newsprint carrier between Canada and the United States.

FALCON Wrecked on the Dune Sands—In 1919 Lake's business had their tern schooner, *Eileen Lake*, under construction in Fortune with John Lake as master builder. Since the work could not be finished without more material, in November the company sent the *Falcon*, an 80-ton two masted schooner, to Shelburne, Nova Scotia, for timber.

With her crew of Captain Tom Murphy, his son Ambrose, of Grand Bank; cook Harry Evans and two other Fortune sailors, the *Falcon* left Nova Scotia laden with hardwood pine planks. By December 11, Captain Murphy intended to head down Langlade Reach to Fortune, but a strong inset of northerly tide combined with strong wind pushed the schooner onto the treacherous western Dune Sands.

Not many schooners unlucky enough to strike the Dune Sands withstood the damage inflicted by its shores; like many others, the *Falcon* broke up. In the mishap Evans, a crippled, heavyset man, lost his life. After a heroic rescue by the Larranaga family, resident farmers of Langlade, who pulled the remaining crew to shore from the freezing waters, the exhausted men were cared for in the Larranaga farm home. As the *Falcon* went to pieces, much of pine plank cargo drifted ashore.

Not wanting to lose their valuable cargo, Lakes sent their schooner *Alice Lake*, skippered at this time by George 'Ki' Noseworthy of Fortune, to help salvage it. Pine planks were taken from the stormy western side of Dune Sands across to the eastern side, a more sheltered shore.

Noseworthy's crew and the men from the *Falcon* hired a team of horses from the Larranagas, hauled the timber across the narrow strip of sand and loaded it on the *Alice Lake*, anchored offshore. A small tern, the *Alice Lake* could not accommodate the long, heavy planks in her holds and the cargo was stacked on deck. After several trips from Langlade to Fortune, the hard pine was finally landed in Fortune and construction of the 164-ton *Eileen Lake* was completed.

Eileen Lake's life was short; on January 19, 1922, leaking and sinking, she was abandoned in the Atlantic. Captain Ki Noseworthy and his crew—Silas Blagdon, George Buffett, Reuben Galton and cook George Forsey—on a bitterly cold winter's night, took to the lifeboats and rowed for the nearest land, St. Pierre, over sixty miles away.

Wet, cold and hungry, the shipwrecked men rowed for three days and nights in an open boat until they were sighted by the Belgian steamer *Persian*. By that time it was already too late for Forsey, who had died of exposure the night before.

Abandonment of the GERTRUDE—Before the year 1919 ended another Fortune schooner went to the bottom. *Gertrude* headed to Fortune with a cargo of Sydney coal, sailing into the full force of a midwinter storm. Seas swept the schooner's deck continuously, damaging the steering gear. Soon the *Gertrude*'s seams opened under the strain of seas and the weight of coal.

Captain Brushett ordered his men to the pumps making every effort to save his sinking schooner. About 30 miles southeast of St. Pierre, a freighter was sighted, the S.S. *Watuka*. *Watuka* answered the distressed schooner's signals for help and, despite the heavy seas, succeeding in rescuing the entire crew—Brushett, mate Berkley Morris, cook Israel Buffett, seamen Wesley Pierce and Thomas Bemister. The latter four were Fortune residents.

Watuka, an ore carrier, continued to Bell Island; Gertrude's men arrived in St. John's from Bell Island on the S.S. *Mary* on December 23, 1919. Morris survived this wreck, but disappeared five years later with his shipmates, Captain Robert Hollett, Morgan Hollett, Max Adams and Max Batten, when the Burin schooner *Roy Bruce* was cut down in mid-ocean in March 1924.

Most towns along the South Coast depended on small schooners like the *Gertrude* to bring food and supplies from mainland ports; the vessels usually made these voyages during the late fall after the fishing season ended. Averaging twenty to forty tons, they served several purposes: they carried fish collected from the small towns to the larger centres; they transported food, supplies and other basic necessities of life, and they also carried an occasional passenger to and from the isolated communities.

So it was with the *Louis H.*, owned in Bay L'Argent by Thomas West and built at Little Bay, Fortune Bay, in 1906. West's cargoes were provisions and passengers carried from Grand Bank to Bay L'Argent and around Fortune Bay. On her last voyage the schooner had sailed from Sydney with provisions to Belleoram, discharged some cargo there and on December 23, 1919, continued to Stone's Cove. That evening she was tied securely to the Stone's Cove wharf; her crew and passengers, including some young girls who attended school in Belleoram and were now returning home, had gone ashore.

Courtesy of Michael Harrington

D. P. Ingraham standing by the wrecked *Elizabeth Fearn*. The 246-ton *Elizabeth Fearn* went ashore at Quidi Vidi. Captain Vatcher and his 8 crewmen rowed ashore safely.

During the night the wind intensified. The next morning, to the residents' surprise, the *Louis H.* was gone; apparently, she had drifted out the harbour and disappeared. Examination of the mooring lines showed them to be chafed and broken.

Despite inquiries throughout Fortune Bay and beyond, the fate of the schooner could not be determined. No one had salvaged or even seen the vessel. The easterly wind must have blown her out of sight of land and probably she struck a rock and sank.

ELIZABETH FEARN, D.P. INGRAHAM A Tug and her Tow—Built in Placentia in 1917 by Palfreys, the tern schooner *Elizabeth Fearn*, having completed a stormy voyage from Bahia, Brazil, grounded at 5:00 a.m. on February 12, 1921, near Quidi Vidi. The steam tug *D.P. Ingraham*, sent to assist the *Fearn* and perhaps pull her off, could do nothing. Shallow water prevented the tug from getting too close and the tern quickly broke up.

Tug *D.P. Ingraham*, built in 1864 in Philadelphia with the best American white oak, was owned by the Newfoundland Tug Co. operating out of St. John's. She had several associations with South Coast vessels; in 1907 she had searched Fortune Bay unsuccessfully for the missing schooner *Vesta*. On December 5, 1921, the *Ingraham* towed the coal-laden Grand Bank tern schooner *Jean & Mary* down the Straight Shore on Newfoundland's Northeast coast.

During a violent storm that night the tug was wrecked with no loss of life on North Penguin Island— her tow, the *Jean & Mary* was lost with crew on South Penguin Island: James "Di" Francis, Henry Lee and John Gould, Grand Bank; Charlie Follett and William Tapper, Grand Beach; Captain Abe Tom Cluett of Belleoram.

Escape from Death on the SPARKLING GLANCE—
Belleoram, a town on the west side of Fortune Bay, has
a history dating back to the early years of the eighteenth
century and possibly earlier. The French once used the
area around Belleoram extensively and referred to it on
their maps as Bande de l'Arriere. With the signing of the
Treaty of Paris in 1713, the French were forced to leave
and the English settlers called the harbour Belorme's
Place, after an early French family who once lived there.

Famed English explorer and cartographer Captain
James Cook mapped the area in 1765, noting Belleoram
as "...a very small but a snug place and conveniently
situated for the cod fishery...." The early economy, as
today, depended on the fishery and one of the first firms
to extensively catch, cure and export cod was John
Penny's business.

Belleoram, a picturesque town, shown in the heyday of sail. Many seamen of this port had trying
experiences with the sea. One well-remembered tragedy, told in story and song was that of the
Belleoram-built tern *John Harvey*.

On January 10, 1912, she grounded on an offshore ledge at Gabarus, Nova Scotia. Two young
Belleoram men, John Foote and John Keeping, died of exposure after taking a line to the shore so as
Captain George Kearley and the rest of the crew could reach land safely.

The bank fishery at Belleoram reached its peak in 1908 when eighteen vessels, many owned by St. John's business Harvey and Company, employing 282 men, sailed out of the harbour.

By 1937 Harvey's had terminated its Belleoram operations; the store and remaining vessels taken over by W. G. Nott who in turn sold out to R. Drake. Other businesses—J. M. Fudge, Burdock and Son, and Kearley Brothers—continued to wrest a living from the cod fishery up to the nineteen fifties.

It is said that any town which sends a fleet of vessels to the sea pays a price in lost and missing ships and men. Belleoram, with its long maritime association, has many tales of hardship, tragedy and heroism, especially in the age of sail.

One of the most thrilling escapes from death on the ocean was told by a crew of Belleoram sailors: Captain Reginald Keeping, navigator Harold Baker, James Buffett, William Cluett, Samuel Poole, Stanley Bond, and Henry Carter. Their schooner was the three-year-old Shelburne built *Sparkling Glance*, a 217-ton tern owned by Harvey and Company of St. John's, although Benjamin Keeping of Belleoram managed the schooner's business.

Early in February 1921, the *Sparkling Glance* left Belleoram laden with 4,000 quintals of fish destined for Oporto. Progress was fine until she ran into a spate of mid-ocean storms on the 5th of February. All that night hurricane force winds howled, but Captain Keeping kept her head into the wind and waves. Keeping hoped that by the next morning the weather would moderate. Cook Carter later told of the storm and the damage it did to the *Sparkling Glance*:

Such a blizzard never raged as it did that morning. During the awful storm the ship's bowsprit rigging was torn to shreds and carried away. Immediately afterward the schooner became unmanageable as a result of her rudder being completely smashed.

When the crew realized the terrible predicament they were in, signals of distress were put up to the masthead. They knew help had to come soon or they would never see home again. Every mountainous sea that tore down on the doomed craft made her tremble from stem to stern, then wallow in the trough only to be lifted on each succeeding foam capped wave.

The drenched sailors somehow managed to keep themselves from being washed overboard by clinging to the rigging. Eating was out of the question and nothing was consumed for two days. The cabin, flooded with water, had some soggy food, but it was impossible for the men to get to it. As the storm abated somewhat, the seven weary men snatched a few moments of sleep.

Clearing weather continued until the eighth of February. Captain Keeping in the meantime managed to improvise a device to steer the rudderless schooner. That afternoon the storm broke again with renewed fury. At daybreak, each man knew the *Sparkling Glance* was on her last hours.

Flare signals, in the form of signal fires on the masthead, and flareguns were kept going in the hope that some steamer would see them. Then to the relief of the apparently doomed men, their signals were answered by a bright flare from some ship a mile or so distant. Throughout the terrible night of February 9, the two bobbing craft on the wild ocean kept in contact by means of signals.

At daylight, a lifeboat from the *Liberty Lord* battled the elements for an hour until the fatigued crew left the

Sparkling Glance. Keeping, before abandoning ship, set fire to the schooner so that the derelict would not be a menace to navigation. The *Sparkling Glance* went to the bottom at 46.52 North latitude, 37.28 West longitude, about 650 miles southeast of St. John's.

Liberty Lord landed the shipwrecked sailors at Bermuda. Later in February they arrived in St. John's, Newfoundland, where they joined the steamer *Kyle* en route to the South Coast and finally reached home on March 9, 1921.

For Captain Keeping and his navigator Harold Baker this was the third shipwreck in four years: in 1917 their schooner *Thomas* was destroyed by German subs, the *William Morton* went to the bottom in 1918 and now they had again escaped the hungry ocean while abandoning the *Sparkling Glance*.

ELSIE Ordeal by Frost

—Fourteen years later another shipwreck nearly resulted in tragedy for Belleoram crewmen when the *Elsie* sank off St. Pierre.

Built in 1910 in the Arthur Storey yards at Essex, the 106-foot long *Elsie* netted ninety tons. Designed for speed to and from the banks and for racing, in 1931 the *Elsie* competed for the International Fishermen's Trophy Race held annually between Canada and the United States. By 1934 she had outlived her usefulness as an American banking schooner and was sold to Captain Levi Kearley of Belleoram.

In December Kearley brought herring to Gloucester; by January 13, 1935, the *Elsie* headed back to Belleoram striking the usual winter storms. Five days of successive heavy seas and high winds pounded the schooner and on the 18th, she began to leak. Pumps failed, seams opened near the stern and Kearley and his five men, after pumping for nine hours without a break, abandoned ship in two dories.

In a biting northerly wind which constantly sprayed cold sea water over the men, they set out for the nearest land—St. Pierre forty-eight miles away. During the ordeal one dory was abandoned and the seamen crowded into the other. On the night of January 21, after two days at the oars, they arrived at the French Islands. They were close to death by exposure and had to be carried to the hospital.

All suffered from frozen hands and feet—Horatio Kearley had to remain under medical care for some time. Captain Kearley's feet were so badly swollen and scarred he was unable to put on shoes until August.

COUNTY OF RICHMOND Lost with crew—On February 21, 1921, this message of another major tragedy came over the wireless from the South Coast of Newfoundland and was received by the Deputy of Customs at St. John's:

> Schooner *County of Richmond*, St. John's to Burgeo, found about 7 miles from Ramea with only her stern out of water. She has been sighted here since the 14th, but too stormy for anything to get there. No sign of the crew.

Built in Johnstown, Cape Breton, Nova Scotia, in 1919, the 245-ton tern schooner *County of Richmond* had been bought by J. T. Moulton's business of Burgeo. In the overseas trade it was well known that the *County of Richmond* carried her load of fish well, but was not a fast sailer.

According to reports out of St. John's the tern left St. John's headed for her home port in company with another of Moulton's terns, the *Gordon E. Moulton*. The

Moulton, with Stephen Collier, master, arrived in five days and everyone expected the *County* to return within a day or so. Both schooners had been together off Placentia Bay, two days before.

Then a partly submerged derelict was sighted anchored, full of water, a little south of South East Rocks near Ramea. Suspicions that the waterlogged hulk was the missing tern later proved to be correct and it was assumed the *County of Richmond* had struck rocks off Ramea. Her crew had apparently left for land in their boat but drowned getting there.

Lost, almost within sight of their Burgeo homes, were: Captain Leonard Hare and his little son who had gone with his father on the trip; cook Norman Hare; mate Wilson Spencer and his brother Charles; a relative of the captain, James Hare; and Joe Benson. All were Burgeo residents except Benson; he belonged to Portugal and had joined the schooner to visit his homeland on the *County*'s final and tragic voyage to and from Portugal. Several days later the derelict drifted to land breaking up along the rugged shore.

As for the *Gordon E. Moulton*, built in 1919 in Dayspring, Nova Scotia, she survived the rigours of the Atlantic for another three years. In early March 1924, the Newfoundland coastal steamer *Glencoe* discovered her afire and abandoned twenty miles off Burgeo; Captain Steven Collier and his Burgeo crew had rowed safely ashore.

NINA LEE, QUEENIE B and Other Victims of the Deep—The 1920s saw the loss of many schooners: for example, in a three month period from December 1920 to March 1921, sixteen foreign-going Newfoundland vessels were abandoned in the Atlantic. Two were lost with all crew—the *County of Richmond* and Samuel

Harris' *General Horne*, out of Grand Bank. In December 1920, while en route from Catalina to Change Islands, a short run often made by fishermen in open trap skiffs, the *General Horne* capsized with the loss of seven crew.

Fifteen days out from Oporto, Portugal, another of Samuel Harris' schooners, *Queenie B*, ran into stormy weather. This vessel, built only two years before at Belleoram, netted eighty-three tons.

For eight days she ran before a heavy April wind with a jury, or makeshift, foresail since all her canvas had blown away. *Queenie B* was sinking when the S.S. *British Marshall*, bound for Texas, saw the wreck and rescued the crew. Waterlogged and laden with salt, the *Queenie B* went under at 37.5 North, 44.9 West. Weary but otherwise none the worse for their experience, the five men were landed at Bermuda and then set sail for Saint John, New Brunswick, on the steamship *Chaudiere*, arriving there early May 1921.

Nina Lee was once owned by the Foote business of Grand Bank and called after the daughter of her captain, Harry Lee. Foote's had sold this schooner to a St. John's business several years before. A seventy-nine-ton, ninety-foot long vessel built in Allendale, Nova Scotia, in 1913 she was bound from Piraeus, Greece, where she had discharged fish. On November 29, 1921, the *Nina Lee* was wrecked in the Mediterranean Sea.

On October 31, 1921, the banker *Linda Pardy* drove ashore at Moria Gut near Sydney, Nova Scotia, while under the command of Captain Peter Mullins of Harbour Breton. The sixty-nine-ton *Linda Pardy* was originally owned in Grand Bank by Fred Pardy who later sold her to Mullins with shares held by Salter's business of North Sydney. While trying to make North Sydney, she encountered heavy winds and anchored off False Bay Beach. Her anchors dragged and the schooner was driven up on the beach.

Around ten years later, Peter Mullins; his two sons, Roland and Ronald; James Tibbo and cook Fred Moores of Jersey Harbour disappeared while returning to Harbour Breton from a fishing trip in Sydney Bight. His schooner was the twenty-one-ton *Martha E*, built in Marystown in 1906 and owned in Burin. Although it was thought the wreck happened near Isle aux Morts, no debris or other indication of the fate of the men and ship was ever positively known.

A Bumper Catch for the MARION BELLE WOLFE— In 1922, when the fishing season ended, Captain John Thornhill had broken all catch records up to that time when he landed a total of 6500 quintals of fish at La-Have, Nova Scotia, from April to September, in the schooner *Marion Belle Wolfe*.

Marion Belle Wolfe, a ten-dory banker, had a late start at fishing that year. Usually the first trip to the

Courtesy of PANL

Perhaps one of the most unusual pictures taken of a schooner, the *Marion Belle Wolfe* anchored in Burin harbour with a home displaced in the November 29, 1929, tidal wave tied to her main boom and stern. In 1933 this vessel was sold to Barbados; her eventual fate is unknown.

banks was under way by early to mid-March, but for some reason it was on or about April 10th before Thornhill left Grand Bank to begin his season. His first stop was St. Pierre for supplies. One popular ship broker on the French Islands was the Folquet Brother's firm and when Thornhill transacted business there he inquired how other banking schooners frequenting St. Pierre were faring. Folquet told him he had heard of good fishing on the southern edge of the Grand Banks.

Acting on that sound advice Thornhill sailed the *Marion Belle Wolfe* south southeast for 240 miles to the area the bank fishermen called 'muddy grounds.' The banking schooner arrived at night. While the men baited up gear, filled the trawl tubs and dories, and waited for daylight, Captain Thornhill prepared a handline with several baited hooks on it and dropped the line to the bottom. This would indicate if fish were plentiful.

When it was pulled up, there was a large fish on each hook. It is said that the dorymen slept for 8 hours from Monday to Saturday, but caught up on sleep on Sunday since, as was the custom, no fishing was done on that day.

After the dories came back to the schooner with their bounty there was still no rest; the fish had to be dressed and salted away in the holds. When schooners like the *Wolfe* were into good catches the weary men grew delirious from lack of rest. At the splitting tables set up on the deck of the schooner some strange yet amusing actions happened.

One man knocked on the splitting table with his knuckles and called out "Jennie" several times. He later explained he thought he was home rapping on the door and calling to his wife to let him in. Another man bent over half asleep weaved his knife back and forth in a split cod. Someone asked what he was doing and he sheepishly said that he was cutting out a pattern for his daughter's dress. Another was seen throwing away the fish and saving the heads and guts. The ship's mascot dog lay down on the quarter deck causing one man to say, "If that man can lie down and have a nap, then so can I" and no one could convince him otherwise.

Thornhill's crew had salted away 1900 quintals when the *Marion Belle Wolfe* was forced to return to Newfoundland to replenish food supplies and to get fresh bait.

Thornhill landed at Epworth, near Burin, and wired Grand Bank to say he had 1900 quintals. The telegraph operator wired back asking if there was some mistake in the number. While in Epworth one of his crewmen asked Captain Thornhill how deep the schooner lay in the water. He took out his matches and placed one over her side, showing the water was one match length from her scuppers.

Another LaHave schooner was in Grand Bank; Thornhill went there to tranfer a thousand quintals to the LaHave schooner. *Marion Belle Wolfe* quickly left for the productive grounds again. Thornhill made several voyages to southern edge of the Grand Banks, bringing in bumper loads each time. During that particular summer, Thornhill was paid, through the LaHave business, the captain's share of one dollar per quintal of cod landed giving him $6,500; while the dorymen on the *Marion Belle Wolfe* cleared $600 a man.

Thornhill's prowess as a banker captain enabled him, with his earnings, to buy part shares in another LaHave banker, the *Vera P. Thornhill*, named for his daughter. John Thornhill thus became one of the few fishing captains on the South Coast who was a vessel shareholder. Skill, hard work, fierce determination and

Marion Belle Wolfe, in the fall of 1922, with fish caught by hook and line on deck. This schooner, captained by John Thornhill, a veteran fishkiller born on Brunette Island, Fortune Bay, landed her fish at LaHave, Nova Scotia.

a relentless motivation of his men soon put the *Vera P. Thornhill* and other schooners commanded by Thornhill at the top of the cod fishing fleet.

Thornhill was a major shareholder in this LaHave banker and landed his catches at Grand Bank. Whenever the *Vera P.* sailed into Fortune Bay heavily laden with fish, he would have his ship's flags flying, indicating another good trip. But fish was not the only product Captain Thornhill brought into Grand Bank harbour.

In 1917, when Thornhill was building the Thorndyke, as he called his spacious home, he had heard reports of an abandoned schooner drifting somewhere between the French Islands and the South Coast of Newfoundland. He set out to find it.

A day or two later he came into harbour towing the derelict *Sadie Holmes*; a schooner laden with building materials from Quebec—a substantial amount of which went into Thornhill's new house. After her usable cargo had been salvaged, the *Sadie Holmes* was pulled up on a beach near Grand Bank and eventually went to pieces.

Chapter Five

Going to Davey Jones' Locker

T HE YEAR 1923 began with the wreck of a fine South Coast schooner, but before the year ended it was only one in a virtual epidemic of ship losses.

CLINTONIA's Crew Asked to Jump Overboard— When Captain Gillies of the transatlantic liner *Empress of Scotland* was called to bridge to observe another ship not far away, he saw a waterlogged schooner about five miles off. She flew her ensign upside down—a signal of distress—with her sails shredded and bulwarks washed away.

Empress of Scotland left Southampton, England, for New York in mid-January 1923 with 127 passengers. About 100 miles south of Sable Island, after steaming near the wallowing schooner, Captain Gillies asked Chief Officer McMurray with ten seamen to row over in a lifeboat. At the time the sea was heavy, but little wind.

It was the *Clintonia*, a two-masted schooner sailing out of Belleoram and captained by Aaron Kearley of Belleoram. As officer McMurray neared the sinking schooner, he saw that waves were breaking over the *Clintonia* as she lay so low in the water. The rescuers could not reach the schooner without jeopardizing their own safety.

Clintonia's six men were asked if they could jump into the water and be pulled to the lifeboat. This they agreed to and lines were thrown over. Each man tied on the rope and was pulled through the sea to the liner's boat. Before the last man, Captain Kearley, left he set fire to his schooner.

Chief Officer McMurray reported that it was dangerous rowing back to the liner in a head sea, but his men were excellent sailors. It was not considered safe to hoist the lifeboat up the davits again, so it was abandoned. Rescue at sea was not new for McMurray; several years before he had been given a silver cup by the Emperor of Japan for saving the crew of a sinking Japanese steamship in Formosa Channel during a Pacific typhoon.

The six Belleoram men were able to climb the ladder to the ship's deck. After a cleanup and a hot meal, they were in good shape. Kearley told how the *Clintonia*, bound from Fortune Bay to Halifax with a cargo of salt fish, had her seams opened by a severe gale and was pushed out to sea. By January 29, 1919, they arrived in New York.

BOHEMIA, GLADYS M. HOLLETT Crushed by Ice—Arctic pack ice rarely drifts as far south and west as Fortune Bay and the South Coast; however, the spring of 1923 was an exception. From late February to April, great pans of ice filled the Atlantic south of the Avalon Peninsula and into Fortune Bay. Coastal steamers were unable to get through the ice jam to land mail or food, and some communities ran short of the necessities of life.

In April 1923, four Newfoundland schooners went to the bottom as a result of encounters with the extreme ice conditions: the *A.B. Barteau, Rita M. Cluett, Bohemia* and the *Gladys M. Hollett,* the latter three owned on the South Coast.

Bohemia had been found ice bound and sinking by the American schooner *Admiral Drake* off Green Bank. Owned by Samuel Harris of Grand Bank, the *Bohemia* was set afire and abandoned on March 18. Her crew were later transferred to the S.S. *Arawa* en route to Nova Scotia.

While travelling from Louisbourg to St. John's in the spring of 1923 the steamship *Sable Island* came upon the icebound schooner *Gladys M. Hollett* about 36 miles southwest of Cape Race. Owned in Burin by W. and T. Hollett, the *Gladys M. Hollett* slid off the ways from McKay's yards at Shelburne. At 122 feet in overall length and 203 tons, this tern was one of the first to be equipped with gasoline driven deck engines.

On the day this vessel was launched, May 10, 1917, there were five Newfoundland master mariners present: sealing veteran Abraham Kean and Captain Lodge of the *Little Stephano;* merchant William Forsey of Grand Bank; Captain Abe Tom Cluett and Hollett, owner of the *Gladys M. Hollett.*

A year later in an encounter with a German U-boat off Halifax, Captain Cluett, mate Mike Brown and her crew were ordered off the *Hollett* and the vessel shelled. She fell over on her side but did not sink. After the crew had rowed to Halifax and reported the incident, the schooner was towed in and repaired.

Five years later she went down in the Atlantic westbound to Newfoundland. The salt-laden *Gladys M. Hollett* was sixty-five days out from Oporto headed to her home port when she became stuck in Arctic drift ice in mid-March. For weeks the schooner was battered in floes until planks near her bow weakened and she began to leak.

Hollett's Captain Brown, presumably the same Brown who was mate during the U-boat incident, ordered the crew to man the pumps continuously. On March 29, water in her holds was four feet high; the next day it was discovered the schooner's rudder case had split. After the *Gladys M. Hollett's* crew was provisioned by the steamer, for during the time they were ice-bound food had run short, a tow line was attached in the hope the schooner could be saved. The men worked hard to save their ship, but the final blow came when the tow hawser from the *Sable Island* to the waterlogged vessel parted. Captain Brown decided to abandon ship.

Taking whatever personal belongings they could, the Burin crew lowered the dory while her captain prepared to set her afire. When the *Sable Island* came back to re-attach the towrope, she picked up the weary mariners and took them to St. John's.

Loss of the RITA M. CLUETT—If any decade had to be chosen as the most devastating years for the loss of schooners, it would have to be the 1920s. By 1923 local papers were despairing over the disappearance of Newfoundland's foreign-going schooners. An editorial in *Evening Telegram* of April 7, 1923, claimed: "During the past couple of years Newfoundland's foreign fleet has been sadly depleted and unless we get better times, the losses will scarcely be made good. The latest to go to Davey Jones' Locker is the splendid schooner *Rita M. Cluett.*"

The article went on to say no one even knew this particular tern was in difficulty until messages came through the Cape Race Marconi Station stating that she had been abandoned and set afire at latitude 39.55 N., longitude 55.51 W.

Red Cross liner *Rosalind* spoke with the beleaguered tern about 135 miles West Southwest of Cape Race, supplied her with food and water and sailed on. Then the storm stripped her sails and rigging, broke the rudder and water seeped into opened seams. Food again ran short and the *Rita* had to be abandoned.

Eight other vessels passed without answering signal flares, until the *President Fillmore* came by. All rescued crewmen were well except crewman Louis Mills. According to the message from the *Fillmore* to Cape Race, although he was seriously ill, it was hoped his life could be saved.

The eighty-five-ton *Rita M. Cluett* had been built in Shelburne, Nova Scotia, in 1917, and was conjointly owned by Steven Vatcher Cluett of Belleoram and Harvey & Co., St. John's. When abandoned she was westbound from Oporto with a cargo of salt.

Captain Randell of the *President Fillmore* later contacted the American cutter *Tampa* bound to Halifax and the shipwrecked crew—Captain J.F. Cluett, mate John Buffett, cook William Evans, John Dodge, Charles Blagdon and Mills—was transferred to the inbound ship. Mills later recovered in the Halifax Victoria General Hospital.

By early October an intense wind storm swept along the South coast and left several wrecks in its wake: on October 3, 1923, the *Norman W. Strong*, owned by James Strong Ltd. and captained by Fred Wiseman, was wrecked off Castle Hyde near Little St. Lawrence; the *Natalie J. Nelson*, owned by Steven Fudge formerly of Belleoram, piled onto the rocks at St. Pierre on the sixth; and the next day, George Bennett of Port au Bras lost his

Courtesy Yvonne Andrieux

The *Natalie J. Nelson*, built in 1903 at Essex, Massachusetts. On the black rocks of Pointe Blanche, St. Pierre, the *Natalie J. Nelson* lies broken in half. A schooners grounded at high tide usually broke in two when the tide fell and her weight was not supported by water.
Nelson's debris, included part of her cargo of illegal liquor she was carrying, lies between the schooner and the shore.

schooner the *Alice Roberts*, when she was wrecked near Burin.

Fortune's Unsung Hero of the VERA B—The wake of a South Coast schooner, in the owner's quest for cargoes and work, took them to many ports along the eastern seaboard. In the fall of 1923, the 60-ton schooner *Vera B* sailed from North Sydney for the Magdalen Islands in the Gulf of St. Lawrence with a cargo of coal. Her captain and owner Hezekiah Gillard had two crew from his home town of Fortune: mate Saul Mosher; cook Hedley Snook; seaman John Warren hailed from St. Barbe. *Vera B* was built in Wesleyville, Bonavista Bay, in 1914.

On October 23, the vessel met with a wild storm and Gillard decided to make for Cheticamp, Nova Scotia, or some other haven between Nova Scotia and Prince Edward Island. He and his crew reduced sail: single reefed riding and foresail and let her run through the stormy night. Sometime throughout the storm the *Vera B* missed the harbour. That night the crew dropped anchor to try to ride out the wind until morning when their exact position would be determined.

In the night the wind veered, forcing Captain Gillard to change tactics. Anchor chains were slipped to let her drive ashore, hopefully on a beach. But the *Vera B* grounded far from shore.

With the tremendous seas sweeping her decks all the four men could do was climb the rigging. For six hours they waited for the seas to abate somewhat. A life-saving station could be seen some distance away, but due to breakers rolling on the shore, little help would come from there.

Gillard said, "I don't see any chance of saving our lives unless we loose the spars and try to get ashore on the wreckage."

Hedley Snook saw a solution. "Captain," he said, "if you lash me to a lifebuoy, I'll try to get to land." Gillard was doubtful, but finally agreed.

Snook, young and strong at age twenty-two, reassured his captain. "It's just as well to take the risk as it is to stay here and perish in the rigging." With those words, after waiting for three big seas to pass by, he said good-bye to his shipmates, jumped over the side into the boiling sea and made for shore.

Snook was driven under, rolled and tossed, beaten to shore on the rollers tumbling onto the rocks, but finally made land more dead than alive. When he regained consciousness he found himself in bed in the home of a French Canadian family named Ludley.

All at once he remembered the wreck and by some superhuman effort dragged himself to the well-intended rescuers on the beach. He made them understand he wanted a stronger rope attached to the line he had brought ashore. The heavy rope was attached to a dory which Gillard, Mosher and Warren pulled to the *Vera B*.

Only one man could come at a time: Warren first, then Mosher and Gillard pulled the dory back; finally the captain was left alone to pull the heavy dory back to the wreck. It was hours before all were safe on shore where residents cared for them. None received the battering Hedley Snook endured.

Vera B eventually went to pieces. The last three off the wreck went home, but Snook remained in a Halifax hospital all the winter of 1923-24. While there he had sand and kelp pumped from his stomach. In April he returned to Fortune where the resident doctor at Grand Bank treated him for some time.

After three months in other hospitals, he was finally pronounced fit and able to continue his sea-going life—almost a full year from the time of his heroic deeds. However Hedley Snook never fully recovered from his ordeal and he received no medals or recognition for his selfless bravery, only the satisfaction of doing what he could in a seemingly hopeless situation, saving his own life and the lives of three others.

On January 14, 1924, the schooner *Annie M. Parker* was abandoned at sea while on route to Burin from Oporto, Portugal. Built in 1901 at Essex, the 100-ton vessel had been purchased by Gabriel Hollett in 1920. The owner put her in charge of Captain Joseph Hollett of Great Burin with a man named Hoben, cook. On her final voyage two calamities struck: her crew developed smallpox and a severe snow storm blew the *Annie M. Parker* out to sea just as she was within sight of her home port.

In the prolonged battle with the elements and disease, one of the crew died and was buried at sea. Battered into submission, the *Parker* sank hours after the *S.S. Grooteneyk*, a liner bound for Holland came by. Upon arrival in port, the rescued crew were detained in hospital.

ARGOS A Norwegian Ship Lost at Burin—Cat Island near Burin was the scene of a shipwreck on June 22, 1925, when the *Argos* stranded there while en route from Argentia to Canada.

Formerly called the *Salen*, the 1586-ton Swedish ship *Argos* was built in 1899 and owned in Gothenborg, Sweden. She was 313-feet long, over twenty feet deep and used to carry coal from Wales to Newfoundland's rail and steamer depots.

After discharging coal at Argentia, the *Argos* sailed for Miramichi, New Brunswick, to load logs for England. On the night of sailing, it was dark with very little sea running although fog was dense. About twelve-thirty while travelling at a moderate speed she grounded on Cat Island, near Burin. Immediately *Argos* began to sink by the head.

Argos' crew took to the boats. Not being familiar with the coast, they were unable to land and stayed in the vicinity of the ship all night. At daylight, seeing their ship had not settled any farther, they again boarded the wreck. Little could be done to save the ship. Officers quartered in the aft of the ship collected their belongings, but the sailors who slept in the forward part lost all they had.

The crew then rowed to Burin where the people took them in with all kindness. Captain Bengtson wired the following message to Newfoundland's Deputy of Customs:

Forehold and engine room full of water; after
bulkhead holding stern of ship afloat. Have wired
to get *Argyle* to try and tow ship off and to safely.

The S.S. *Argyle* failed in her attempt to move the
Argos, for by this time everything forward from the
bridge was under water. Bengtson and his men left for
Argentia and then to St. John's.

Late the next day, June 29, after the *Argyle* left, local
salvagers went aboard the wreck. Many of the ship's
fixtures had already been removed when, without
warning, the ship broke in two, slipped off the ledge
and sank. Still on board were Fred Abbott and Bert
Thorne of Port au Bras; Richard Moulton and James
Dicks of Burin Bay—all went down with the *Argos*. Two
bodies, Dicks and Moulton, were recovered; the other
two were in the ship, now lying in ten fathoms of water.

HUBERT MACK Drifts out of Fortune—On October
26, 1925, another vessel succumbed to the rocky shores
of the Burin Peninsula. A two-masted cutwater
schooner built in 1908 at Fortune, the *Hubert Mack* was
tied onto the Fortune wharf laden with Sydney coal for
her owners, Johnny Paul and William Keeping; Paul
skippered the *Mack* with Keeping as his mate.

A northwest gale came up, surging the schooner
back and forth until she parted her lines. One of her
crewmen, Fred Mario, a Portuguese sailor who had
stowed away years before and at that time lived in
Fortune, was on the *Hubert Mack*. Mario, the last man
aboard, jumped ashore on the eastern wharf as the
schooner drifted out the harbour. *Hubert Mack* stranded
and broke up in First Gulch about one mile east of
Fortune.

Abandonment of the MAXWELL HORTON, BIEN-VILLE

On the next page, the log of the *S.S. Dakarian* dated March 28, 1926, describes abandonment of the Grand Bank tern *Max Horton*.

6.00 p.m.
28/3/26 Lat. 40.32.N. Long 47.36.W. (approximate)
Observed schooner to northward flying signals of distress.

Bore down towards her she proved to be the schooner *"Max Horton"* official No. 138832 of St. John's, Newfoundland from Cadiz with salt ballast, bound to Burin, Newfoundland.

The crew had already left their vessel in their boat and were taken on board.

The Master, Heber Keeping reports having experienced heavy westerly gales and the schooner's rudder post broken since March 18th. The vessel becoming unmanageable and leaking and fearing vessel foundering should another gale spring up, it was agreed by the master and crew to abandon ship while there was a chance of rescue.

She was therefore set on fire to avoid her becoming a menace to navigation.

The following is a full list of the Crew: Six in number. Heber Keeping, Master; James Whiteway, Mate; Benjamin Clarke, Cook-Steward; George Witherall, Sailor; Charles Clark, Sailor; Benjamin Riggs, Sailor; T. J. Mercer, Master; G. Bonfeld, Mate.

Signed Heber Keeping, Master (*"Max Horton"*); James Whiteway, Mate (*"Max Horton"*).

... ny 1 entry in Official Log Book. s/s. *Dakarian* 145891.

... ... Lat. 110. 37. N. Long 17.36. W. (approximate)

Observed schooner to northward flying signals of distress.
Bore down towards her, she proved to be the Schooner "Max Horton"
Official No. 138832 of St Johns, Newfoundland from Cadiz with
salt ballast, bound to Burin Newfoundland.
The crew had already left their vessel in their boat and were
taken on board.
The Master, Heber Keeping reports having experienced heavy
Westerly gales and the Schooner's rudder post broken since
March 18th the vessel becoming unmanageable and leaking
and fearing vessel foundering should another gale spring
up, it was agreed by the Master and crew to abandon ship
while there was a chance of rescue.
She was therefore set on fire to avoid her becoming a menace
to navigation.
The following is a full list of the crew: Six in number.
Heber Keeping, Master. James Whiteway, Mate. Benjamin Clark, Cook-Steward.
George Withers, Sailor. Charles Clark, Sailor and Benjamin Riggs, Sailor.

Signed
{
F. J. Mercer.   Master
J. Bonfield   Mate.
Heber Keeping   Master ("Max Horton")
James Whiteway   Mate ("Max Horton")
}

Copies of this entry have been furnished to the Master of the "Max Horton"
and the following signatures appended:—

Copies
{
Heber Keeping   Master
James Whiteway   Mate
Benjamin Clark   Cook-Steward
George Withers   Sailor
Charles Clark   Sailor
Benjamin Riggs   Sailor.
}

Copy of log entry of S.S. *Dakarian*

South Coast schooners have been visiting the French islands of St. Pierre and Miquelon for centuries. Many schooners were lost on its rocky shores; few French schooners were wrecked on Newfoundland shores near St. Pierre. However on December 13, 1926, *Bienville*, a vessel of 160 tons and built in 1919, owned by C. P. Chartier and Company of St. Pierre, went ashore at Point May near Lamaline on the Burin Peninsula with the loss of one life.

Madeline Stacey, a resident of Point May, remembered the incident:

> When I was a young girl and still in school a ship called the *Bienville* came ashore. She was carrying half general cargo and half liquor from France to St. Pierre. There came a gale here along the land and blew all her sails away. She was blown ashore and wrecked.
>
> The first crewman to come ashore was a sixteen year old boy known on the ship as a 'mousse', a crewman assigned to do the cleaning jobs on ship. The boy jumped from the ship even though he was warned not to because the *Bienville* was still moving toward shore and his chances to get off safely would be better. He was carried to my father's house (Michael Hennebury) where spent two weeks recuperating from an injured knee. One man was swept overboard about 500 yards off Short's Cove, near Point May. His body was recovered the next morning by men from Point May: Joseph Hennebury, Thomas Stacey and Thomas Cousins.
>
> My father had two barns—one big enough to keep 15 head of cattle. They took out the cattle and shifted them to the small stable. The big one was packed full from top to bottom with liquor. There were two big stores down on Lories Beach and they

were packed full and there must have been 50
puncheons of wine besides.

Constable Daniel Wade of the Newfoundland Constabulary stationed at St. Lawrence—for Point May was
under Wade's jurisdiction—came to guard the shipment until authorities assigned another St. Pierre ship
to take the cargo away. The wreck happened just before
Christmas and some of the salvaged goods remained in
Point May. Several bottles were hidden as they were
being transported from the ship to the storage sheds.
The wrecked vessel was purchased at a low price by
Point May fishermen who used the wood for house
foundations and fishing shacks. Thus, the ill luck of the
Bienville brought good fortune and cheer to many
others.

The same storm claimed another schooner near
Fortune: the *Loyola* laden with fish was stranded and
became a total loss.

ELLA M. RUDOLPH One Survivor—Of the nine persons aboard the *Ella M. Rudolph*, only one, the Captain's
son, survived the night of December 6, 1926, when a
sudden storm drove the schooner onto the rocks near
Catalina.

In 1915 the *Ella M. Rudolph* was brought down from
Nova Scotia to Grand Bank for Felix Tibbo's salt fish
industry. For three years the small, six-dory banker,
under the command of John Cluett of Garnish, had
carried her complement of fourteen or fifteen men to the
banks without incident.

In 1918 she was sold to Charles R. Steele of St.
John's, and then passed through various owners until
1925, when Eleazer Blackwood of Port Nelson, Bonavista Bay, purchased the *Ella M. Rudolph*. On the Northeast
Coast—Trinity, Bonavista and Conception Bay—

schooners went to the Labrador to catch cod in what was known as the 'floater' fishery.

This was an inshore fishery; the crew lived aboard the schooner, caught fish by cod traps and stored the salted product in the schooner's holds. Each of these schooners carried a couple of boys, usually family members, and also had on board a girl who cooked for the fishermen. In late summer they returned to their home ports, cured their fish, then came to St John's to sell their product and buy food and supplies for the winter.

While returning to Port Nelson from St. John's, laden with winter supplies and provisions, the *Ella M. Rudolph* met with disaster. Eight people drowned: Captain Blackwood; two of his three sons, Bert and Harry; Joseph Vivian from Hare Bay; Samuel Carter, Port Nelson; Noah Vivian, Shambler's Cove; Walter Attwood, Safe Harbour and a lady cook, Mary Jane Abbott, age 18 from Hare Bay.

The *Daily News* of December 8, 1926, reported that the *Ella M. Rudolph* left St. John's at 6:30 a.m. on Monday, December 6. That night a typical late fall wind storm and blizzard reduced visibility to practically zero. Sometime on the following night, the *Ella M. Rudolph* was dashed to pieces on the cliff head at Brook Cove, North Head, near Catalina.

As far as could be determined by the lone survivor, every crew member was thrown into the icy water or against the rocks, killing or drowning all except Marmaduke Blackwood, the captain's young son.

This excerpt from the *Fisherman's Advocate* of December 7, 1926, describes the end of the *Ella M. Rudolph* and tells how Blackwood survived:

...Marmaduke had been below for a cup of tea and had just reached the deck at the instant the schooner struck. He saw one of his brothers jump over the bow into the sea. The brother did not get hold of the rocks and the sea carried him out. When the sea went out Marmaduke jumped into the water over his brother's body and when the sea came in, it took him and landed him on a cliff of rock. Another sea subsequently landed him on another ledge from which he was able to scramble to safety. He narrowly escaped being killed as the bowsprit of the schooner crashed into the cliff only a few feet from his head.

...Blackwood said that it was only a matter of seconds and the ship was matchwood. He remained on the spot for five hours and when the weather abated started to look for houses...After a while he reached a hill and from it saw Port Union lights...About four a.m. he reached the Daltons' home at Little Catalina.

Immediately, at four o'clock in the morning, an all-out search and rescue party left for the scene. There

General Maude, one of Samuel Harris' 14 tern schooners named for World War One generals, was abandoned in the Atlantic on March 26, 1926. Of Harris' fleet of '*Generals*' six were abandoned at sea, three lost with crew, two wrecked and three sold to foreign owners.

were no other survivors. One body was recovered that night—Mary Jane Abbott, the lady cook. Later all bodies except two were found.

COLUMBIA's Newfoundland Connection—On August 24, 1927, an unexpected gale, a lashing from the dying tail of a tropical hurricane, swept the banking grounds off Sable Island. Several Nova Scotian schooners from Lunenberg went down with crew, including the *Joyce M. Smith* which had among her crew fourteen men from the Burin area.

Columbia of Gloucester, Massachusetts, one of the few schooners to ever come close to taking the Fisherman's Trophy from the great Canadian racer *Bluenose*, also disappeared in that terrible August gale. She failed to return to port; then on September 12, 1927, five of her dories were found washed up on the sandy beaches of Sable Island. Months later another wrecked dory confirmed the loss of the schooner with Captain Lewis Wharton and his twenty-two men.

Built in the Storey yards at Essex, Massachusetts, in 1923, *Columbia* had been a well-known visitor to Newfoundland. During the years prior to 1930, when herring teemed in Fortune Bay waters, American banking schooners came to the South Coast to buy the highly desired bait fish. In his frequent trips to Harbour Breton, *Columbia*'s Captain Wharton had met and married a girl from Harbour Breton, Francis Boyce. Captain Newman Wharton, Lewis' brother, was married to Florence Jensen of Harbour Breton.

When the *Columbia* disappeared, three of her twenty-two crew were from Burin: Joseph Mayo, his eldest son Albert and his youngest son, George Henry. At the time of their deaths, however, they had been residing in Halifax.

SUNNER ex OVER-THE-TOP Goes to the Bottom—
Built in 1919 by W.G. French at Birchy Bay, Notre Dame
Bay, the tern schooner *Sunner* was first christened *Over-
The-Top*. After World War One ended with an Allied
victory, several ships built in the Maritimes were given
war-related names: *Over-The-Top, Armistice, Victory
Chimes* and *Winthewar*. *Sunner* was sold and resold;
finally coming under the register of the Halifax business
of J.C. Penny, a former resident of Ramea.

In the summer of 1927 the owner, knowing Captain
Harry Thomasen of Grand Bank was experienced in the
Brazilian trading routes, hired him to command the
Sunner. Thomasen found the 166-ton *Sunner* a fine sail-
ing ship and she handled well.

In the latter part of August *Sunner* loaded half-
quintal drums of dry fish at St. John's and set out on an
approximate two thousand mile trip to Pernambuco
and Maceio, Brazil. Captain Thomasen had five crew
with him: mate Bill Christopherson, a Norwegian who
lived in St. John's; Wallace Smith, from Placentia Bay;
Thomasen's brother-in-law Charles Hickman, Grand
Bank; Joe Mullins and one other St. John's seaman. Also
making the voyage was the captain's wife, Mrs.
Thomasen and their two sons, aged five and three.

On the southward voyage the *Sunner*, for the most
part, had fair weather except for one severe storm. As
the schooner weathered a tropical hurricane, the captain lashed himself to the wheel and guided the
schooner safely. Although the tumultuous trip of the
Sunner happened almost seventy years ago Captain
Thomasen remembered the incident:

> The schooner was pitching and rolling so violently
> during a Saturday's meal of pea soup, that the
> sliding boiler and soup bowls had to be placed on

the floor. No one could eat with the table at a steep tilt.

During the storm the foremast was damaged, but exactly what the problem was could not be determined until we reached Brazil. After sixty-six days of sailing we reached Pernambuco where half the cargo of fish was discharged.

A survey of the foremast showed it had to be replaced. As no new mast was available at Pernambuco, Captain Thomasen asked port authorities for a Certificate of Seaworthiness. This certificate had to be paid for, but it gave *Sunner* the clearance to sail to Maceio. Perhaps there a stick suitable for a mast could be stepped.

At Maceio, as the fish cargo was discharged and a sand ballast was put aboard, Thomasen searched for a suitable mast; again, nothing suitable could be found. Before leaving Brazil for the West Indies, *Sunner's* crew worked on the damaged foremast. They moved the foretop down so that the foretop overlapped the mast and strapped both together with chain and clamps.

Before the tern could leave port, another slip vouching for the schooner's seaworthiness had to be purchased—Thomasen realized by this time it was a money making ploy for Brazilian ports. Now the *Sunner*, with its foremast fished, or strapped up, could carry no balloon jib nor fore topsail and this meant a slower voyage homeward. The northward journey, and as it turned out the final journey of the *Sunner*, began in December 1927.

Knowing his vessel would be at sea during Christmas Day, Captain Thomasen bought a young pig at Maceio before he left port. The pig was kept behind the wheel box; it became a game and routine for his two sons to feed and watch the pig grow until it was killed for Christmas dinner.

In the new year 1928, *Sunner* stopped at Barbados to land mate Christopherson who had malaria. While there, the cook also fell sick. Both men had to be discharged and Negro crewmen replaced them. Captain Thomasen eventually learned Christopherson died a few days after hospitalization.

Sunner sailed on to Turk's Island, discharged her sand ballast and loaded salt for Lunenberg, Nova Scotia. Thomasen knew by this time, February, the hurricane season was over. Bad weather was not expected, but the elements are unpredictable and soon strong winds lasting for several days buffeted the tern. Then one night a rumble and crash told the crew the damaged foremast had broken off. This put extra pressure on the mainmast and it broke as well.

When the foremast fell, it caused irreparable damage. The splintered edge somehow went through the schooner's deck, lodged in the bottom and could not be removed. This split or jarred the planking and the *Sunner* took on water. Every crewman worked that night to clear away the tangled rigging and broken spars littering the deck. Broken masts and spars would punch larger holes in the vessel's sides if not removed and allowed to drift away.

In addition to this work the pumps had to be manned constantly, for sea water rising in the holds could not be kept in check. By March 9, 1928, Thomasen knew the wrecked *Sunner* had to be abandoned.

The heavy lifeboat was on the deckhouse. Rigging and tackle used to lift it off had gone overboard with the masts. The only recourse was to take the lifeboat down on deck manually. With the combined effort of all six men, it was finally secured on deck. There was no way to get the lifeboat over the side, so Thomasen took the ship's axe to cut away the stanchions and bulwarks. The craft could then be pushed through the breach.

Sunner's crew and passengers now faced the daunting prospect of stepping off their sinking schooner hundreds of miles from land with no immediate hope of rescue.

As the lifeboat was being laden with food, water and supplies, one of the sailors asked the captain to look at a banking schooner off in the distance. Thomasen could hardly believe it for they were far from shipping lanes and fishing grounds. Captain Thomasen went about his work again, but sailor persisted.

But miraculously the schooner came down alongside. It was the Nova Scotian banker *Palitana* headed for the banks. Thomasen recalled the encounter:

> *Palitana's* captain asked why our schooner had distress flags up. "You can see what we want," I replied. "We are sinking and want to be taken off." "Why don't you drop your anchor? It would make the transfer easier. You're on Brown's Bank, a fishing ground," *Palitana's* captain (Frank Meisner) called as the schooner drew near.
>
> I told him the water was too deep; there are no fishing grounds here. A dory from the rescue vessel came over and carried Mrs. Thomasen, the two boys and a sailor from the *Sunner* to safety.

When the dory came back and the rest of the crew had been taken off, they discussed the ship's position on the charts. Still disbelieving he wasn't over the relatively shoal waters of Brown's Bank, Thomasen convinced the captain of the rescue schooner to throw the sounding line over.

> He said, "I'll do that. But it was only yesterday I left Halifax and I know I'm on the banks." One of his men lowered the sounding line full length and lost

it without finding bottom. Only then was the *Palitana*'s captain satisfied his course was wrong and was indeed in deep water, far from his intended destination.

To the captain and crew of the abandoned *Sunner*, the arrival of a rescue schooner when they were so far from shipping lanes or fishing grounds was hardly believable. For the captain, who had not only his own life to care for, the miraculous delivery of his wife and two small sons could only have come through divine providence.

CATHERINE B Abandoned at Sea—In June 1923, when Grand Bank merchant Samuel Harris closed out his branch store in Change Islands, he sold several of his vessels, including the *Howard Young* and the *Catherine B* which had operated around the Northeast Coast. The latter, a 45-ton schooner built in 1919 in Marystown, was purchased by Frederick Short of Hant's Harbour, Trinity Bay. In 1929, she was ten years old and, in terms of the life of a schooner used in the Labrador fishery, would have been considered seaworthy.

On Friday, November 29, 1929, under the command of Ellis Janes, the *Catherine B* left St. John's for Hant's Harbour with a cargo of winter provisions. With Captain Janes was his crew of Charles Green, Wilbert Short, James Loder and four passengers, Freeman Francis, Wesley Short, Frank Strickland and Frederick Short, the vessel's owner. All were residents of Hant's Harbour.

Within a few hours out of port, the schooner encountered a southeast gale, with high seas and a blinding snowstorm, which later increased to winds of hurricane force. The first portent of disaster happened at eleven a.m. when the *Catherine B* lost her mainboom.

Crew and passengers of the *Catherine B*. Back row (l-r) Charles Green, Freeman Francis, Captain Ellis Janes, Wesley Short, Wilbert Short. Front (l-r) James Loder, Frank Strickland, Frederick Short. Insert at bottom left is the *Catherine B* entering Hant's Harbour some time previously to her abandonment.

With all hands working, the men managed to heave to under a doublereefed foresail and drift to the southeast keeping the schooner outside of Baccalieu Island.

Then the wind veered northwest with severe frost, dashing any hopes of swinging down into Trinity Bay; *Catherine B* was driven to sea. The storm increased in velocity for two days as the schooner was continually swept by high seas. At the gale peaked, the mainsail was ripped to pieces, the halyards were blocked with ice and when the wind shifted again, the foregaff and the foresail went over the side.

At six-thirty Sunday evening, after more than two days of being driven before the wind, the lights of a steamer were sighted. It proved to be the *S.S. Holfplein*, an ore carrier that had left Bell Island some hours earlier

for Rotterdam. The crew of the distressed schooner lit a
flare as a signal of distress. The steamer, commanded by
Captain Schaap, came down near the *Catherine B* on the
weather side.

Holfplein's second mate and four crewmen volun-
teered to go the rescue in a small lifeboat. About 9:30
p.m. the lifeboat came up beside the *Catherine B* and her
crew jumped into the lifeboat one by one. The last to
leave his schooner was Captain Janes. Before he left he
had kerosene oil poured on her decks, but there was no
time to set it afire when the lifeboat called for him to
jump. Janes figured from the condition of the *Catherine
B*, she sank soon after.

After the lifeboat reached the *Holfplein's* side, all
members of the crew except one jumped for and
climbed the ladder hanging over the side of the steamer.
Frederick Short, aged 74, was hauled aboard the ship by
a rope tied around his waist.

Holfplein continued on to Rotterdam, but three
hours after the rescue, she ran into a terrific storm that
lasted for thirteen days. Everything moveable on the
deck of the steamer was washed overboard—Captain
Schaap claimed it was the worst Atlantic storm he had
ever experienced.

For one of the crew, the voyage to Holland was
especially memorable. On December 8, Freeman Francis spent his nineteenth birthday on the *Holfplein*. Three
days later the steamer arrived at Rotterdam and the
British Consul there made arrangements for the Hant's
Harbour men to be transported home.

HIRAM D. McLEAN   Rum Runner Goes Down—A
large three-masted schooner of 447 tons, the 152-foot
long *Hiram D. McLean* was owned by Penny's business
of Ramea and operated out of Sydney, Nova Scotia.

In late January 1929, after the *McLean* discharged her load of Sydney coal at Carbonear, she sailed for Turk's Island in the West Indies for salt. Captain Abe Thornhill of Fortune had a Newfoundland crew: bosun William Snook of Fortune; mate John Pauls; cook John Green and John Barrett of Carbonear; and Ron Young from Bay St. George. In later years bosun Snook described his duties on board the *McLean*:

> I was cook on the *McLean* for a few days, but since they couldn't find a bosun I took over that work. Then a fellow from Carbonear (Green) living in Sydney went cook. As bosun I took orders from the mate and passed them on to the men; organized watch shifts, supervised painting, spliced gear, mended sail and other shipboard chores.

Captain Abe Thornhill of Fortune was a veteran seaman. Years before he had command of large tern schooners *Flowerdew* and *Emily H. Patten*. When he was

In 1924 the American Coast Guard, patrolling for rum running vessels, had the *Hiram D. McLean* under surveillance and took this picture of her.

Courtesy United States Coast Guard

skipper of a two-masted banking schooner out of Grand Bank, he had only left that port when he lost a man, Fred Witherall of Fortune. When the wind slacked off, Thornhill had ordered his men to lower the mainsail, and Witherall, on the leeward side of the mainboom, was knocked into the sea and drowned.

During World War Two Captain Thornhill and his son George lost their lives when their tern schooner *Mildred Pauline* disappeared in the Atlantic in 1942, supposedly torpedoed by a German submarine.

Shortly after the *Hiram D. McLean* left Turk's Island headed for LaHave, Nova Scotia, she ran into a typical North Atlantic storm with high winds and heavy seas. Built in Economy, Nova Scotia, ten years before, the *McLean*'s aging timbers and planking needed repair: the strain of salt and the pounding of waves opened her seams. Captain Thornhill ordered his men to the pumps, but the nemesis of salt laden vessels plagued the schooner—her pumps clogged with salt and were useless.

Ten days after leaving Turk's Island, the *McLean* had sailed to within two hundred miles east of Norfolk, Virginia, when on February 23, the crew knew the schooner was soon going to the bottom. Seaman Snook remembered the experience:

> After the weather got the better of the schooner, we couldn't keep her free with pumps choked with salt and that's all we could do about that.
>
> We were looking out for a rescue ship a couple of days before we abandoned her, but without luck. We had the distress flag up half mast. This day a tanker came along close to us to see if she could help. Her crew came near in a large lifeboat and we jumped one at a time for the boat. We saved nothing only the clothes we stood in.

On the evening of February 23, 1929, the American tanker *Swift Scout* bound for Curacao, Dutch West Indies, for oil rescued the weary sailors. Before the six Newfoundland crewmen jumped into the lifeboat, Captain Abe Thornhill ordered the *McLean* set afire, so that the waterlogged derelict would not be a threat to shipping.

However, the rough seas presented another problem to the rescue sailors manning the tossing lifeboat. In the choppy seas, the little craft took a sudden lurch and one man was thrown overboard. Captain Abe Thornhill, nearest the struggling man in the water, grabbed him by the hair and collar and pulled him aboard. Snook recalled this and the experience he and his mates had climbing aboard the ship *Swift Scout*:

> A little lop caused the sailor from the *Swift Scout* to lose balance and he fell overboard. Abe grabbed him and several men in the lifeboat pulled him in.
>
> The lifeboat went to the tanker's leeward side where a big wooden ladder had been lowered over the side. When the tanker dipped down in the trough of the sea and the boat was low enough, one of us would grab the ladder. When she'd roll back up the ladder was ten or twelve feet away from us. As we climbed up to the rail the ship's crewmen pulled us aboard.

Rescue over, the *Swift Scout* finished her voyage and then returned to the United States, stopping at Four Rivers near Boston. The six Newfoundlanders found a passage to Halifax, and from Halifax to St. John's on the *S.S. Rosalind*; Thornhill and Snook finished the final leg to Fortune on the *Portia*.

LATONA A St. Jacques Tragedy—Less than a year later another South Coast ship was wrecked three miles east of Isle aux Morts, when the banking schooner *Latona*, headed for the Labrador fishery, struck an offshore reef.

Owned by S.J. Young of St. Jacques, this 64-ton schooner had been built in 1899 in Massachusetts, measured 80-foot long and carried four or five banking dories. The small Fortune Bay community of St. Jacques had seen fishing companies, mainly Dyett's and Burke's, come and go since the 1800's when the town first began to grow and prosper. Beginning in 1880, three brothers, Samuel, John and Randell Young harvested the bountiful banks and established a company. In 1930 Gordon Young, son of one of the owners, commanded the *Latona*.

At 9:30 p.m. on June 8, 1930, the *Latona* struck an offshore reef awash with heavy seas and immediately went to pieces. Three St. Jacques men drowned—James Cox, his son John and Archie Cluett. It is said that Stephen, Archie Cluett's son, was rescued from drowning twice by his father before Archie himself was washed off the wreck and drowned. Seven survivors reached land; three to Burnt Island, four to Isle aux Morts.

Courtesy Marine Archives, Memorial University

The *Dazzle*. Abandoned eight miles off Ramea in November 1930, the *Dazzle's* Captain Reid and crew were rescued by Morgan Giles in his small boat and taken to Ramea. The schooner left Halifax, but ran into foul weather which opened her seams and carried away the rudder.

In February 1930, the *Sentinel*, a banker once built and owned in Grand Bank, was damaged in a storm at Rose Blanche. When lost, she was registered to Absolum Thomas of Harbour LaCou.

Chapter Six

Prohibition and
the Great Depression

IN 1919 THE UNITED STATES adopted National Prohibition making the production, sale and distribution of liquor illegal. Enforcement of the law through the Volstead Act spawned a new and turbulent era on America's east coast in the people's pursuit of hard-to-get alcohol, a period of lawbreaking that lasted fourteen years until Prohibition was repealed in December 1933.

The French islands of St. Pierre, a few miles off Newfoundland's South Coast, took on a major distribution role supplying rum, whisky and wine to Newfoundland, Canadian and American smugglers. Often Nova Scotian or Newfoundland schooners, several owned and manned by South Coast sailors, took the products to the 12 mile limit off the eastern seaboard of the United States. There they were met by liquor buyers who took the goods back with them.

This was a lucrative trade, but later as the U.S. Coast Guard increased in strength and surveillance techniques, it became dangerous and virtually impossible to continue. High speed chases and gunfire became more common. On January 21, 1931, William

Cluett of Belleoram was shot and killed by gunfire from a coast guard vessel off Ambrose Light. Cluett, who had survived the arduous abandonment of the *Sparkling Glance* in 1921, captained the rum runner *Josephine K*, laden with $100,000 worth of liquor when he and his crew were apprehended. Cluett died in the Marine Hospital on Staten Island, New York.

Profitable employment, other than rum running, for foreign-going and coasting schooners was getting more and more difficult to find, due in part to the Great Depression. For a few years after the Great War ended, freight and foreign exports were profitable for Newfoundland shipowners.

Courtesy of Jack Keeping and Gordon Thomas Collection

The *Saladin.* By the 1930's many schooners lay idle in South Coast harbours. With the bottom out of fish exporting markets, many bankers were tied up unwanted and unused or reduced to coasting. The 109-ton *Saladin*, built in Essex in 1902, fished or coasted out of Fortune for several years for owners John and Albert Tulk. By 1937 she had been sold to Blackwood's business in Bonavista Bay.

When markets declined salt fish, like most goods, was worth very little. All the great terns owned along the South Coast by Moulton, Harris, Hollett and Wareham were idle. Their stores were full of salt dried cod; people owed them money but merchants only had fish to pay them. Fish was worthless since financially stricken countries like Spain and Portugal were unable to pay for imported goods. As many Newfoundland firms went bankrupt, schooners and men had no work. Sailing ships lost at sea were seldom replaced.

CHAPEL POINT   A Rum Runner Burns—After William (Bill) Snook of Fortune had lost his ship the *Hiram D. McLean*, he was again looking for employment. He had found part-time work in a Toronto factory, but in the 'Dirty Thirties' as Newfoundlanders called the Depression Years, steady employment was hard to come by even in the larger centres, and he decided to go home.

When Snook arrived in Sydney on his way to Newfoundland, he met Captain Ben Snook in the schooner *Bessie MacDonald* and hitched a passage to Fortune with him. Seaman Bill Snook recalled:

> I was home two days. Construction had started on the western wharf in Fortune harbour, so I went to see the overseer, Mr. Pynn. He promised me a job by the next day. But that evening about 4 o'clock, I received a message from St. Pierre wanting to know if I would go on the schooner *Chapel Point* with Captain Clarence Williams. George Walters, who was later lost on the *Mark H. Grey*, Amos Cluett, Bert Thornhill, Sam Keeping and myself who all lived in or belonged to Fortune joined the *Chapel Point* in St. Pierre. The other crew were the two engineers, John Pierce from St. Jacques, the

other a Scotsman; her supercargo was from Quebec—nine crewmen in all.

Built in Essex in 1917 in the Storey yards, the *Chapel Point* had a long colourful career: fish freighter, movie vessel and rum runner sailing under three names. She was a 262-ton tern with topmasts, no bowsprit and equipped with two 100 horsepower crude oil engines carried for auxiliary power. Originally named *Gaspe*, she often carried fish cargoes from the Newfoundland and Canadian coast to America.

In February 1922, she was chartered for use in the making of the whaling movie, *Down to the Sea in Ships* and fitted with whaling boats and a crow's nest. By 1923, she was sold to French interests, renamed the *Beatrice* and later resold, in 1928, to John Burdock, Edward Fudge and Captain Kenneth Fudge of Belleoram. Fudge renamed her *Chapel Point* after a point of land near Belleoram and used her as a fish freighter and rum runner.

In November 1930, Bill Snook and his shipmates loaded the *Chapel Point* with St. Pierre liquor, cleared for open seas and left for ports known only to her captain and supercargo. Supercargoes, not the captains, controlled the liquor, made the sales, handled the transfers and kept the books. Snook recalled:

> Our first stop was in the Panama Canal; we passed through the locks, then headed to Los Angeles, a forty day trip. There at Los Angeles, our destination, we lay 50 miles off the coast and couldn't go any closer. Dealers trying to beat the American prohibition figured on America's west coast more money could be made and since less smuggling was carried out there, chances of apprehension was not as great.

A small boat came out at night to get the liquor, three or four hundred cases at a time. A large bill of money, probably a thousand dollar bill, was examined, one half produced by the supercargo; its serial number to be matched up with the other half carried by the men receiving the booze. If the serial numbers could not be matched, no liquor would be transferred. This was to prevent the valuable cargo from falling into the wrong hands.

We had over 4000 cases of whisky, rum and brandy, and were awhile getting it transferred properly. We arrived off Los Angeles in July and we were discovered and driven away by the United States Coast Guard sometime in November with some 1000 cases of liquor still in the holds.

In late November, Captain Williams took the *Chapel Point* off the coast of Mexico—international waters where the schooner could not be arrested, but in effect the *Chapel Point* was trapped. She could not dock in Canada nor in the United States; passage through the Panama Canal was out since that was patrolled by the United States. Too small for long ocean voyages, she had no way to return to Newfoundland by any route. Soon most of the crew tired of this cat and mouse game, being watched constantly by the Coast Guard.

On December 9th the end came while she was moored off Cape Colinet, Mexico. *Chapel Point* caught fire in her engine room.

The official report of the American Coast Guard vessel *Montgomery*, dated Tuesday, December 9, filed by her boatswain at San Pedro, California, states:

At anchor picketing *Chapel Point*. Weather fair, clear, sea calm. At 1545 *Chapel Point* caught fire in engine room, due to Delco generator backfiring. Crew of *Chapel Point* almost immediately abandoned ship in dory and came alongside

Montgomery; the master of the schooner requesting that he and his crew be taken on board this vessel as they were afraid to return because of the fear of drums of gasoline and fuel oil exploding.

Immediately sent boat crew away from *Montgomery* to board schooner, to investigate and if possible obtain papers or documents. Took crew of *Chapel Point*, nine men in all, including master Captain Clarence C. Williams on board.

Boarding party unable to get into after compartments of schooner due to smoke and fire; however they managed to take hatches off number one hold and saw that there were several hundred cases of liquor in that hold.

They remained aboard the schooner about five minutes then returned to *Montgomery* bringing a small dog that had been left behind.

None of the vessel's papers nor any of the crew's personal belongings was saved. At first it was believed that the vessel had been set on fire purposely, however after several hours talking with the crew, it became evident that such was not the case. They left in the scantiest of clothing, one without shoes, another without a shirt.

William Snook remembered the Coast Guard cutter taking him and his shipmates off and landing them aboard an old five masted schooner, the *Malahat*. The crew stayed aboard this vessel for several days, past New Year's Day, 1931.

Meanwhile the *Montgomery* finished its report on the burning schooner with these words: "Continued cruising close to *Chapel Point* throughout the night, that vessel burning fiercely with intermittent explosions of varying violence. On Wednesday, December 10 at 1930 hours, the derelict having burnt to water's edge sank in forty fathoms leaving three masts, two large oil tanks, and small debris floating."

MONTGOMERY
San Pedro, Calif.,
19 December, 1930.

From: Officer in Charge MONTGOMERY
To : Commander,California Division(via Commander, Section Base 17).

Subject: Report of cruise of MONTGOMERY, 7 December to 18 December,1930.

Enclosure: (1) Track chart of subject cruise.
(2) Three(3) snapshots of CHAPEL POINT and crew.

1. Sunday December 7th 1930 at 0005 unmoored and stood out on patrol to relieve MCLANE picketing British schooner CHAPELKAPOINT off Cape Colnet, Mexico. 0020 Tom Pedro Light close, set course 150°(T) standard speed. At 2105 stopped, made contact with and relieved MCLANE picketing three masted auxiliary schooner CHAPEL POINT of ST. JOHNS, Newfoundland, position lat. 30°47' N long. 116°23'West. Cape Colnet Mexico bearing 14° (T) distance 18 miles. Black it anchor in forty fathoms . Lay to, drifting close to black throughout night.

2. Monday, 8 December 1930. Underway, drifting close to CHAPEL POINT. at 1625 came to anchor close to black. at 1645 Mexican patrol boat S.A.P.-1 passed close, bound south. No other activities this date.

Reproduction of United States Coast Guard report of activities of the *Chapel Point* written by boatswain on the cutter *Montgomery*.

Captain Williams, Snook and the other men were
then transferred to a steamer and carried to Vancouver,
arriving there on January 5, 1931. When he knew the
men were in Canada, Edward Fudge, the part owner of
the *Chapel Point*, living in Halifax, tried to get the
government to pay for the crew's passage home. The
Canadian government would have none of that since
the *Chapel Point* and her men had been on illegal business. A court inquiry on the activities of the schooner
and its owners proceeded in Vancouver. Snook
recalled:

> Anyway I had an aunt, my father's sister, living in
> Vancouver. I stayed with her, but every day I had
> to report to authorities. We were witnesses for the
> prosecutors and would not be sentenced.
>
> On the last day of court, Fudge's lawyer looked
> at the list of names he had there. "I have a name
> here, a Snook," he said. "Where do you belong, Mr.
> Snook? I know you're a Newfoundlander because
> that's on your report."
>
> "Sir," I said, "I belong to Fortune."
>
> "Well, Fortune," he laughed. "That's where I
> was born, Fortune, Newfoundland. Do you know
> or are you related Robert Snook and George
> Snook?"
>
> "Robert Snook is my grandfather and George
> Snook is my father."
>
> He looked at me. "I once lived next door to
> them," he said.
>
> Our lawyer explained to me that he was a
> Penny, born in Fortune, but when his mother died,
> had been raised by Dr. Haddock and taken to
> Vancouver when his foster father, Haddock,
> moved there.

Inquiry over, the next day the crew left for Halifax.
It took eight days to cross Canada by train and when

they arrived in Halifax, Edward Fudge paid them off. The Newfoundland sailors took the passenger boat *Rosalind* to St. John's, and then transferred to the *Portia* for Fortune.

William Snook summarized his life aboard the several tern schooners he had sailed on:

> Pay was good for those times, depression years—one hundred dollars a month and found. Food was the best: vegetables, meat, tinned goods. We often kept live hens or turkeys in a lifeboat on deck to be killed when needed. When sailing down south we always had fresh fruit aboard. Sleeping quarters were good, sometimes on the larger three masters we had store bought mattresses.
>
> On some schooners I was the youngest aboard and was assigned the foremast; the more experienced men, because of seniority, handled sail on the other masts. On the foremast sheets had to changed and there was more work. But that was the life I sailed from age fifteen.

End of the GYPSY QUEEN—Arrival of winter brought wind and snowstorms that proved fatal to the *Gypsy Queen*, a schooner built in 1905 in Burgeo. Owned by Clement and Company of Burgeo, she had been abandoned near Fox Island, four miles off Ramea Island, and the crew of five rowed to Ramea. In a blinding snowstorm on the night of December 15, 1930, the *Gypsy Queen* lost her sails after she had passed Francois.

In an effort to prevent her from driving onto Fox Island, both anchors were dropped and the schooner abandoned while the storm was at its height. She was later found totally wrecked with both anchor chains parted, on the western end of Ramea Island.

LUCY M. CORKUM   A Wreck on Bob's Rock—*Lucy M. Corkum*, built in Lunenberg in 1923, was bought by John Parrott and Sons of St. Bernard's, Fortune Bay. Parrott put her under the charge of Parminias 'Min' Banfield, a veteran captain from Bay L'Argent. On May 7, 1931, while returning from the Grand Banks laden with fish, the *Lucy M. Corkum* struck Bob's Rock situated between St. Pierre and Point May on the Burin Peninsula. The 125-ton schooner filled with water and sank.

Throughout his career as schooner captain, Banfield became involved in several calamities of the sea: on the night of September 24, 1917, he skippered the *Lottie Silver* when she was rammed on the high seas by the Fortune schooner *Margaret Lake*. Captain Banfield abandoned ship in the *Silver's* dory and at daylight he and his crew were rescued by Captain H. B. Clyde Lake and the *Margaret Lake*; in May 1933, Banfield's schooner *Dorothy Melita*, owned by Patten of Grand Bank, went to the bottom after she struck an iceberg 125 miles off Newfoundland. One crewman, Chesley Grandy of Bay L'Argent, died in the mishap.

PARTANNA   A Memorable Voyage in 1931—In the days of trawl fishing, South Coast schooners, to finish their season's catch, made the long journey from Newfoundland's southernmost point, the Burin Peninsula, all the way north to the Labrador coast. This fishery, which lasted from mid-August to October, usually centred around the Batteau/Black Tickle area, prolific cod producing grounds.

Although a profitable venture, at least for the merchant, it was not without danger, hardship and disaster for vessels and men. Powerful insets of tides along the Labrador coast, spectacular but deadly icebergs, rocks and shoals in unfamiliar waters, and sudden, intense, localized storms were added threats to a schooner's perilous existence upon the stormy Atlantic.

By October 1931, the banker *Partanna* had completed her season's fishing and prepared to leave the Labrador coast and head for home. Usually South Coast schooners travelled the shorter route through the Straits of Belle Isle but on that particular season her captain, Charles Anstey, took the longer, more hazardous journey along Newfoundland's north east coast.

On this voyage her crew were all South Coast bank fishermen: mate John Legge, Fred and Walter Grandy, Adam Rideout, all of Garnish; cook Igol Green, his son, kedgie Waterfield Green, Nathan Kelland, Samuel Fox, Tom Burfitt, Manuel Cox, William Joe Smith, Berkley Breon, Grand Bank; Walter Matthews, Grand Beach; Harvey Cox, Will John Savoury, Belleoram; Frank and George Cox, John and William Mitchell, Terrenceville; Morgan and Mike Bungay, James Snook, Stan Skinner and Aloysisus Drake of Sagona.

Also on board were several floater fishermen, their wives and children returning from the Labrador to Trinity and Conception Bay for the winter. Some years the Conception Bay fishermen and their families who had fished all summer on the Labrador coast would not have their catch dried and shipped when the coastal boat *Kyle* arrived in early October. Rather than wait two more weeks for the *Kyle* to return, they often purchased a passage for themselves on a banking schooner.

It had not been a particularly good trip for the *Partanna* that fall, so the small fee charged would augment the schoonermen's meagre earnings. Captain Anstey agreed to transport the several families which included two or three women who went to the Labrador as cooks as was the usual custom in the floater fishery.

Each family of 'shoremen' as the South Coast fishermen called them, brought their fish and supplies aboard the *Partanna*—two families had their large skiff boats. Both boats were tied on the stern that evening and it was planned that the next morning before leaving the coast they would be taken in on deck using the mainboom and foreboom tackles.

During the night the wind came up from the northeast blowing a virtual hurricane accompanied with heavy snow. A fierce wind drove the blizzard across the water and over the *Partanna's* decks reducing visibility to nil and making it near impossible to stand let alone work on deck.

But work was a must for the schoonermen that evening. *Partanna's* crew had two anchors out to hold against the mighty seas which threatened at any moment to drive the schooner in on the Labrador rocks. During the night the men mustered on deck to bring out another cable and bend on a third anchor. Only after the extra anchor grabbed the bottom did the schooner hold against the wind—while driving bowsprit into the seas whipped up to a frenzy near Black Tickle, Labrador.

By daylight the storm had abated enough for the men to move about on deck as preparations were made to sail for Newfoundland. Before any work could be done the men had to shovel several feet of snow off the deck. Then they had to raise the two boats which had filled with water during the night — only six inches of their stems were visible above water. To rectify this problem both were bailed out, towed ashore, hauled up on the beach and minor repairs were made before the skiffs were taken aboard and lashed down on deck.

In the run off Newfoundland's northern coast headed down to Conception Bay, the wind had moderated to a lively sailing breeze and the *Partanna* made a good time along with the four lower sails reefed.

Yet even in times of relative quiet, the dangers of the sea threaten and survival was often a matter of luck combined with good navigational skills and judgement. During one dark night about forty miles off Fogo, tragedy almost claimed the heavily laden schooner.

The Funk Islands, with no lighthouse or foghorn, lie in that vicinity, almost in a direct line between Black Tickle and Conception Bay. For some unknown reason the helmsman allowed the *Partanna* to yawl off course far enough that she came within a stone's throw of hitting the heap of isolated rocks.

About two o'clock in the morning, all hands were hastily summoned on deck. As the man at the wheel saw the waves breaking near the schooner, he called through the gangway for help. With every man at the ropes, the *Partanna* was brought to and out of danger; but she came so close to striking the Funk Island rocks the white surf thrown up from them came in over her quarter.

Without any further incidents, the floater fishermen, their families and the season's catch were landed in Brigus, Clarke's Beach and Harbour Grace. Around October 18, the *Partanna* arrived in Grand Bank, discharged her fish and lay up for the winter.

Such struggles against nature's elements were typical for the hardy fishermen who manned the banking schooners. For five more years the *Partanna* continued her take from the bountiful banks, bringing home good catches for her owner Grand Bank Fisheries Company. But the relentless sea demanded its toll and in April 1936, the schooner and her crew were lost near Trepassey Bay. At the time of her loss only Captain Anstey remained of the men who experienced the

The Daily News

MONDAY, MAY 4, 1936

FURTHER EVIDENCE OF LOSS OF THE SCHR. 'PARTANNA'

Wreckage Picked up in Trepassey and St. Mary's Bay—Grand Bank Abandons all Hope

Saturday, the Department of Posts and Telegraphs had further partic- ulars as to the loss of the banker

This is how the newspaper of May 1, 1936, reported the wreck of the *Partanna*.

trying voyage to the Labrador. For the poem 'Loss of the *Partanna*' see Appendix D.

GEORGE AND MARION at Mistaken Point—Captain Freeman Lawrence of Bay L'Argent was part owner, along with Lake and Lake of Fortune, of the *George and Marion*. On September 11, 1931, she was totally wrecked at Mistaken Point on the Southern Avalon while bound to the Labrador for the fall fishery. Lawrence and his crew of 23 rowed safely to shore.

WILSON T A Rum Runner Disappears—Several pieces of wreckage found on the shores of the islands of St. Pierre indicated another schooner had foundered there.

By November 6, 1931, the *Wilson T,* a rum running schooner owned in New Brunswick, but crewed by Burin men, was long overdue. Built in Port Elgin, New Brunswick, in 1925, the 61-foot long *Wilson T* netted 37 tons and was owned by Oswald and Patrick McFadden of Buctouche, New Brunswick. *Wilson T* had been fitted with a powerful engine to aid in eluding the American and Canadian patrol vessels looking for probable rum running schooners. On June 12, 1928, she had been apprehended off Lunenberg by the Preventative Service Cutter *Bayfield,* but when released, she again resumed illegal activities.

Under the supervision of agents in Sydney and other mainland ports, *Wilson T* was engaged in the smuggling of liquor from St. Pierre to 'Rum Row,' a strip of water twelve miles off the American seaboard where the cargoes were often transferred.

While returning to St. Pierre from one such mission, the *Wilson T,* commanded by Fred Myles, had been wrecked taking her crew to their deaths—Myles, age 37; his son, Philip, 16; Charles Keating; Leonard Shave; Charles I. White; and Thomas Hartson.

Early November 1931, the *Wilson T* left St. Pierre with one hundred cases of alcohol and Canadian Club whisky destined for the American seaboard. In the Gulf she was apprehended again by the government cutter. Authorities from the cutter boarded her and, when told by Myles the schooner was short of fuel, they allowed the schooner to return to St. Pierre for fuel.

That night it was blowing hard and foggy. *Wilson T* ran upon the Seal Rocks, a treacherous ledge barely awash west of St. Pierre, and was lost with crew. Oswald McFadden searched in vain for evidence, finding only a dory and life belt that had drifted ashore on the western side of Miquelon.

Although Captain Fred Myles resided in Burin, he was born in St. Malo, France. Many years before as a young 'gravier' or working boy on a French fishing vessel, he and some other boys had jumped ship on the eastern side of the Burin Peninsula. Myles walked to Frenchman's Cove and was taken in by a family there.

Later, when he married a young lady of the area, he discarded his French name, Harmon Gilliard, and preferred to be called Fred Myles. Eventually the young Frenchman proved his worth as a seaman rising through the ranks to become a schooner captain. But in 1931 he disappeared with his son on the *Wilson T.*

A Coastal Trip on the ARGINIA—In early December 1931, Robert Hillier joined the schooner *Arginia*, a two-masted sailing schooner built in Shelburne, Nova Scotia, in 1908. In the 1930's she was operated by the Dixon business of Fortune. It was Hillier's first trip on a schooner and he not only learned the work of a deck hand, but saw the problems, big and small, that preyed on Newfoundland seamen a half century ago.

Hillier, a resident of Point aux Gaul on the eastern side of Newfoundland's Burin Peninsula, knew the vessel's owner, Gilbert Cake and asked him for a chance to sail to St. John's as a working passenger. His friend agreed. Dixons were the principal shareholders, but Cake and the schooner captain, Harold Ayers of Fortune, had bought a few shares in the 90-foot long *Arginia*. Hillier's brother Lewis was a crewman along with mate Jim Ayers, son of the captain; Frank Foote of Lamaline and cook Lewis Kendall of Fortune.

Captain Ayers headed for St. John's with intentions of obtaining a load of 'relief' flour—a brown flour, unwhitened and cheaper, issued in one hundred pound bags and distributed by the government in the Depres-

The St. Pierre ferry Rodco

Many schooners like the *Arginia* travelling to other ports or the fishing grounds often stopped at St. Pierre to obtain cheap cigarettes, liquor and ship supplies and sometimes carried passengers destined for St. Pierre. In later years vessels like the *Rodco* (above) ran a regular ferry service from the South Coast to the French Islands.

Built in Bracebridge, Ontario, in 1942, the *Rodco* netted 61 tons and was 112 feet long. On the St. Pierre run she was skippered by Edwin Vallis of Grand Bank. She ended her days in Garnish where she was dismantled by Sam White. Photo property of the author

sion years, the Newfoundland 'Dirty Thirties.' Ayers had telegraphed officials in the capital city to confirm his cargo and his expected arrival date.

Hillier joined the *Arginia* in Fortune, her home port, and from there sailed to St. Pierre to purchase a few ship supplies and cheap cigarettes. This was Hillier's first voyage by schooner, and although he went as a nonpaying passenger, he was considered one of the crew. He stood his turn at watch with another crewman, learned to handle sail, loaded freight and willingly did his share of ship duty.

During the voyage, Hillier discovered one scourge of sailors on small wooden ships—bed bugs and biting insects. *Arginia* was moving with bugs. He slept in the forecastle with the other deckhands (the captain and his son shared the after cabin), and as he lay in his top bunk Hillier saw how plentiful bugs were. He ran the blade of his pocketknife between the deck seams over his head and when he withdrew it, it was full of crushed insects and blood.

While the oil lamp was turned up, the pests would stay hidden, but when the lamp was screwed down at night, they would come out, crawl over sleeping men and bite. Bites were often around the eyes and neck leaving a red, itching welt which usually swelled up. Hillier remembers a shipmate who woke up one morning, his face so swollen he was scarcely recognizable.

When insects became too numerous, infested schooners were 'smoked out' or fumigated. The forecastle or after cabin would be sealed up—seams of the doors, portholes and other openings blocked with cloth or old rags. The captain would then set a bucket of whitish sulphur powder on the floor, set it alight and leave, sealing the door behind him. The heavy sulphurous smoke would kill most of the bugs which were then swept up and thrown overboard.

From St. Pierre, the schooner sailed along the Southern Avalon. A typical December wind storm forced Ayers to shelter in St. Mary's Bay before he finished the voyage past Cape Race and northward to St. John's. Since the *Arginia*'s first stop had been St. Pierre, a foreign port, she first had to clear St. John's harbour customs before tying up at one of the many finger wharves.

To Ayers' disappointment he learned that the two day storm delay in St. Mary's Bay had cost him his load of brown flour. John Puddister, who oversaw the issuing of relief supplies, was not available. Captain Ayers went to the government office but learned Puddister left St. John's the day before. Other schooners were in port ahead of the *Arginia* and she went on a waiting list.

After several days of waiting Ayers tried to make up a paying freight of whatever goods he could get at various St. John's firms—several puncheons of molasses, potatoes, turnip, a few bags of white flour, other foods and household supplies.

When Ayers thought he had gathered enough to pay for his trip, he left St. John's on December 21, hoping to make home before Christmas Day. On departure morning there wasn't a draft of wind and the *Arginia* had to be towed out of harbour. Ayers had realized his margin of profit on the voyage would be small and did not engage the harbour tug to pull them out. Sails were set and one of the men attached the schooner's dory to the bow.

Hillier and three crewmen climbed aboard the dory and bent their backs to the oars until they rowed out past the Narrows pulling the 60-ton schooner and her partial load of supplies behind them. When the wind filled the *Arginia*'s sails, the men climbed back aboard.

By the next day after the schooner rounded Cape Race the wind picked up from the north east progressively worsening until the *Arginia* reached St. Lawrence on the evening of December 23. Even after the schooner anchored in St. Lawrence harbour, the crew feared she would part her chains in the wind storm and drive ashore. To reach land safely that night the crew threw off the dory and slacked themselves ashore with a rope attached to the schooner.

The following day the weather improved and the schooner escaped undamaged. Her round trip nearly over, the *Arginia* sailed for Point aux Gaul, the home town of Hillier and his brother. Before Hillier left ship he helped discharge some of the freight sold to Gilbert Cake's general merchandise store.

Arginia anchored off Point aux Gaul, for the town had no natural harbour, and while there the schooner was beset by yet another accident. This was Christmas Eve and some of the crew were in good festive spirits. One man stepped on the sprocket chain attached to the running deck engine, fractured his foot and received a nasty cut as well. He was taken to nursing station at Lamaline where Nurse Dorothy Cherry examined the break, then transferred the injured man to the Banker's Hospital at Grand Bank.

For Hillier his voyage on schooner was over. Perhaps he saw the problems and setbacks life in the coasting schooner trade had to offer and decided it was not for him. He earned his living closer to home in the inshore fishery.

As for the *Arginia*, she continued her work as a freighter along the South Coast. In December 1933, she came from Sydney with coal in a storm of wind and could not make Lamaline harbour. Captain Ayers berthed in St. Pierre for six days from December 23 to the 29th, then attempted Lamaline again.

While the coal was being offloaded, another gale pushed the *Arginia* ashore. A small boat came out to take the men off, but they refused and the schooner grounded in Muddy Hole, Lamaline. All coal was taken out. *Priestman*, a dredge stationed in Fortune, came to Lamaline, towed the *Arginia* off and escorted her back to Fortune for repairs.

Again refitted and seaworthy, the *Arginia* sailed and freighted for another ten more years until she went ashore to total loss at Devil's Bay, near Rencountre West, on June 30, 1943.

FLORENCE E. Wrecked and Looted on the Labrador—In the mid-1920's G.& A. Buffett's business in Grand Bank purchased a large banker, the *Florence E.*, at Essex, Massachusetts. The business was heavily involved in bank fishing and larger, more competitive vessels commanded a better share of the market. At this time the American schooner fleet at Gloucester and Essex was in decline as steam trawlers replaced wooden sailing vessels. Bankers like the *Florence E.* were bought by Newfoundland interests at bargain prices.

Built in 1920, she netted 119 tons and measured 105 feet long, 24 feet wide and 11 feet deep. On her final voyage she carried twenty men; eighteen to man her nine dories, the cook and captain—Sam Ridgley of Little Bay, Fortune Bay.

Like most South Coast schooners in the fall of the year, the *Florence E.* finished the fishing season with a voyage to the lucrative Labrador fishing grounds. The schooner left for the North in mid-August and was slated to return to Grand Bank the second week in October. However the productive *Florence E.* never made it back home, but ended her days wrecked and looted on Double Island.

In the early evening of August 31, 1932 the *Florence E.* was anchored and fishing off Battle Harbour, near Double Island. Her dories were off from the schooner; each doryman was doing well with the catch of cod when a sudden shift in wind coupled with the strong Labrador current, overpowered the sailing craft and pushed her toward shoals.

Her bottom nudged the rocks off Southwest Point, Double Island. Water poured into her holds faster than pumps could keep it out and the *Florence E.*, already partly laden with salt fish, grounded.

At first Ridgley assumed it might be possible that with some repairs and work at the pumps, the schooner could be salvaged. Apparently the crew felt otherwise. The schooner was in danger of breaking up if the wind and waves intensified during the night. All twenty men left the vessel for the Labrador mainland leaving the *Florence E.* unmanned and a prey for looters.

For vessels unlucky enough to have struck the reefs off Newfoundland and Labrador's rocky shore, landsmen in the area did what they could to save lives. That became their primary concern. But when human lives were not in danger people swarmed to the crippled, stranded vessel making good use of spoils of the sea.

When a ship was abandoned, these looters, termed 'wrackers,' usually took whatever could be lifted and carried away—food, ship's fittings, sails, gear, equipment, and articles of cargo become especially desirable. Wood, if of no immediate use, was stored for home fires later. Many wrackers operated within the legal limits, on permission, or reported their bounty, but others disregarded the law taking what they could despite the captain's warnings.

After the turn of the century the Newfoundland government tried to control unlawful looting. In December 1903, fifty-seven wrackers were arrested for unlawfully looting the schooner *Bessie Williams*, lost that fall at Stag Harbour Run with 1200 quintals of fish aboard. People had boarded her before she was properly abandoned, taken her sails, fittings and made a complete wreck of the schooner.

When Magistrate Penny and a police constable arrived at Stag Harbour from St. John's, they conducted a full investigation resulting in many arrests and convictions. Five ringleaders received six months in jail, others paid fines and all goods taken from the vessel were seized by authorities and returned to the vessel's owners.

In the case of the *Florence E.*, no court action was undertaken. Captain Ridgley's report to the schooner's owners in Grand Bank informed them their banker was filled with water and could not be refloated. To add to Ridgley's disappointment and frustration, he also indicated in his message that the *Florence E*, despite his vigorous protests, was being stripped and looted by wrackers.

Their season's livelihood lost, he and his crew joined the *S.S. Sagona* and came to Newfoundland via the West Coast arriving at Curling on September 14. From there they connected with the *Glencoe* at Port aux Basques for their homes in Fortune Bay.

The life of a South Coast schooner could end in many ways and this is how the news of the loss of the *Florence E* appeared in the September 2, 1932, edition of *Evening Telegram*:

Landsmen Raiding Wrecked Vessel

The following message was received by the Marine and Fisheries Department yesterday from Mr. S W. Brazil, J.P., Battle Harbour:—"Florence E. from Grand Bank, owned by G. & A. Buffet ashore southwest point Double Island. Full of water and captain says impossible to get off. People raiding against captain's protest.

Newspaper clipping on the loss of the Florence E.

Before the year 1932 ended, another banker in the overseas trade went to the bottom. *Frank Baxter*, owned by Alberto Wareham of Spencer's Cove near Harbour Buffett, began to leak south of Cape Race. The 142-ton banker measured 113 feet long and 27 feet wide and was launched at LaHave, Nova Scotia, thirteen years previously. Wareham's put her in charge of John Murphy, a veteran captain. Murphy was a resident of Bobby's Cove and his crew belonged to other small settlements near Harbour Buffett: mate Thomas Hayward, Davis Cove, near Bar Haven; Pat Whelan, Bobby's Cove; Louis Upshall, Cornish Cove; Tom Mulrooney and Tom Welsh, Red Island.

Frank Baxter left Cadiz, Spain, on November 2 and had a few days of fair weather. On the 9th storms came and four days after sails were stripped. At that point her crew began an unequal fight to save their schooner.

Shorn of canvas, *Frank Baxter* floundered until a jury sail was rigged. This helped make her more manageable and headed into the wind. On December 6 at sundown, the crew sighted the lights of the first ship. Due to distance that ship missed them; then another freighter missed the sinking schooner's signals. By day Captain Murphy ordered distress signals and at night set up signal fires on the masthead.

By now, December 12, they had been out of port forty days; they were about 300 miles south of Cape Race and were getting discouraged. Then the smoke of freighter *Clan Alpine* appeared on the horizon at about 3 p.m. Three men below deck came up to have a look at the rescue ship.

When asked later if they were excited or let out a cheer when the freighter came alongside, *Frank Baxter*'s crew replied, "Well no, we just waited for her to come

Samuel Harris Ltd. of Grand Bank owned vessels which were employed in Northeastern Newfoundland catching and transporting salt fish to his branch business at Change Islands managed by Elliots. On November 18, 1932, the *Howard Young*, built at Lunenberg in 1906, drove ashore at Keels, Bonavista Bay.

near. Of course we were glad because we were afraid we would never get home for Christmas."

Captain Murphy signalled to *Clan Alpine* he had a lifeboat left and would cross in it. The freighter made a protecting lee and the six men rowed over after setting the *Baxter* afire. To fire the schooner to prevent her from becoming a menace to navigation, Murphy and his men dipped blankets in kerosene and ignited them. The last view of the Harbour Buffett schooner showed her burning furiously amidships.

They landed in New York on December 20 where arrangements for transportation home were made by the British Consul, hopefully in time for Christmas.

Chapter Seven

Schooners 'Come to Grief'

B Y THE 1930s Newfoundland's involvement in the salt fish trade with schooners carrying the Labrador and Grand Banks catches to Brazil, Europe and the West Indies was nearly at a standstill. The few firms still in the foreign trade found it difficult to make a profit. John Parker in his book *Sails of the Maritimes* says that high building costs made many of the schooners incapable of paying the owners a fair return on their investments.

In addition to high costs, other problems plagued the schooners. Parker claims many were of poor quality, light design, poorly fastened and many were badly overloaded with their heavy cargoes: salt, salt fish, coal and freight. In an attempt for efficiency and speed, owners resorted to installing engines in vessels that were designed to carry sail. Poor fittings and the extra weight often hastened the schooners' demise.

Inferior materials, poor design, bad fastenings, overloading to the point of strained timbers, and schooners wrecked through navigational errors meant many owners lost one or two boats a season. These were seldom replaced and the small shipyards at Belleoram, Bay d'Espoir, Marystown, Fortune, Burin, Placentia, Grand Bank and Garnish gradually closed out. The white wake of schooners leaving the South Coast ports of call was coming to an end.

EXOTIC Stranded in Bonavista Bay—Patten and Forsey's fish exporting business in Grand Bank began after the turn of the century and lasted until 1922 when both men, J. B. Patten and William Forsey established their own separate firms. While in partnership one of the first banking schooners they obtained was the 78-ton American-built *Exotic*.

In time Patten and Forsey, requiring larger, ten dory bankers, sold the *Exotic* to the Northeast Coast. Here she was lost laden with fish while on the way from St. Julian's, on the Great Northern Peninsula, to Carbonear in November 1933.

On board were Captain William Kelloway, his crew of thirteen men and two females, who were probably cooks. Kelloway later related his experiences on the loss of the *Exotic* in the newspaper *Evening Telegram*.

Early in the voyage wind and snow slowed progress. On November 18 the *Exotic* reached Seldom Come By near Fogo, remained there for eight days and, the weather improving, left for Carbonear. A little after dark the *Exotic* passed the Penguin Islands until around seven miles south of the Cabot Islands, as Captain Kelloway related, he and his crew decided to make for Shambler's Cove, near Bonavista:

> We saw the light on Puffin Island and Shoe Cove, with the wind and snow increasing. Very soon the lights closed in and the *Exotic* was entirely surrounded by breakers and we were forced to drop anchor about 4 o'clock in the morning.
>
> After giving her forty-five fathoms (300 feet) of chain, she brought up or stopped drifting. We

sounded and found the water to be very shoal. We then made preparations to leave the *Exotic*.

However the water was too rough to launch the life boat and to leave the stranded schooner safely. The men and women were forced to remain there until 6 a.m.; by that time the snowstorm had increased to a blizzard. *Exotic* dragged her anchors. With the lives of all fourteen aboard in jeopardy, Kelloway saw no way out of his predicament except to run the schooner over the reef to the beach beyond. He wrote:

> Not knowing where we were we slipped our chain, hoisted our jumbo and the vessel swung around. Very soon she was in a cove, where we dropped our port anchor and made two lines fast to the shore in hopes of saving crew and cargo. We then proceeded to land, and decided to cut away the foresail and make a camp on shore. After camp was prepared I and another man decided to travel and find out where we had come to grief.

This was not as easy as Kelloway and his shipmate thought. Facing a blinding snowstorm, stumbling over rough and unfamiliar terrain, the two were forced to turn back and make preparations with the rest of the shipwrecked crew for the coming night. Dry wood was gathered and a roaring fire lit outside the ship's sail tent. They had little food—mostly bread and that soaked by salt water. Water was plentiful, but, as Kelloway recalled, it was too cold and stormy to eat or drink:

> When daylight arrived, we left with four others of our crew, and after travelling over hills and through valleys, around ponds and across rivers, we came to telegraph poles and found a road that we decided to follow.

Very soon we discovered we were travelling out of Shambler's Cove. Knocking on the door of the first house we came to, we were met by an old friend and acquaintance, Captain Daniel Bragg. In as few words as possible I told him of our trouble and the rest of our crew which had stayed behind at a spot which proved to be Fox Harbour.

Not long after, two motor boats went to the rescue. All were taken safe and sound to Shambler's Cove. While Kelloway gratefully acknowledged his rescuers—Daniel and Wilfred Bragg, Peter Ford, Tom Carter, Moses Newman, Silas White and Wilfred King—he did not name his shipmates in the shipwreck. *Exotic*, built 49 years before in Gloucester, was reduced to debris near Shoe Cove Point on the Bonavista Peninsula.

Courtesy of Robert Stoodley, Grand Bank

Above, the banking schooner *Democracy* which struck a rock ledge near Fortune on May 5, 1933. Captain George Handrigan and his crew of twenty escaped in dories. The 100-ton banking schooner, built at Lunenberg in 1919, broke up in the wind storm.

A month later the 102-foot long schooner *Iron Head*, owned in Belleoram by Loren Nauss Cluett, sprang a leak while en route from Sydney and sank off Miquelon. Crew was saved and landed at St. Pierre.

CHARLIE AND ERIC A Wreck on the Labrador—
Before the fishing season of 1933 drew to a close,
another aged banker was wrecked, this one about 20
miles east of Hopedale, Labrador. Formerly called the
Mystery when built in Gloucester in 1904, the 103-net
ton *Charlie and Eric* had once belonged to Felix Tibbo at
Grand Bank and he renamed her for his two sons.

Tibbo sold this ten dory banker to H.E. Petite's
business at Mose Ambrose. Petite put her under the
command of George Paul, a resident of Mose Ambrose
but born in Femme, Fortune Bay. Tom Evans of Femme
was second hand, or mate; Phil Paul of Rencontre East
was cook and the remainder of her twenty-three crewmen hailed from Bay de L'Eau, Femme or Terrenceville.
After a summer fishing off the South Coast, on September 2 she left for the Labrador fishery.

Off the Labrador cod were caught by jigging, two
men to a dory but, catches for that season were low. On
the morning of September 22 her dories had rowed a
short distance from the schooner to fish; but about nine
or ten o'clock disaster struck. For Captain Paul these
were unfamiliar waters; the *Charlie and Eric* struck an
uncharted rock and grounded on a reef.

Paul fired the swivel, a small cannon-like gun used
to signal the dorymen, and the ten dories came back. By
this time the schooner had partly filled with water and
nothing could be done to save her. Sails were never
lowered, except the foresail was removed and stored in
one of the dories. The captain figured the canvas might
be needed if camp had to be made once the crew
reached land. All clothes and personal belongings were
collected and the crew, in ten dories, left to row to the
nearest headland behind which lay Hopedale, a small
town with about 100 families. Before the men left the

scene of the wreck, swells had rolled the schooner over on her side.

In the morning the weather was good, but before nightfall the wind veered northeast with heavy snowfall. John Barnes of Femme, a doryman on the *Charlie and Eric*, remembered the loss of his schooner:

> Just as my dory mate, John Bartlett (of Femme), and I were about a half mile from the *Charlie and Eric* we saw her tip up headlong about to slip into deeper water off the reef. We had no time to stay around for wind was picking up and we wanted to reach land in daylight, if possible. By the time we made Hopedale about 8 to 10 hours after, there was a foot of snow on the ground. The people put us up in the Grenfell Mission School.

We had no money to pay for food, lodging or good clothes to replace rough fishing wear, so we sawed up the winter's wood for the Mission people and stored it in sheds. Ten days later the coastal boat *Kyle* arrived.

The ten dories were left behind in Hopedale; there was no way the *Kyle* could accommodate them. This was the last run for the coastal boat before winter set in and several hundred 'floater' fishermen and their families were returning on the *Kyle* to their Trinity and Conception Bay homes. Leaving Hopedale on the *Kyle* was the first stage of Barnes' journey to Fortune Bay. He recalled:

> The coastal boat had a load of northern fishermen, their families, fish, everyday living supplies, food even to their goats and hens. There were people sleeping everywhere. As the *Kyle* stopped in various ports, we (the *Charlie and Eric*'s crew) helped the floater fishermen pull up their skiffs and trapboats for the winter.

We eventually arrived in St. John's. Dr. Mosdell, our government member for Fortune Bay, arranged for transportation by train for Port aux Basques. We were on train for 21 hours until we arrived at Port aux Basques; then we connected with the *S.S. Glencoe* making her run down the South Coast to Fortune Bay.

Courtesy John Millett King, Fortune

The *John Millett.* When launched this tern was named the *General Jacobs,* but was renamed when John King bought her. In August 1933, the *John Millett* sank in the Atlantic. Her crew—Captain John King, Robert Anderson, George Elford, Samuel Boomer, Elias Strong and George Walters, all of Fortune—was safely rescued by the freighter *Sangaspar* and taken to Puerto, Mexico.

EXCELLENCE Abandoned in the Atlantic—In a story *Last Voyage of the Excellence* by Charles Woodsworth, the desperation of a schooner's crew is described:

Crashing seas. Torrents of rain. Glaring lightning. A trip-hammer wave that smashed in several of the starboard bulwarks and broke the water butts on deck.

Reid, taking his turn at the wheel, was temporarily blinded by the lightning that swept the inky sky in brilliant and almost continuous flashes. He was unable to see the compass dial and had to be sent below to recover.

Dicks, 21-year old sailor and youngest man on board, who followed him was similarly affected. Shortly after, Manning, the bosun reported water getting into the cargo. *Excellence* was beginning to 'go by her head.'

Water was pouring in from great cracks in hull and decks. All hands, captain and cook, took their turn at the pumps. Ten minutes pumping. Ten minutes rest. Pumping! Pumping! Till hands were mere lumps of gnawing agony and shoulders and backs ached dully.

An hour or two sleep in a day—not more. November first went by. Still no sign of the gale blowing out.

Several days before the above incident, the *Excellence* had left John Moulton's business at Burgeo on October 14, 1933, bound for Oporto, Portugal, with a cargo of dried cod. A two-masted schooner of 140 tons, she was built in 1918 at LaHave, Nova Scotia, and purchased by Fred Wareham of Harbour Buffett only four months before.

In command was Captain Alex Rodway, with him five Harbour Buffett crewmen—mate Neil Masters; bosun Jack Manning; cook George Gregory and sailors Dick Reid and Ralph Dicks.

Born in 1898, in Kingwell on Long Island, Placentia Bay, Rodway began a life at sea at age 14 and survived fifty-two overseas voyages and five shipwrecks in his lifetime. In 1921, at the age of twenty-three, he took charge of his first schooner, the 84-ton *Edith Pardy*, owned by Patten and Forsey at Grand Bank, and crewed by Ben Courtney of Woody Island, Les Inkpen and Bill Pike, Burin. Later in his sea going career, he made several trips overseas to Italy in the Harbour Buffett schooner *Elizabeth Rodway*, a 100-ton vessel built in Codroy and later abandoned in the Atlantic in February 1922 by Captain Robinson.

Excellence went along well on the first few days, a lively northwest gale driving her along under double-reefed foresail. Then on October 27th another gale accompanied by an intense electrical storm temporarily blinded the men handling the wheel. In those days there were no wheel houses on small Newfoundland schooners and the helmsman stood exposed to the elements.

Water poured into opened seams and Rodway ordered the fish cargo jettisoned. Twenty-five tons of fish were brought up armful by armful and thrown into the boiling sea. By November first, still with no letup in wind, lights of a passing ship were sighted. From the course the other ship was holding she would pass to the windward.

Rodway ordered flares lit and fired as the ship drew nearer, then bitter disappointment as the unknown ship slowly passed by, unseeing and perhaps uncaring. By this time all the crew knew, as the wallowing *Excellence* filled with water, they could not make the Azores; their only hope was to be picked up. They toiled on at the pumps.

Early on the morning of the fourth lights of another ship appeared behind them. Carefully Rodway guided the staggering craft across her track. The steamer closed in. In response to a hail from the steamer's bridge, Captain Rodway shouted, "We're leaking! Waterlogged!"

An English voice with a heavy accent came back. "Can you use your own boat?"

"I think so!" *Excellence's* crew hastily cut the lifeboat ropes and got her out. There was no time to take anything, only the captain grabbed his chronometer and sextant.

As the little lifeboat bumped and scraped against the steel side of the steamer, one by one each man went up the rope ladder hanging down her side. Although the sheltering side of the ship calmed the waters somewhat, it was too rough to save the lifeboat and it was set adrift.

It was the Norwegian ship *Hild*, bound from Chicago to Cette, France. From there the crew went to Gibraltar, then to England and across the ocean to Newfoundland and their Harbour Buffett homes.

Harbour Buffett Ships Early Misadventures—Harbour Buffett, found on the southeastern side of Long Island in Placentia Bay, had a long sea tradition; its early economy was based on the inshore fishery, especially lobster, herring and cod. Perhaps the original name of the settlement came from the French—Havre Bouffee. However, local historians claim it is so named because of a flat edge of land resembling a buffet or flat-topped piece of furniture. On the chart prepared by English cartographers Captain James Cook and Michael Lane in 1767, Harbour Buffett and the outlying settlements are shown.

Like most Newfoundland towns, the first date of settlement is not known, but by 1836, according to the first official census, Harbour Buffett had a population of thirty-eight. The population rose to 313 by 1857 and peaked in 1921 with 498 people recorded. During this period Buffett, as it is frequently called, became a service centre, supplying goods and services for other Placentia Bay towns. Newfoundland government's resettlement program began in 1961 and this factor caused a steady decline until the town was abandoned in the mid-seventies. Settlement centred around four areas: the Harbour, North East, the Tickles and Coffin's Cove. Early fishermen worked directly for the merchants or traded their fish for food and supplies. By 1857 there were four large vessels owned in the town and 39 smaller boats.

After the turn of the century merchants and fishermen were engaged in the offshore bank fishery using schooners of between 70 to 90 tons. Salt fish exporting businesses, including Alberto Wareham of Spencer's Cove on Long Island and W. W. Wareham of Harbour Buffett, exported the dried fish directly to Europe and the West Indies in their own vessels. Many of these were large terns, like the *Dazzle, Mabel Frye, Stina* and the four-masted *R.R. Govin,* and were purchased in Scandinavia or eastern United States.

Often ships from European countries came to Harbour Buffett to collect fish or to discharge salt and these too were involved in misadventures at sea. In early February 1923, the Danish schooner *Centaurus* arrived at Buffett to load fish. While in port an argument broke out among the crew; *Centaurus'* captain shot and killed one of his crew. The captain was held in custody by local authorities. Rather than leave shorthanded, the foreign vessel shipped another man from Merasheen Island and slipped out of Harbour Buffett. Oporto, Portugal, was her intended destination, but the Danish ship never arrived there nor, as far as could be determined, any port. By July 16 that year, the *Centaurus* was posted as 'lost with crew'—presumed to have gone down taking one Placentia Bay man with her.

Other Buffett schooners were lost at sea with happier endings; like the *Mildred Adams* and the *Stina*. *Mildred Adams*, Captain Ernest Collett, left her home port on New Year's Day 1932, headed for Sydney to load coal. W. W. Wareham owned this schooner, a large one at 147 net tons and 114 foot long. She was constructed at Mahone Bay, Nova Scotia, fifteen years previously.

Blown across the Atlantic for twenty-three successive days, the *Mildred Adams* sank about seven miles off the Azores and her crew was rescued with great difficulty. For the last seven days of that dangerous journey, the crew—Collett, mate Uriah Gilbert, George and Thomas Upshall, all from Harbour Buffett; cook Stanley Wareham, Kingwell; and Patrick Hounsell, a resident of Bay Roberts—only had a small ration of bread and water for each meal. Food stored for ten or twelve days had to stretch to last twenty-eight days.

From the Azores the crew was taken to England on the steamer *Arundle Castle*; from there across the Atlantic to Halifax on the S.S. *Melita*. Wareham's schooner had been insured for $6,000.

Throughout the 1930s, scores of Newfoundland schooners—stripped of sails, leaking, pumps clogged with salt—were abandoned during foreign-going voyages. Fortunately most crews were rescued by ocean going liners. To stop and carry out a rescue during a voyage had its disadvantages for the large ships: delays in reaching ports, extra pay for the crew, cost of heavy oil poured overboard to calm seas, the food and accommodations shipwrecked crews required.

A rescuing ship received no compensation in case a distressed ship was lost, but owners were justified in demanding payment if another vessel was salvaged or towed to port. Usually large liners stopped, knowing the situation at sea was a life and death struggle. Veteran seamen realized that any time the treacherous ocean could make them the next victim. Captains and their officers forgot schedules, payment and extra expense to ships carrying on the tradition of mutual aid.

The STINA Goes Down—So it was a matter of help without payment for another ocean liner and a helpless Placentia Bay schooner.

Early in 1934, after the loss of the *Excellence*, Captain Rodway went to Sweden for Wareham's business at Harbour Buffett to purchase a three-masted schooner called the *Stina*. Back in Harbour Buffett that summer repairs were made on the 216-ton *Stina*: the rotten jib boom repaired, a broken rudder fixed and topped with a new coat of paint. The mainmast badly needed replacing but the owners decided, since no new stick was

Courtesy Marine Archives

The *Stina* tied up by Wareham's wharf and stores in Harbour Buffett. In the centre (behind schooner's foremast) are flakes for drying fish. The two-storey building on the right is the Church of England two-room school and parish hall.

available, to 'fish' or strap up the old one. That decision perhaps proved to be the *Stina's* undoing.

In the fall of 1934 the *Stina* collected a fish cargo of 5,100 quintals at Grand Bank, Fortune and Burin destined for Europe, but the schooner or cargo never completed the voyage. East of the Azores heavy southeasterly winds hauled around to the southwest; Rodway ordered the foresail reefed as the tern lay to.

During the storm the *Stina* pitched down into a trough, and the three masts, already weak and rotten, broke off in the heavy gale. Rodway had with him a veteran group of hardworking seamen who knew the ways of a vessel; some had sailed with him previously: Jack Manning, Ralph Dicks, George Gregory, Willis Wareham and a sailor from Sweden, Holger Erickson.

Driven before the wind, out of control, the *Stina* drifted out of steamship lanes. Without masts and sails there was no way of controlling the direction and speed of the schooner. Captain Rodway knew the *Stina* didn't leak much, so he put a drag out to hold the headlong progress of his tern.

For three days Captain Rodway and his crew somehow kept the *Stina* before the wind, then, miraculously a steamship appeared—an Anchor-Donaldson line ship, the S.S. *Coracero* carrying fruit from South America to Scotland. The men on the *Stina* were fighting for their lives; ironically, their lives were saved by death on the rescue ship, the *Coracero*.

When the *Coracero's* engineer became ill, he was to be landed at the Cape Verde Islands and the ship changed direction for that port. But the engineer died before he reached Cape Verde Islands, and the ship's course was again altered for Cape St. Vincent off Portugal and then to England. This put the steamer on track for the sinking *Stina* and ultimate rescue for Rodway and his crew. On October 27 they landed at Liverpool, England, to await transportation home.

At Liverpool, as in most major seaports—Halifax, St. John's, New York, London, Boston—there was the Seamen's Institute, an important place for sailors, especially those shipwrecked or awaiting transportation home. Not only was the Institute a place to relax, play cards, get mail and meet other sailors, but for mariners stranded, it provided a place where one could shower, shave and wash clothes. Many had a dormitory where clean beds were available at little or no cost.

Debris from the MONICA HARTERY—On the evening of December 24, 1933, the discovery of debris— boards, planking, part of a stern and railing, torn sails—in the sea around Petites, near Rose Blanche, could only mean another schooner had been lost.

Examination of the flotsam showed the break deck aft to the taffrail had been separated from the main part of a schooner which floated bottom up nearby. The broken nameplate on this wreckage identified her as *Monica Hartery*, a coasting vessel well-known along the South Coast.

Built in Cape Broyle in 1927, the *Monica Hartery* was owned by Leo Button of Lead Cove, Trinity Bay, who had bought the 57-ton auxiliary schooner from Bowring Brothers. Sailing on the *Hartery* were Button and four residents of Channel: Captain Alexander Keeping, Samuel Rideout, William Strickland and Albert Neil.

Two fishermen of Rose Blanche tending nets found wreckage near Black Rock about two hundred yards from the Rose Blanche fog alarm and reported at that time the weather was strong north east winds with snow flurries. Police constable Parrott, stationed in Rose Blanche, gathered a crew for the schooner *Joseph*

Patrick and left to search the wreck site and to salvage materials.

Speculation as to whether some of *Monica Hartery's* crew might have escaped to safety ended at 3 p.m. Christmas Day, when three bodies, those of Keeping, Rideout and Strickland, were found.

As relatives retraced the journey of the schooner, it was learned she left Port aux Basques on December 17 for Sydney, Nova Scotia, loaded cargo and sailed for the South Coast. Early on the morning of December 24, during a wind storm, she probably struck Black Rock and broke up.

Chapter Eight

Cut Down
by Transatlantic Steamers

THE DANGER OF COLLISION with transatlantic liners was an ever present threat to fishing schooners on the Grand Banks. A fifteen thousand-ton steamer would cut through a small schooner like a hot knife through butter. Even if the schooner saw a liner coming, it would be practically impossible to make enough noise to attract the attention of anyone on the larger ship. In the dense fog which often covers wide areas of the banks fishing vessels, often at anchor on productive grounds, would be neither seen nor heard.

Over the years, many schooners were rammed and sunk by ocean liners. In 1886 the *Flying Arrow*, a Harbour Grace vessel with Captain Parsons, was run down in the Grand Banks fog by a large Nova Scotian barquentine. The crew of the *Flying Arrow* saved their lives by climbing on the bobstay of the vessel that rammed their schooner. Nova Scotian schooner *Mahaska*, which had several Newfoundland dorymen among her crew, was run down the French trawler *Remy Chuinard* in 1929 and two men died, one from Nova Scotia and William Hardy of Rose Blanche, Newfoundland. Leo Hackett of

English Harbour East jumped from the *Mahaska* into a fishtub to save himself. In the tub was a hand gaff, an iron hook used to handle fish, which went through his foot resulting in an injury which never completely healed.

South Coast schooners, too, had their share of misadventures from collisions. In 1890 a three dory banker from Burin, the *J.M. Martin*, was run down on the Grand Banks. Two men, Frank Martin and Robert Childs, were drowned. The rest of the crew, Captain John Martin, George and Tom Martin were rescued. Three other Burin schooners met the same fate: *Antelope* in 1894, two men lost; *Roy Bruce* in 1924, all five crew lost and *Vibert G. Shave* collided with a steamer in 1930 and five people died.

VIBERT G. SHAVE, ETHEL COLLETT Two Tragic Collisions—A schooner of forty-eight tons net and launched earlier that year at Metategen, Nova Scotia, the *Vibert G. Shave* was owned by Thomas Shave of Burin. However on her final voyage, September 1930, she was commanded by his son Chesley with his four crewmen. Since the run was a relatively short one and the weather good, the captain's wife travelled with him.

On Saturday, September 27, the *Vibert G. Shave* left St. John's laden with shop goods and supplies destined for her home port. Being new, the schooner was well equipped, all running lights burning and in good order.

According to Captain Shave's testimony later, the weather even up to 11 p.m, was pleasant with moderate winds, a smooth sea on a clear night. A little after twelve, the man on watch John Broydell, called the captain telling him a steamer was right into them. Crewmen on another schooner sailing about a mile away at the time, the *Mary J. Hayden* commanded by James

The Burin schooner *Vibert G. Shave* probably taken in the spring of 1930 showing pans of ice in Burin harbour. On her first voyage she fished off Codroy on the West Coast. That fall she was run down off Ferryland resulting in the death of 5 people.

Hadyen, saw the port light of the *Vibert G. Shave* and the lights of the steamer. They followed both lights up to the point of collision, but were too far away to warn either ship or prevent the accident.

Captain Shave rushed on deck, saw the approaching hull and foam of the steamer and within one minute witnessed the *Haugerland* colliding amidships with his schooner on the starboard side. The Burin schooner sank immediately with the loss of the captain's wife and the crew—Broydell, Joseph Brushett, William Gosling, Philip Vincent, all residents of Burin. The captain later related that he knew his wife was about to come up the companionway behind him, but she never made it.

Thrown overboard at the moment of impact, Captain Shave drifted along the starboard bow of the steamer, then clutched a piece of dory thwart to keep afloat. *Haugerland* came to stop, lowered a lifeboat and picked up Shave who by this time had been in water over thirty minutes. Although a thorough search was made of what little wreckage remained, no bodies were seen.

S.S. *Haugerland*, a Norwegian ship of 3560 net tons with a crew of thirty-five, had left Sydney, Nova Scotia, for Bell Island to load iron ore. According the Marine Court Inquiry held at St. John's in December, the *Haugerland* erred in navigation: she was undermanned and travelling at an excessive speed in much frequented waters; entries in the log book were incorrect; the man at the wheel at the time of collision was fifteen years old with seven months sea experience; and the lookout at the bow did not report another ship's light although it was determined he had time to do so.

Most grievous, *Haugerland*'s officer, minutes before collision, ordered full speed astern. The inquiry determined that had the steamer kept going ahead at a reduced speed she would have kept the schooner afloat for some time possibly saving some crew members. By backing off, the *Haugerland* withdrew from the *Shave*, leaving a gaping hole and she sank immediately.

Four years later, a little after midnight on June 11, 1934, just outside St. John's harbour, another schooner—once owned on the South Coast—met virtually the same fate,. The steamer *Silver City*, out of St. John's and bound for Hickman's Harbour with another vessel, the *I'm Alone II*, in tow smashed into an unidentified schooner.

Silver City's Captain Vardy and crew called out to the schooner asking her to heave to so as he could send a lifeboat to her. Vardy then heard someone shout, "We're sinking!" Voices were heard calling for help in the darkness when the schooner apparently sank about 200 yards from the *Silver City*.

One of the lifeboats was lowered halfway down, waiting for the steamer to reduce speed. The lifeboat's crew finally pulled to the place where cries were coming from, but by the time they arrived no one could be seen.

The steamer and lifeboat continued to search until daylight and then reported the accident to St. John's authorities. The harbour police combed the site and found among the debris a piece of bulwark, an overturned lifeboat and an oily streak on the water. They also located a single suitcase which identified the owner and the missing schooner.

The small boat was taken in tow and the suitcase examined; it contained a suit of clothes, topshirts, a tie and collar, socks, personal letters and shipping bills. The bills were addressed to schooner *Ethel Collett*, Harvey and Company, St. John's. Another receipt, dated May 15, was addressed to Martin Ford, Hare Bay. A postal telegraph to Hare Bay confirmed the worst fears—a Bonavista Bay schooner had been sunk with all hands about five miles off Torbay.

Ethel Collett had left Harbour Grace for St. John's several hours before. That night the light wind was southeast, the night dark but otherwise clear. Lost were Captain Martin Ford, John Curtis, Marshall Wells, Walter Collins, all of Hare Bay; and Michael Bridgeman of St. Brendan's, Bonavista Bay.

Launched in Lunenberg, Nova Scotia, in 1892, the oak built sixty-ton schooner, originally named *Pandora*, was brought to Newfoundland in 1915 by Ernest Collett of Harbour Buffett, Placentia Bay. Collett had her rebuilt in St. Pierre, renamed *Ethel Collett* and then some years later sold her to Collins' business in Hare Bay.

Fortunately not all rammings were as tragic; many South Coast schooners were sunk by larger ships without loss of life. On August 9, 1921, the Italian liner

Valierei collided the 74-ton schooner *Stanley and Frank* while the latter was anchored on Misaine Bank. Owner and captain George T. Bond of Bay L'Argent and his crew were brought to St. Pierre by the liner.

Pauline Lohnes, Captain Mik Augot of Harbour Breton, was rammed by the Belgian steamer *Jean Jadot* on the Grand Banks in 1937; *Eva U. Colp*, Captain Will Thornhill, owned by Forward and Tibbo, Grand Bank, run down by the *S.S. Aun* off Sydney in July 1942; *Miss Glenburnie* of Grand Bank, struck by a steamer off Halifax in 1955; and the *Freda M*, Captain George Follett, was sent to the bottom by the *Manchester Merchant* on October 7, 1961. Her crew—mate George Keeping and his son Chesley Keeping, engineer Martin Parrott, his brother cook George Parrott, Edgar Bonnell, and Jim May—escaped without injury.

These are but a few of the many documented and reported collisions; many relatives of sailors 'lost without a trace' swear their loved ones' ships were cut down and the accident never reported.

A passenger on the transatlantic liner *City of Paris* once said that one night as the steamer was crossing the Grand Banks in a storm, watchmen on the bridge noticed something odd on the forecastle head. On close examination, it was discovered to be ten feet of a schooner's mast lying on the deck. This was reported to the captain who presumed that in the storm they had cut down a schooner and part of her mast had fallen on deck. Not one person had the slightest knowledge or had heard any noise to signal such a tragedy. The fate of the poor schooner's crew can only be imagined.

BEATRICE VIVIAN Encounter with an Ocean Liner—On June 12, 1936, the Burin schooner *Beatrice Vivian* was run over by the 17,000-ton *California* about twenty-five miles off Cape Race.

Built and launched in Burin in November of the previous year, the 100-ton *Beatrice Vivian* was into her first season on the Grand Banks and on the second trip, the caplin baiting. Her crew numbered twenty-six: Captain Jim Gosling and his nephew, George Gosling, mate Jim Way, Edward Smith, Frank Foote, James Legge, Frank Inkpen, Arch and Philip Brushett, Eli Green, Sam Moulton, Sam Cleal, James Keating, George Gosling, all of Burin; Austin Antle, Joe Foote, of Foote's Cove; Austin Myles, Frank Whittle, St. Bernard's; engineer Clyde Hollett, Great Burin; Sam Mayo, James Govier, Gordon Welsh, James Brushett, Marystown; Arthur Rideout, Little Harbour; Ambrose and Charles Synard, Parker's Cove.

Earlier in the week *Beatrice Vivian* had put into Placentia for fresh caplin and had tied up by another Burin schooner *Bruce and Winona*. It was later learned the *Bruce and Winona* sailed from Placentia the same day as the *Beatrice* to obtain bait at Garnish, struck a rock near Corbin Head in the fog and sank that same day.

Beatrice Vivian returned to the banks, resumed fishing and, by late evening, was feeling her way along in the dense fog that often enshrouds the banks south of Cape Race, when the *California* loomed up on the port bow.

Around 5:00 p.m. many of the schooner's crew were on deck; others were aft preparing to go on deck and several were sitting around the forecastle table waiting for supper when the liner cut into the head. These men in the forecastle climbed out of the skylight or up the companionway. If they had been asleep in the forecastle, many would have been killed or drowned.

California sliced through the schooner's bow near the forepeak on the port side—the foremast fell, spars were thrown onto the liner's deck thirty feet above. Part of the schooner's anchor chain and rigging wrapped around the liner's propeller clanking against the steel hull until it was freed hours later. Captain Gosling, in a Halifax newspaper interview, said that:

> The crew rushed to the dories on the starboard side and threw off six. Some men had time to grab a few belongings in the five minutes before the aft section sank, but most of us lost everything. *California* put about immediately to look for a buoy that had been put out at the time of the collision. She had been going at about 12 to 15 knots.

Beatrice Vivian's engineer, Clyde Hollett, who climbed out of the engine room where he had just finished oiling the engine, remembers the disaster:

> When the foremast fell, wires and rigging fell over the dories, so the men used their heavy bait choppers to clear the rigging. These same choppers were the ones the fishermen cursed up in heaps when cutting bait because they were so big and clumsy, but now saved their lives since the dories were cleared quickly. As the men lifted out the dories by hand, no one spoke. There was no confusion or panic.
>
> I was one of the last off and it was the first and only time I ever jumped up into a dory from a schooner. Within 7 to 8 minutes the level of the deck where I stood was under water and I reached up to catch the gunnels. Captain Gosling wanted to get the schooner's papers, but saved nothing; I

managed to grab my oil skins and small clothes chest. The ocean was smooth as a millpond.

Beatrice Vivian hung there for a minute or so, but when the compressed air inside blew out her timbers, she went straight down.

While in the dories the men stayed together and sounded their location with the small foghorn kept in each dory. Without this, it would have been very difficult for the liner's men to find the five dories in the thick Cape Race fog. Within fifteen to twenty minutes the Burin men climbed aboard. Seamen on the *California* lowered straps to hook onto each dory and lifted them on deck.

Gosling was at a loss to explain how the accident happened for although the schooner blew her horn continuously and the steamer's whistle was set on automatic, neither vessel heard the other. Bound from Glasgow, Scotland, to New York, the *California* put into Halifax to transfer the men to the Halifax harbour tug and then continued on to New York.

In Halifax most men were housed in the Seamen's Institute until they made connections with the steamer *Portia* going to Port aux Basques and along the coast to home. Captain Gosling stayed with his son John, a resident of Halifax. When Engineer Hollett returned to Burin, he spent the rest of the summer salvaging the engine from the wrecked *Bruce and Winona*. Eventually he moved to Nova Scotia to work on and then to captain the schooner *Leah Beryl*.

For Captain Gosling it was his second shipwreck in four years. He had been returning from a successful fishing voyage off Domino, Labrador, on September 24, 1932, in the *Marjorie E. Backman*. Although owned in Lunenberg, the ninety-nine-ton schooner operated out of Burin and carried twenty-three Burin crewmen: Captain Gosling, mate William Gosling, George Gosling, Walter Gosling, Thomas Gosling, James Watts, Sam Moulton, Bert Marshall, Max Beazley, Joseph Periera, Joseph Foote, Tom Lundrigan, Norman Brown, George Hamilton, Frank Inkpen, Dick Inkpen, Philip Brushett, Charles Foote, Michael Cheeseman, Len Broydell, Rex Inkpen, Earl Kirby and Isaac Parsons.

Marjorie E. Backman had been fishing on the Labrador since August 8th and was returning to Burin via the eastern route around the Avalon Peninsula when a plank warped off below water line on the vessel's stern. The men pumped for a day hoping to get the *Backman* to shore, but the leak became so bad they were forced to abandon ship. While some pumped, others under orders from the captain, had the dories prepared. Each dory was outfitted with two anchors, three new lines of 300 feet each and all the oars on board the schooner, as well as extra thole pins and sails. The *Newfoundland Quarterly* carried the details of the abandonment as recalled by Joe Foote:

> They knew, as the day wore on, that nothing they could do would save the schooner so all six dories were tied together and slacked astern and the Captain put the crew in the dories and set the schooner on a course toward the land, which probably towed the dories from 8 to 10 miles; when she was up to her deck in water they cut themselves clear. The last Joe saw of the *Backman* was the top of the main boom.
>
> That was about 8 o'clock Saturday night and the long, hard row began without knowing where they were for sure, especially when they made land which none of them had seen before.

The *D.J. Thornhill*, launched in Grand Bank in November 1936, was owned and skippered by John Thornhill. On her deck are relatives and town dignitaries.

Her first crew in 1937 was: Thornhill, cook Charlie Parsons, Am Thornhill, Alex Price, Albert Elms, Alex Bond, George Barnes, all of Grand Bank; Matt Cluett, Steven Cluett, Frank Hoben, Frank Bond, John Cluett, Frenchman's Cove; George Hickey, Pat Hynes, George Saunders, Joseph Hackett, English Harbour East; William Fudge, Belleoram; Reuben Pardy, John Pike, Bay L'Argent; Wilson Dodge, Lally Cove; Albert Grandy, George Cluett, Garnish; and engineer Reg Buffett of Fortune.

For Walter Gosling, the evening he pulled at the oars for land was his birthday, but spent his time battling the elements with his shipmates. Crewman Norman Brown survived that wreck but lost his life four years later when the banking schooner *Partanna* was shipwrecked near St. Mary's Bay in April 1936.

With a strong breeze blowing offshore it took the 23 men, rowing in shifts, thirteen hours to reach Change Islands, twenty-five miles away. When they arrived at the wharf of W.J. Torraville, a prominent businessman in the community, the residents of Change Islands rushed to their assistance, provided food and lodging and even hired the community hall for a social for the shipwrecked men.

After a few days in Change Island homes *Backman's* crew left for Lewisporte on the S.S. *Prospero* and were taken to St. John's by train.

MABEL A. FRYE's Crew Rescued by an American Steamer—On October 7, 1936, the crew of the schooner *Mabel A. Frye* was brought into New York by the S.S. *American Merchant*. The men, all from Kingwell, Placentia Bay, told how their blazing kerosene-soaked blankets had been sighted by Alfred J. Moore, Captain of the *American Merchant*, while both ships were 350 miles off the Newfoundland coast.

Mabel A. Frye, purchased that year by Captain Alex Rodway at Boothbay Harbour, Maine, was a four-masted vessel, grossing 1,151 tons. She was in bad shape and had not been on dry dock for years, but her owner thought he could earn enough in a few trips to pay for repairs to make her more seaworthy.

Rodway, thirty-nine year old master of the *Frye*, and his crew—his brother and mate John Rodway, cook Fred Wareham, seamen Cleverly Ingram, George Slade and Tom Burton—were bound to Conception Bay with Nova Scotian coal. High winds pounded the schooner for five days, sails were torn from the masts, then the masts went overboard. As the seams began to spread, the *Mabel A. Frye* took water for two days as she drove farther asea.

Possibly the crew might have kept the schooner afloat, but coal dust soon clogged the pumps rendering them useless. *Mabel A. Frye* was sinking slowly by the head. Then, as the weary crew realized they could keep the sinking schooner afloat no longer, a rescue ship appeared.

As Captain Rodway remembered: "We sighted the *American Merchant* and she looked mighty fine to us. We had no flares. The seas were running high, but we could see the steamer's riding lights. So I dashed below, grabbed all our blankets and fired them with kerosene."

Captain Moore sent out the *Merchant's* lifeboat with Chief Officer Christensen in charge. In heavy seas and in the dark, it took only an hour before the five Placentia Bay men were taken aboard. When the steamer docked in New York, Rodway and his crew went to the British Consulate to seek assistance for transportion back to Newfoundland.

Rodway lost nearly everything he owned in the *Mabel A. Frye*: his financial investment, money, sextant which he had since he became master in 1923, chronometer, barometer, binoculars and like the rest of the crew, his extra clothes.

Loss of the ALICANTE and other St. Bernard's Schooners—John F. Parrott's firm of St. Bernard's had been in fish collecting and general merchandise business since the 1920s, servicing communities at the head of Fortune Bay. Many schooners were purchased in

After Captain Parminias Banfield of Bay L'Argent lost the *Lucy Corkum* in May of 1931, he was sent to Lunenberg to bring down the *Marie Spindler* for Parrott's business. Built at Lunenberg in 1924, the *Marie Spindler* was lost on November 15, 1937, when she went ashore on a ledge of rock five miles from Curling, near Corner Brook.

Nova Scotia and eventually lost: *Lucy Corkum, Hornet, Marie Spindler, R.M. Symonds* and the 130-ton *Alicante*, built in Lunenberg in 1917 and sold to Parrott in September 1928. Captain Stephen Lawrence, sent to Lunenberg to bring the *Alicante* down, went to Halifax on the trip to Newfoundland to load general cargo. She struck rocks near Boxey Point, Fortune Bay, on September 30 and was wrecked. Another banker employed by Parrotts in the bank fishery was the sixty-ton *J.B. Badcock*. In 1955 with the bank fishery in decline, there was no further use for her. *Badcock* was tied up at English Harbour East and finally sank at her moorings. At low tide she can be still seen today, the last of Parrott's schooner fleet.

MILLIE LOUISE An Unusual Cargo—For two years or so, in the late 1930s, fish processors in Canso, Nova Scotia, contracted Newfoundland firms and schooners to carry dogfish from Newfoundland to Canso. The raw product was ground into fishmeal for fertilizer. The dogfish were taken from Newfoundland waters, thrown on the wharf in the sun; when enough accumulated, they were loaded into the holds of schooners. In the heat, without any means of preservation—salt or refrigeration—the tons of decaying fish attracted flies with their larvae or maggots. Cargoes of reeking dogfish made for some very unpleasant voyages.

John R. Dixon's business in Fortune had a contract to supply the Canso plant and collected their fish from Kilfoy in Little Bay, Placentia Bay, and from Shave's business in Burin. One schooner engaged by them for this trade was the *Millie Louise*, owned by George 'Ki' Noseworthy of Fortune.

An eighty-ton schooner built in 1906 at Mahone Bay, Nova Scotia, the *Millie Louise* was once commanded by Captain Keeping of Ramea. In 1934 Noseworthy bought her from Joseph P. Salter in Sydney; Noseworthy and his son, Gordon, managed the little schooner's affairs for several years. In late June 1938, Gord Noseworthy skippered her and remembers the final voyage:

> *Millie Louise* had no rope lanyards in her rigging, but turnbuckles, a metal screw turned manually to shorten or lengthen rigging. When there was any strain on the sails there was no give or slack like there would be with rope lanyards and she would pull her seams apart in the strain. But we managed all that type of rigging well.
>
> The crew of the *Millie Louise* all belonged to

Fortune: Frank Piercey, Tom Thornhill, George Collier, Mark Blagdon and myself.

In Canso when we took out the fish, the workers wore gas masks to avoid poisoning from the odour and ammonia. Because they lived and slept in the fumes, often crews of schooners carrying dogfish had to go to the doctor when they reached port. Strength of ammonia in bilge water was so strong that it cut the oakum out of the *Millie Louise*'s seams. There were so many schooners lost those years for the same reason.

After the dogfish were offloaded, the schooner went to Sydney and loaded 180 tons of coal for Catalina on Newfoundland's northeast coast. The stevedores refused to trim the coal, such was the smell in the holds, so the crew had to trim, or level back, the coal themselves.

On July 2 the schooner left Sydney. Thirty miles from Scaterie, off Nova Scotia, she started to leak, settling around the sternpost. She went down within a few hours. Captain Gord Noseworthy recalled the loss of his father's schooner:

We got in the small dory she carried, five of us and the schooner's mascot, a big Newfoundland dog. We tied the dog onto the risings of the dory so he wouldn't jump or make her rock.

We saw the *Millie Louise* sink, stern first. We rowed off to keep a little distance away so we wouldn't be carried down by her suction.

The weather was civil with only a small draft of southeast wind. We were rowing toward Scaterie or Sydney when we met another schooner, the *Betty Zane* owned by Ben Lou Inkpen of Burin. He was headed for Nova Scotia and carrying dogfish as we had done only a week or so before. We went up along side of her and asked if they would take us aboard.

Captain Inkpen said, "Yes, but I'm sinking too. We can't keep the water out of her. You can come aboard just the same." We got aboard; then, our crew and his crew kept pumping day and night and the *Betty Zane* stayed afloat. We got into Sydney harbour and tied onto the ballast heap, a place where Newfoundland schooners dumped their rock ballast. Later Inkpen put her on the slip and examined her bottom only to discover all the oakum was gone out of her—rotted by her cargo.

With the problem caught in time Inkpen saved his schooner and later sold her to Warehams; unlike the *Millie Louise* which sank from a combination of reasons: old age, her unusual rigging, lack of oakum in her seams caused by the dogfish cargo and the weight of coal on her final voyage.

MARY SABINA, S.S. CAPE PINE Two More Victims—When Joshua Caines' schooner *Alice Garland* tied up at North Sydney on the night of June 15, 1938, she carried a cargo not listed on her registry—Captain Paddy Dober and his four crew of the *Mary Sabina*. A two-masted schooner built in Lunenberg in 1917, the *Mary Sabina* was registered to Dunphy of North Sydney, Nova Scotia.

Dober had left Fortune Bay three days before with a load of fish destined for Curling on Newfoundland's West Coast. He ran into adverse weather and the 'shifting' boards gave out. These boards separated the heavy mass of loose herring stored in the holds and kept it from sloshing around. With no restraining boards, the herring shifted causing the schooner to list. Extra pressure on the planking opened the schooner's seams; then to add to Dober's problems, the broken boards in the holds damaged the pumps.

In a short time the rail was awash, enabling the crew to walk on it as they tried in vain to distribute the weight of the barrels and cases of freight on deck. As the weather deteriorated, *Mary Sabina's* crew was forced to stop work for it was impossible to move about on the sloping deck.

Daylight the next morning saw the five men huddled in the forecastle as the schooner took on more water. Then the worst possible happened. The single dory *Mary Sabina* carried was lost and their means of self-rescue was gone.

Alice Garland had been near the troubled vessel some hours previously inquiring if the crew needed help. Dober, thinking it might be possible to trim the cargo and pump the vessel out, asked the *Garland* to wait awhile. In the darkness *Alice Garland* moved away and lost sight of the sinking schooner. At the last possible moment, Captain Caines again spotted the sinking ship and took off the weary crew. A few minutes later the *Mary Sabina* rolled over and sank.

On August 18, 1938, the S.S. *Cape Pine* went ashore at Garden Joe, two miles west of Dantzic Point on the toe of the Burin Peninsula. *Cape Pine*, built in Norway in 1899, and formerly named the *Moss*, was owned by the Newfoundland Whaling Company. She had been under charter by J.R. Dixon to carry dogfish to Canso; however on her final voyage she returned from Nova Scotia laden with coal. Captain Dominey of St. John's commanded this fine ship with his mate John Green. Dominey carried Fortune men as crew: Henry Mavin, Bert Thornhill and Elias Anderson.

Cape Pine's compass malfunctioned and, in the dense fog that often surrounds that area, Captain Dominey mistook the small buoy light on Bob's Rock for the Green Island light. The Fortune crewmen, who knew the area well, warned Dominey, but before the vessel's course was altered, she grounded. Her crew escaped without incident.

The TYEE's Tale—On October 29, 1938, an unusual sea accident took the lives of four seamen from the Lamaline-Allen's Island area: Clyde King, Jim Collins, Maurice and Randell Fleming. The Motor Vessel *Tyee*, once a luxury yacht owned in the United States, was en route to Buctouche, New Brunswick, from St. Pierre with Captain Fred Murphy of Prince Edward Island in command.

Murphy was below deck and the four Lamaline men were in the wheelhouse on deck when, without warning, a huge wave sliced across the *Tyee*'s deck. When Murphy came up, everything above deck was washed away—his four crewmen, the wheelhouse and compass. Murphy scanned the sea around but saw nothing.

Somehow Murphy managed to get the sea-racked hulk to the Newfoundland shore and from there to St. Pierre where Henri Moraze, the part owner, had her repaired.

ALLEN F. ROSE Burned and Abandoned—*Allen F. Rose* had only a relatively short voyage, from St. John's to the South Coast, but winter storms of 1938 pushed her several hundred miles out to sea. It was to be her last voyage of the season and owner Hubert Vallis of Ramea, had obtained a small cargo of supplies destined for Ramea and Burgeo. On November 23, a day or so out of port, the *Rose* met adverse winds.

Built in Belleoram in 1909, the eighty-one-ton schooner grounded and sank near Hatcher's Point near Ramea harbour in 1918. George Penny bought the

Frank J. Brinton, owned in Grand Bank by Harris Export Company and later lost on the Labrador, anchored in St. Pierre harbour.

Over the years many South Coast schooners were lost near Pointe aux Canon in St. Pierre's inner harbour: *Hockomock,* owned by Penny of Ramea, lost January 6, 1931; *Mary D. Young,* 1918; Marystown schooner *Lucy Melinda,* 1955 and Hollett's of Burin lost the *Bohemia* in 1927. Wrecks on September 10, 1932, claimed the *Clara F,* and two schooners from Jersey Harbour: Thomas Hardy's *Admiral Dewey,* and the *Marjorie and Eileen,* owned by Chesley Boyce.

sunken wreck, and had divers raise it. After repairs, Penny used the *Allen F. Rose* until 1920 when he sold her to Hubert Vallis who had just lost the schooner *Stanley Joseph*. Eighteen years later, at the time of her loss, she was under the command of Joseph Keeping of Ramea.

Captain Keeping ordered his leaking and sinking schooner abandoned about 250 miles northeast of Cape Race at latitude 49.40 North, longitude 47.57 West. On November 26, a rescue ship had been sighted and it now stood by. Before stepping off he set the *Allen F. Rose* afire to prevent her from becoming a menace to other ships. The *S.S. Mormacsun*, bound from New York to Sweden, carried the Ramea sailors to Gothenburg, Sweden. Families in Ramea had expected their men home by late November, but they had not arrived in due time. When the news came, weeks later, they were rescued, it was a welcome relief.

The same storm played havoc with other Newfoundland schooners: the *Palfrey*, Captain Baxter Burry, left St. John's and went overdue in the heavy weather, but finally reported in at Glovertown. *J.E. Conrod*, under Captain Arch Thornhill, with mate Garfield Rogers, left her home port of Grand Bank on November 24 for a four or five hour run to Burin. Eight days later another schooner, the *Calvin Pauline*, reported her limping into St. Pierre, storm tossed, with her foresail torn away. She had not reached Burin.

Fox Island Tragedy—Fox Island, near Ramea, had been the scene of a poignant tragedy during the August Gale of 1935. On August 24, the *Annie Young* left Fox Island in company with another schooner the *Man Alone*, both bound for the Labrador fishery.

Penny of Ramea owned the twenty-two ton *Annie Young* and her crew were all of Fox Island: Captain

George Hayman, John McDonald, both married; the rest were single men, cook Bennie Hayman, John Marks, John Warren and three Coley boys. The captain was 34 years old and left three children. Her disappearance is told in song and story in *Come and I Will Sing You*, edited by Genevieve Lehr and Anita Best.

That night as the gale progressed both ships thought they could ride out the storm. From a distance the men of the *Man Alone* could see the other schooner's mainsail was torn away and she was not faring well in the intensifying wind storm.

Before the two schooners parted company, the last words Captain Warren of the *Man Alone* heard *Annie Young*'s mate John McDonald say were, "The rain will be good for the women's gardens. It will help them grow." As the storm grew fiercer the lights of the *Annie Young* could be seen for five hours; then she went down carrying eight Fox Island men with her.

Man Alone barely survived the storm, drifting into Codroy almost a wreck. Her men had been without food or water for thirty-seven hours.

Chapter Nine

Tragedy Along the Coast

MULTIPLE TRAGEDIES and death from drowning came all to often in the days of sail; many were due in part from the risks men had to take to secure a livelihood—transatlantic voyages in small schooners, trips to mainland ports in winter storms and the hazards of bank dory fishing. The only monetary benefit the Newfoundland government could give to the widow or dependant of a man drowned from a banker was a single grant of eighty dollars. To qualify for this insurance the fishermen paid fifty cents each spring when he signed on a banking schooner. Eighty dollars was very inadequate and served, at best, as a temporary relief.

Another form of financial assistance given to widows came from the Permanent Marine Disaster Committee at St. John's. This fund was initiated by John Alexander Robinson, the one-time editor of the *Daily News* and Postmaster General. Widows of men lost on coasting schooners or fishing from dories in the inshore fishery could apply; often the response was affirmative and immediate.

A third charity was community based. Collections of cash and food in the victim's town and surrounding communities often saved starving families as the toll of sea disasters along Newfoundland shoreline continued to rise.

MARY CARMEL Mute Evidence of a Major Tragedy—Sometime around mid-December, 1939, mute evidence of a sea tragedy presented itself in Burgeo-Ramea area: the body of a battered dog drifted ashore on Big Island, Ramea, and then a suitcase belonging to Steven Dolimount was found on Burgeo Beach, near Burgeo. Both dog and suitcase were from the small coasting schooner *Mary Carmel*, owned by Clifford Shirley of English Harbour West.

Earlier in her career when the *Mary Carmel* was owned and captained by Alfred Marshall of Burin, she struck the rocks at Fox Cove near Burin in an October

Courtesy *Those Bright Days*
Souvenir Booklet of St. Jacques/Coomb's Cove, 1992

The final home of the *Mary Carmel* was English Harbour West, on the western side of Fortune Bay. Earliest records for English Harbour West, the 1836 census, show a population of seventeen and numbers reached a peak of 393 in 1971. Always dependent on the fishery, major businesses over the years were those of Job Brothers, J. Petite and Sons, Job Brothers and Clifford Shirley.

Schooners tied up at Petite's premises are: *Jenny Elizabeth*, (left) later sold on the North West Coast and lost on Little Pound Cove Reef, Badger's Quay, July 18, 1959. *Palitana* (middle), the same schooner that rescued the *Sunner*'s crew in 1928, burned and sank at Ming's Bight, White Bay, on June 11, 1957. *Charles L*'s (right) life ended more violently: on April 6, 1969, she hit the rocks on the southwestern side of St. Pierre Island and one young man, a friend of her new owner, drowned in the

The twenty-three ton *Mary Carmel* moored at Burin. In December 1939, she was lost with crew.

storm, 1922. After going ashore, the schooner quickly filled with water and sank. Several residents of Fox Cove witnessed the ship's distress, gathered on the shore to help out and saved Marshall from drowning.

William Brushett, the diver at Burin dock, temporarily repaired the *Mary Carmel* until she could be towed to dock for repairs. Marshall then sold her to the Shirley interests at English Harbour West where she fished for many years under the command of John Jim Brushett of Jacques Fontaine. *Mary Carmel's* work in the spring was to collect lobsters and, in late fall, when the fishing season ended, to bring freight and supplies from mainland ports to the South Coast.

In the fall of 1939 Captain Philip Yarn of Mose Ambrose brought coal from Sydney to English Harbour West and had good weather all the way, making the trip to and from the mainland in good time. By December, when Captain Yarn decided to make a second trip to Sydney, he had pushed his luck too far, for the treacherous weather of early winter came on. He reached Grey River and, seeing the ominous change in winter weather, decided to turn back.

At 3 p.m. on December 11, Penny's schooner *Mary F. Hyde*, on her way to Ramea, passed the *Mary Carmel*, already labouring and making very poor headway. Crew of the *Mary F. Hyde* thought the eastbound schooner would make it to harbour at Francois by dark.

That was the last time anyone saw the *Mary Carmel* or her men—Philip Yarn, age 37; and two men of English Harbour West, Steven Dolimount and George Bishop. Apparently as it grew dark and as the wind increased, Yarn realized it was too stormy to get into Francois and decided to run to sea or to make Ramea.

That night it blew a gale, swinging around southerly with heavy glitter. Residents of English Harbour West remember the extent of glitter when the next morning many found their outdoor radio antennas broken under its weight. In the dark night of blowing snow and ice, the *Mary Carmel* ran upon a rock or offshore ledge. With nothing moveable on her deck and dory and hatches lashed securely, everything went down with the schooner.

From the only two pieces of evidence, it was assumed the schooner struck Little River Rocks or South East Rock near Ramea. South East Rock, especially treacherous, was the scene of the wreck of the *County of Richmond*, lost with crew eighteen years previously.

Captain Yarn's dog, battered and broken, washed up on the beach at high water mark and Dolimount's suitcase were all that remained of the schooner; no bodies or other wreckage of any kind was located.

The tragedy cast a gloom over the small settlements where the men belonged, especially during the Christmas season. Six men went around English Harbour West on horse and sleigh collecting fifty dollars and food. Much of this was donated to the wife and four young daughters of George Bishop.

Mary F. Hyde, a larger vessel at 78 tons, made port safely. Built in Lockeport, Nova Scotia, in 1911 this schooner was first owned by the Patten and Forsey firm in Grand Bank, who sold her to Penny's business at Ramea. At the time of her loss, many years after the *Mary Carmel* incident, she was owned by the Pikes of Port aux Basques.

IRIS VERNA   Burned on the Fishing Grounds—Two men left aboard the *Iris Verna* were left to cope with a shipboard fire while the fishing crew of eight were out in dories. Owned by Warehams of Harbour Buffett, the *Iris Verna* fished off Rose Blanche on February 23, 1940, when the engine backfired, ignited gas nearby and started an intense fire which the captain and the cook could not contain. One of the other four dories took the

Courtesy of Walter Simms

Jean Wakely, moored on St. John's South Side. A 263-ton tern built in 1920 at Essex, Massachusetts, the *Jean Wakely* was first owned by Thomas Wakely of Harbour Buffett. When the Wakely business closed out, the schooner was sold to Petites of English Harbour West. During the Prohibition Era she made many trips to the American east coast carrying liquor from St. Pierre.

two stranded men aboard and after some time all were rescued by other fishing vessels.

By 1939, as the world was once again embroiled in global warfare, demand for Newfoundland salt fish rose and prices improved. Banking schooners, despite the dangers from hostile enemy submarines which once again lurked off Newfoundland, continued to fish the Banks.

FLORENCE Split Open on the Banks—John B. Patten, a salt fish exporting businessman in Grand Bank, owned the 130-ton *Florence*. Built in Nova Scotia over twenty-five years before, the schooner was badly in need of repair. In the spring of 1940, Patten hired Arch Thornhill of Anderson's Cove, a well-known fish killer, as her skipper.

Captain Thornhill chose a seasoned, hard working crew of Fortune Bay seamen for his schooner: cook Cecil Bolt, George Harris and Cecil Elms of Stone's Cove; Win Good, Little Bay East; Clyde Freeborn and Wallace Vardy, Harbour Mille; Phil Grandy, Garnish; Ches Price, Reuben Price, George Price, Allen Hillier, Abe George Hillier and William Price of Brunette Island; and William Riggs, Charlie Francis, Hector Rose and Charlie Fizzard of Grand Bank. William Thornhill of Anderson's Cove was kedgie, or deckboy.

As kedgie, Thornhill would have been assigned the general duties of most kedgies: helping the cook, cleaning dishes, peeling potatoes, catching painters or lines when the dories came back from pulling trawls. A kedgie only went in the dory if one of the two dorymen became sick; then, he was expected to bait hooks and pull trawls.

Even during the long hours when galley work was finished and the dories had not yet returned from their set, the kedgie's life was not idle. Many were known to set a small 'snapper' trawl over the side of the schooner, often catching a few hundred pounds of codfish to augment the voyage.

During her last trip to the Grand Banks, the *Florence* had gone to Dildo, Trinity Bay, to replenish her bait supply. While returning to the banks from Dildo, the schooner was running off before the wind with all sails—aft, fore, jib and jumbo—out and filled. The crew heard something crack with a loud snapping noise, but not knowing what had broken, supposed it to be a spar or mast splitting under the heavy strain of canvas. Nothing seemed out of place and the banker sailed on.

For three or four days in late September the *Florence's* eight dories worked the Grand Banks, but Captain Arch Thornhill decided fishing would be better on St. Pierre Bank.

Fish was more plentiful on the St. Pierre Banks, and by Saturday, September 30, since her holds were almost full, the *Florence* was due to sail for Grand Bank that night to arrive in port Sunday morning. All dories with sixteen men were out trawling; the only three crew left aboard were the captain, cook and kedgie.

Captain Thornhill prepared to pick up dories from the last set. The jib sail was traced up in the jacket and the captain told kedgie William Thornhill to go forward and lower the jumbo sail. When the kedgie reached forward the captain made his jog over to get his fishing dories.

There was practically no wind, but when the *Florence* made her second dip into the slight swell, the jib stay and jump stay—wire or strong rope used to support the masts and spars—burst and the two spars came down with a crash on the deck near the steering wheel.

The two masts came loose and this, in effect, split the *Florence* open.

Captain Thornhill shouted for the kedgie to run back aft to avoid being hit with falling rigging. Both jumped down through the gangway and took refuge below deck. Slight bumps on the swell eventually caused the two masts to work loose and break off—the foremast snapped level with the deck; the mainmast, a foot or two above that.

When the masts fell, rigging, blocks, crosstrees and everything else left aloft crashed onto the deck or over the side. Water poured in through gaping seams opened in the stern and the *Florence* quickly settled lower and lower into the water.

Captain Thornhill stood upon the cabin with a flag tied on to a fish fork and signalled another schooner within hailing distance. This was the *Mahaska* (II), a Nova Scotian schooner built in Lunenberg in 1928, fishing a berth away from the *Florence. Mahaska's* crew, one of whom was a Burgeo resident, Garfield Marsden, had seen and heard the masts and spars falling over and thought the *Florence* had been torpedoed by German submarines known to be operating in that part of the North Atlantic.

Mahaska came down and took off Captain Arch Thornhill, kedgie William Thornhill and the cook, Cecil Bolt. To keep from drifting away from the *Mahaska* trying to reach them, Thornhill had dropped anchor. It seemed as if the *Florence* would sink within a few minutes, but stayed afloat for four hours. No one went back aboard; so in effect, the crew lost all personal belongings except their oilskins.

Dorymen of the *Florence,* spread out a half mile to a mile from their mother ship, were not aware of the calamity aboard their schooner. With her masts gone and the schooner low in the water, they could not see her and they supposed the cracks to be a signal gun. After rescuing the crew, the Nova Scotian schooner went to the dories and picked up each doryman.

Four hours after the *Florence* literally 'fell apart' she sank, still at anchor. When she struck the bottom, the old schooner broke completely apart and both bulkheads, the one forward and the one aft, came to the surface. *Florence*'s two airtight hardwood tanks, which had once held drinking water but were now almost empty, burst out of the sea when they floated up.

The crew went to Sydney on the *Mahaska*, and from there to Halifax where they connected with the *S.S. Baccalieu* headed for Fortune Bay. From the time the *Florence* sank until they arrived back home, the nineteen men were one week overdue.

At the time of her loss, the *Florence* had obtained 600 quintals, but the crew received no earnings. In the days of hook and trawl fishing the men were credited only for fish landed and since their catch was on the bottom of St. Pierre Bank, no one was paid in cash or kind.

Although Patten's business looked after their transportation from Nova Scotia to Grand Bank, from there each man had to find his own way to his place of residence. Kedgie Thornhill asked Captain Sid Harris, who was getting ready to sail the *Pauline C. Winters* into Fortune Bay to pick up crew, for a passage to his Anderson's Cove home.

During heavy wave action, thousands of pounds of pressure per square inch hammer a ship's hull. Wooden schooners often withstood this pressure, but as the ship ages her timbers and caulking, if not properly maintained or replaced, weakened and her chances of opening up during intense gales increased. Experienced

On the left the 124-foot long *Eileen C. MacDonald*, built in Shelburne in 1941 and owned by Wareham of Harbour Buffett, lies tied up in Grand Bank harbour. On November 23, 1966, she was destroyed by fire at St. Kyran's, Placentia Bay.

On the right the deeply laden *Autauga*, owned by Joseph Rose of Jersey Harbour, prepares to dock at Grand Bank. Fourteen of her crew line the bulwarks in anticipation of seeing friends and relatives. In September 1951, the *Autauga* was wrecked near Cape Breton Island. Captain Pius Augot and crew—Jasse Bishop, Reg, Mike and Phil Augot, John, George and Jack Stone—rowed ashore safely.

captains and skilful seamen often endured and survived long and severe ocean storms, kept the schooner's head to the wind to reduce wave action and safely navigated their schooners the several thousand miles to and from Europe or the West Indies.

ELLEN AND MARY Survives the Winter Winds—In late January when weather conditions on the treacherous Atlantic are at their worst, the 129-ton schooner *Ellen and Mary*, heavily laden with salt for Simeon Tibbo's fish exporting firm at Grand Bank, rode out an intense but typical Atlantic gale.

For three days while a thousand miles out from Portugal, the staunch vessel was buffeted and bounced by heavy seas. Although she had lost some canvas, the *Ellen and Mary* came through the storm in relatively good condition. As the wind abated her captain, William Courage of Frenchman's Cove, Fortune Bay, sighted an American passenger liner off in the distance.

After consulting his crew, Captain Courage decided to hoist signals and hail the large steamer. Quite often vessels 'spoke to' each other for several reasons: to verify position; to check compass deviations; to pass on news of each other's whereabouts and condition; and to obtain fresh water, food, or other necessary supplies.

Newfoundland crews used opportunities like these, especially if the schooner's journey had been long or storm delayed, to ask for 'baccy.' Passengers of ocean liners, amazed at the seemingly fragile cockleshells bobbing beneath them, often threw cigarettes or tobacco down to schooners' crews.

The oceanic steamer Courage hailed, steel-hulled and powerful, had sustained damage from the mountainous seas whipped up by the gale. Broken doors, buckled bridgework, missing vents, smashed glass and other minor wear and tear could be seen from the deck of the *Ellen and Mary*.

During the course of conversation the commander of the liner, seeing the decks of the trim schooner were nearly flush with the sea, asked where the *Ellen and Mary* had been during the violent midatlantic storm. Courage could only reply, "Right here, of course. Where else could we be a thousand miles from land?" The American could scarcely believe the 110-foot wooden vessel could stay afloat in such a storm much

Courtesy Capt. John Smith

Not only did schooners like *Ellen and Mary* contend with mid-ocean storms but also with dangers near land. Here she lies aground in mouth of Grand Bank harbour. At high tide and with the offloading of fish, she was later refloated.

less come through unscathed with white water running across her decks constantly.

No doubt a testament was given there to the high calibre skill and judgement of her captain and crew; as well, a tribute paid to the seaworthiness of handsome schooners like the *Ellen and Mary*.

Built in Essex in 1912, the *Ellen and Mary* eventually succumbed to the ravages of rocks in the St. Lawrence River on July 18, 1942. Her captain at that time was Gordon Walters, who with his crew, Gabriel Banfield, Fred Cluett, Carl Grandy of Garnish and Charlie Holley of Point Rosie, rowed safely ashore without personal injury.

JEAN H. ELFORD A Thwarted Prospective Voyage—In August 1942, a two-masted schooner sank in the Gulf of St. Lawrence, that stretch of water separating Newfoundland and Labrador.

Originally called the *Agnes Moulton* and built in Burgeo in 1915 by the Moulton business, she was a six dory banker of forty-two tons. Later C. B. Spencer and George Elford of Fortune bought her, renamed her *Jean H. Elford* and put George Ayers in command. In July 1942, Elford sent her on what was termed a 'prospective' fishing voyage to the Labrador coast.

On this voyage the schooner was insured, at high premiums, for her capacity of 300 quintals of salted cod and would be paid for that amount whether filled or not. For most businesses however, the high cost of this type of insurance was prohibitive and most chose not to insure for a prospective voyage, but took their chances on the fickle fish and unpredictable weather.

Jean H. Elford took ice at Fortune, bait at Dantzic Cove and sailed along the South Coast and around Cape Ray for the Labrador. Off Cook's Harbour in the Straits, the schooner did well. Fish was plentiful. Then a lack of bait and plenty of wind did the old vessel in. Six of the eight crew with Ayers on that final voyage were cook William Spencer, Clarence Pierce, George Buffett, William Forsey, John Major and John Day, all residents of Fortune.

After eight days in Port Saunders waiting for better weather, the *Elford* prepared to return home. Ten miles from Cow Head Bay the schooner was discovered to be leaking heavily. Ayers thought to make the Bonne Bay light, six miles away, but the schooner had settled so badly, he told his eight men to prepare a dory and abandon ship. One of the crew, William Forsey, later wrote of the experience in a song, partly reproduced here:

...Disaster struck our first attempt
Our long boat it did go.
We had to calm the heavy sea with oil
To face that heavy blow.

As the golden sun did sink
Away out in the west
The *Jean H. Elford* dipped her nose
And went down for a rest.

...We made land at Rocky Harbour
At twelve o'clock that night.
May God protect those people there
For they did treat us right.

We cannot forget those family of Dykes
Who were so good and true
Who did so much for us that night
The little shipwrecked crew.

MARIANA Sunk by Weight of Coal—Built by Howard Allen at Sable River, Nova Scotia, the *Mariana* had several Newfoundland owners until John Marshall Fudge of Belleoram purchased her. Fudge bought the vessel from Mr. Haynes of Bonavista in June of 1941 and used her on the coal run to and from the South Coast. His crew hailed from Belleoram: Randell Fudge, Cecil Adams, Tom Dominaux, Stan Savoury and cook Levi John Savoury.

Loaded with coal, the *Mariana* left Sydney in early October 1942. Before she left the dock, the foreman in charge of loading exclaimed, "That schooner is as leaky as any that ever loaded at this coal pier." One of her crew claimed you could wash your feet on her deck. Yet despite the obvious danger, her men sailed the leaky, aged vessel for this was their work and life on the sea.

On the way out through Sydney harbour at four o'clock in the evening, the weather was fine and calm. Captain Fudge read the evening newspaper while sitting on deck. That night as the wind pitched to the southwest and increased in intensity, the rudder was damaged when the helmsman gave the schooner too much wheel. Later the wind rose to gale force, about sixty or seventy miles an hour from the northwest.

Thirty miles from Pass Island on Newfoundland's South Coast, the *Mariana* was leaking severely. By then the crew had pumped so much, they had to put bread bags around the handles of the break pumps so keep from galling their hands. When crewman Stan Savoury, who had gone up the rigging to light the riding lights, came down and entered the forecastle, he went to his waist in water.

This was reported to the captain in the wheelhouse who ordered the schooner brought to. Attempts were made to pump more and bail out the water, but it was of no use—water poured in faster than it could be taken out. Timbers strained under her weight of coal and water; the *Mariana* was going under fast.

Seaman Tom Dominaux was ordered to go forward, get the axe and cut the ropes to the riding sail, foresail and jumbo. With no sails up the schooner would slow enough to get a dory over the side. In his haste to remove the foresail and in the darkness, he missed the halyards and took a gouge out of the foremast. This was the last attempt to lower the schooner's sails and the *Mariana* sank, as her crew described it, with her 'clothes on.'

After Captain Fudge decided it was time to abandon the schooner, his men prepared to get the dory off. He had bought a new dory in Sydney for $140.00, perhaps in anticipation of problems, but this dory was smashed up in the attempt to get it over the side.

Fudge ordered the old dory, smaller and not as seaworthy, put over the side; by this time with the bulwarks almost level with the sea and water ran across her deck, the second dory slid over the side without problems. All six crewmen got in. Captain Fudge said, "Look! She wants to come with us." As the dory ran before the swells, the partly submerged *Mariana*, with her canvas up, was running too and seemed to follow the men for some time before she finally went under.

In a gale of wind, with no light for the lantern had broken and there was no flashlight, they tried to reach shore in a leaky dory. Daylight broke and all that day the *Mariana*'s crew pulled for shore. As darkness approached, they saw land. Captain Fudge, who in later years, recorded his experiences on the *Mariana*, recalled:

> At once I knew that this must be Muddy Hole, a small settlement between Cape La Hune and Burgeo. We must make a landing quickly, for darkness was coming on and the sea was breaking across the shoal-barred harbour. We were tired and hungry, and once in a while one of us would fall asleep.
>
> Determined to make landing, we had been 24 hours without sleep and very little food for 30 hours... if we failed to land there, there was no other hope. The next landing place was twenty miles on our lee, and with night coming on, we would soon fall asleep. Then we would be at the mercy of the sea.
>
> After watching the barred harbour break three times, we passed over a sand bar and into the small harbour in safety. The good folks of Muddy Hole pulled our dory up and took us to their homes.

To reach their homes in Belleoram, the crew hired a motor boat to take them to Pushthrough; there the shipwrecked crewmen found a friend, Captain Ambrose Bond, on the schooner *Gypsy Smith* who was headed down the coast and Bond carried them home.

Chapter Ten

Encounters with the Enemy

THROUGHOUT THE 1939-45 Battle of the Atlantic, many Newfoundland fish merchants continued to send their schooners laden with cargoes of salt cod to ports in Europe without the aid of convoy protection.

Convoys were established to keep open the lifeline to the United Kingdom, but in the Atlantic the Allies still lost 2,603 merchant ships totalling 13.5 million tons, say Terry Hughes and John Costello in their 1977 book *The Battle of the Atlantic*.

Being in a convoy then was no guarantee of safety. Furthermore, the freighters and warship escorts tended to leave smaller craft behind, especially during frequent Atlantic storms when the ships would lose contact with each other and were scattered over a wide area.

ROBERT MAX Face to Face with the Enemy—Four transatlantic crossings were made by the *Robert Max*, a 180-ton wooden schooner owned in Grand Bank, on Newfoundland's South Coast. She set sail on her fifth wartime crossing in late July 1941, under Captain Harry Thomasen with his crew of Newfoundland merchant seamen: Gordon Hollett, Luke Rogers, Alex Banfield, John Douglas and Sam Pardy.

Launched in Shelburne, Nova Scotia, the 136-foot long *Clara B. Creaser* (later renamed *Robert Max*) was termed a knockabout. Knockabouts, with their long overhang and no bowsprit, became a popular schooner style for two reasons: the traditional bowsprit presented a danger to men furling sail and many men were lost working from there. The bowsprit also created manoeuvring problems when docking.

he *Clara B.* waits, in good company, to the left of the *Bluenose*. The *Bluenose* is bedecked with flags with attendant crowds at her launching. *Clara B. Creaser* served two countries well for 22 years until she was sent under by a German shells.

August 4 dawned beautiful and clear; *Robert Max* was 1100 miles from Newfoundland and off the Portuguese coast. A little after midday a German submarine surfaced nearby, fired one warning shot across the stem, one over the masts and ordered the boat to heave to.

Under orders from *U-boat 126* commander Ernst Bauer, Thomasen and two crewmen rowed over while the other three Newfoundlanders sailed the schooner up into the wind and then lowered the jib, a small sail. This allowed the *Robert Max* to drift slowly down near and past the sub. Seaman Sam Pardy recalled:

> From where we were, we could see her flag with the swastika on it. We kept jogging around and after a while we saw the skipper and the two men coming in the dory. They hollered, 'Heave off the lifeboat. We only got ten minutes!' They rowed up

around the port side and tied the dory on against the forward rigging.

Captain Thomasen later related that on board the sub he was interrogated about the *Robert Max*'s cargo and destination. Although the schooner was not armed, the Germans decided to sink her for in their opinion she carried food for Allied nations. Crew members of the *Robert Max* were given 10 minutes to gather personal belongings and move away.

The first four shots were aimed at the two spare barrels of gas and kerosene strapped against the cabin. Almost immediately these exploded and burst into flame. Several shells ploughed into the engine room putting this section of the schooner afire. As a final show of bravado, the German gunners took aim at the forerigging and cut the halyards, causing the foresails to fall. Next the mainmast and mainsail received several rounds.

Under a barrage of 28 shots, the *Robert Max* went under, but as if unwilling to resign herself to the deeps, the schooner sank only until she reached her mast-heads, near the cross trees. From several yards away in the open lifeboat the six Newfoundland seamen watched her for about 15 minutes. Finally she gave her farewell nod and disappeared.

Each man bent to the oars to pull away from the lonesome scene where only an hour before their home and refuge on the sea had sailed. As seaman Pardy recalled:

> This was not a nice experience to go through, but then we rowed away. The submarine came up again alongside, took us aboard and we went up talking to the captain and some sailors. The inside was hot. The sub's crew all had their underwear

and pants rolled up to the thighs and were barefooted.

Captain Thomasen went to the conning tower. I was up three steps and put my hand on the gun that fired at us. I had to take it off quick it was so hot where they had used the shots.

The German commander gave them a course to the coast of Portugal and, in a gesture of humanity, offered to attach a steel cable to the lifeboat and tow the captain and crew toward the nearest land. He added a word of caution: if enemy planes approached while they towed the lifeboat, the sub would have to make an emergency dive and possibly take the lifeboat with her.

Thomasen refused. Then the Germans offered to tie on a rope instead of a wire cable — a rope could be chopped quickly. But fearing an attack upon the submarine by Allied planes or ships, the captain took his chances in an open lifeboat that he knew was well manned and provisioned. Most likely the good weather and favourable wind would push them to the coast. He organized the six crew members into shifts for rowing and keeping watch. As Pardy pointed out:

> We came 297 miles in 72 hours aided by oars, a small sail and a good wind by night. Our hands got shiny on the last of it from rowing and bailing which was necessary because the lifeboat hadn't been in the water for a year. We'd have turns; John Douglas, Gord Hollett and I sitting on the bottom of the boat where we'd bail out water. When we'd get up our rubbers would be full of water. It wasn't very comfortable — six men in a small boat and their hands sore.
>
> The course they gave us wasn't right. It was a long ways out. We were 700 miles from Portugal, but there's three islands out in the ocean, the

Azores. Well, we got to the southernmost one that was about 90 miles long.

The men saw the purple smudge of Santa Maria at 1:30 p.m. on August 6. Its mountains could be seen from quite a distance away. It was not until twelve hours later they reached and anchored off its lee shore. Thomasen, Pardy and the other men had found the port of Ponto Delgado on the island of Santa Maria, Azores:

> We had 120 fathoms of buoy line and an anchor with us, and we put that overboard and lay down to rest. I made a cigarette out of some Jumbo tobacco we had. I tore a leaf out of the old man's *Belcher's Almanac* and made a smoke out of that.

As daylight broke on August 7, they were seen by a local fisherman who guided them through the rocks to safety of the beach. Their odyssey was over.

Pardy reflected on the German sailors he had encountered—young men like himself caught in a drama they had no control over:

> On board the submarine, you know, there was this German about my age and size. He said to me, 'This war no good, Jack. No good for you, no good for me.'

CARIBOU One Man's Fight for Survival—On the evening of October 13, 1942, Mac Piercey joined the gulf ferry *Caribou* en route to Newfoundland. After three years in naval theatres of the North and South Atlantic, he would enjoy the days of relaxation and the time to visit family and friends in Fortune, on Newfoundland's Burin Peninsula.

In North Sydney, Nova Scotia, a few minutes before the ferry slipped her moorings for her final run, Piercey and his hometown friend Hedley Lake, who was also a Royal Navy sailor, were assigned cabin #17

Caribou leaving Newfoundland. Put into the Gulf service in November 1925, she made tri-weekly crossings. Death, destruction and the horrors of war were brought closer to Newfoundland when a German sub sent her to the bottom around forty miles from Port aux Basques.

on C deck, three levels down. Mac was surprised that no one instructed the *Caribou's* passengers where lifeboat stations were located. Perhaps it was believed unnecessary for, as an extra precaution against enemy attack, the ferry was escorted along the 96-mile voyage by an armed minesweeper, HMSC *Grandmere*.

As he made his way below to his room, Mac noted, with an instinct that came with his years in the navy, where all exits and potential obstacles were located. Once the ferry was at sea there were no portholes to see through. *Caribou*, like all Allied vessels, travelled under the rigidly enforced 'lights out' war regulation and had her windows painted black. Passenger accommodations were dimly lit rooms accessed only by a labyrinth of darkened companionways and corridors.

But at 3:40 a.m., a few hours after the *Caribou* left port, a German U-boat torpedo slammed into the ferry, destroying her and taking 136 of her crew, civilians and servicemen to the bottom. Of the twenty-five Newfoundland members of the Royal Navy on the *Caribou's* last trip, thirteen died.

When the ferry shuddered and ripped apart under the impact of the enemy explosives, Mac leaped from his bunk only to find his cabin door stuck. By the time he braced his feet on the jamb and forced it open water was already knee high. Clad only in shorts, he had no time to dress nor to look for help—then the ship's lights winked once and went out. In the confusion he had no idea what had happened to his friend and roommate, Hedley Lake.

With only seconds to determine which direction led to safety, Mac decided to walk back against the surge of water rushing down the corridor. To go with the tide was easier, but it would only take him to a bulkhead, a dead end. The water pouring in had to be coming from the outside. Stumbling up stairways in total darkness he fought against the flow forcing his way up.

When he reached the main staircase, already approaching a horizontal tilt, sea water was two feet from the ceiling wires and pipes and he gripped these to keep from being swept back. In the black confusion the only glimmer of light he could see was the phosphorescent glow of ocean waves somewhere ahead.

Cold sea water poured like a miniature Niagara Falls down over the staircase; it was here the strength and agility acquired during basic naval training literally pulled Mac through. Mustering the last ounce of remaining strength he shimmied hand over hand along the overhead pipes using the handrail as purchase for his feet. His upper body, head and neck held above the crush of water pressure, he pulled himself over and under the torrent and up on the deck.

This final struggle up from the ship's mangled bowels he fought alone, for during those life and death moments Mac saw no one else attempting to get out. In the blackout with tons of water rushing down through exits and stairways, the ship's officers were unable to guide disoriented passengers to safety; in fact thirty-five of the *Caribou's* 46 officers went down with their ship.

Having gained the deck, Mac hesitated for a moment to get his bearings—to boldly rush forward could have been disastrous. He hadn't rescued himself from the bowels of a burning, sinking ship to fall headlong through a shattered deck or into a cargo hold where the *Caribou's* steam pipes, like broken lances, spewed scalding steam.

By now other indistinguishable human forms groped around jagged planks, steel, rigging cables and ropes littering the deck in jackstraw profusion. He reached ship's iron railing and made his way along the edge, but was unable to see the black sea ten to twenty feet below.

The young seaman didn't jump. To leap from that distance Mac might have struck debris, another person or the side of the ship, breaking his leg or back and reducing the chances of survival. He climbed to the outside of the rail and waited.

Within a few seconds the water came level with the tilted deck and he pushed off swimming as well as he could from the threatening vortex of the doomed vessel. In the darkness he felt a piece of drifting debris, a section of a hatch cover, and kept himself afloat, still clad only in shorts, in a choppy October sea. At five degrees Fahrenheit, it was barely above freezing.

As he kicked away, two images etched themselves into long term memory: flames licking up at the ship's flag as the *Caribou'*s rudder and spinning propeller lifted out of water; but more tragic, two lifeboats, partly filled with people, still strapped to jammed davits when the ship took her final plunge. Glancing at his wrist, Mac noted his watch had stopped, but knew that from the deathtrap of Room 17, C deck to the cold Atlantic had taken three or four minutes at the most.

A lifeboat, occupied by a few men, was nearby and pushing his support ahead of him, Mac reached the side and swung in over. To his dismay he found water almost level with her gunwales; the lifeboat was going under perhaps to the same fate as the *Caribou*. Someone offered the end of a shirt to stuff the plug hole. Mr. Spencer of Port aux Basques, the man who had helped lower the lifeboat from the *Caribou*, had on a pair of rubber boots and both were used to bail. As the lifeboat floated higher, the several men aboard rescued other

Courtesy of Clyde Forsey

In the war years many South coast shipwrights and carpenters were employed in Nova Scotian shipbuilding yards. Clyde Forsey, Max Grandy, Ambrose Matthews, Clarence Hickman, Roy Grandy, George Moulton, of Grand Bank; Lloyd Lake and Reg Ayers of Fortune helped build the freighter *Walter G. Sweeney* at Lunenberg.

On November 1, 1961, the *Sweeney* sank off Cape Breton—her Newfoundland crew including Samuel Power of English Harbour West—was rescued by the naval tug *St. John.*

struggling survivors until 34 exhausted and bewildered souls crowded aboard.

Dawn came a little after 7 a.m.; rescue planes roared overhead looking for and locating survivors. At 9:30 HMCS *Grandmere,* the *Caribou'*s escort vessel, picked up Mac and other lifeboat occupants. But for 136 out of two hundred and thirty-seven people on board the gulf ferry it was too late; they had disappeared only 40 miles from Port aux Basques and home.

While in hospital in North Sydney, Mac learned Hedley Lake had also survived.

The Long Voyage of the ANGELUS Lifeboat—In the spring of 1943 when the war in the Atlantic was at its peak, the Canadian barquentine *Angelus* left Barbados headed north with a cargo of molasses. Her captain was Edward Jensen of Lunenberg, Nova Scotia, with his crew: Frank Walsh and Walter Boudreau, Moncton; cook John Boyd, Vancouver, B.C.; John Brunette, Montreal; Cecil Hardiman, Grand Bank; and four seamen from Belleoram, mate Arthur Holmans; his 20-year-old son Alexander; John Hillier and Clarence Mullins.

Angelus' destination was Halifax and for three weeks her voyage was uneventful. On Wednesday, May 19, she met her fate in an enemy submarine which sent her to the bottom with only two survivors of her ten crew.

On that day, the lookout Alexander Holmans reported a submarine on the surface about 4 miles away and the captain immediately gave orders to make the lifeboats ready for launching. *Angelus* was at this time about 350 miles southeast of Cape Sable, Nova Scotia.

As lifeboats were being prepared, the U-boat fired a shot that fell on the ship's port side. The German commander ordered all hands into one lifeboat and to come alongside the submarine. Captain Jensen was ordered to come aboard where he was questioned about his destination, nationality and type of cargo he carried. All the while Jensen was aboard, the U-boat's men kept several machine guns aimed at the lifeboat.

The commander then gave the crew twenty-five minutes to return to the *Angelus* to get water, food and navigating equipment. This Jensen refused as the lifeboat was well-stocked. Ordering Jensen to get out of the way, the sub fired twenty rounds into *Angelus* before she rolled over and sank.

With sail raised, the lifeboat made for the American coast and good progress was made for four days. But as was so often the case on the stormy Atlantic, a strong wind howled around the lonely craft. By the end of the fourth day and after the men had covered about 200 miles, the wind increased to a full-blown gale. Heavy seas were so rough the lifeboat capsized and the occupants were thrown into the water and had a difficult time uprighting her.

To pile on the agony, as Newfoundlanders often say, they lost all food except a case of corned beef and some tins of condensed milk. The lifeboat overturned a second time, Captain Jensen disappeared, but before they could think about that tragedy, the tiny boat rolled over a third and a fourth time. The last time it was only after a long and exhausting battle with the cold sea that the remaining eight men were able to right the lifeboat.

Cold water, their prolonged struggle to keep afloat, and the lack of food and drinking water took its toll: one of the Newfoundlanders died from exposure and within twenty-four hours six more died and were buried at sea. This left only mate, Arthur Holmans, who had seen his son die in his arms, and Boudreau. These two were very weak and disconsolate.

On May 24 they heard a plane, but were too exhausted to signal; however the plane had seen them. Within a few hours an American warship picked them up and landed the two survivors of the *Angelus* at an American port.

Four months before their death on the high seas, Clarence Mullins and John Hillier, two young residents of Belleoram, had been involved in a dramatic rescue when they helped save twenty-six crewmen from an American war vessel. On January 16, 1943, subchaser *S.C. 709* left Portland, Maine, headed for Argentia, Newfoundland. Four days later in a freezing gale, she iced up and grounded while attempted to harbour at Louisbourg, Nova Scotia.

Many attempts to get a rescue boat and lines over the reef and to the stranded ship failed and *709*'s men were exposed on the upper deck for twenty-four hours in sub-zero temperatures. Icy spray coated their light clothing as they dared not go below for fear of the *S.C. 709* keeling over from the weight of ice on her. Many had no shoes or gloves and wore thin jackets.

The American sailors were freezing to death when help came first from the *Angelus*, anchored in Louisbourg harbour. Mullins and Hillier and two other crewmen from the *Angelus*, Walter Boudreau and Joseph Chaisson, took two dories to Burying Ground Point near Louisbourg and launched them. Contending with the wind and sea, they managed to get the dories through the slob ice and past the reef to the stricken ship. *Angelus'* men made two trips taking eight American sailors each time until a Louisbourg fishing boat completed the rescue.

Although they received no official recognition, in the eyes of the U.S. naval department and the commanding officers of *S.C. 709*, Mullins and Hillier, as well as the other members of the rescue team, were heroes for their efficiently in saving the lives of all the crew.

MARGARET K. SMITH and Other Ships Overdue Presumed Lost—With the loss of the passenger ship *Caribou* off Port aux Basques in 1943, the sinking of unarmed schooners and the enemy submarine attacks on Bell Island the horrors of sea warfare came closer to home. Its dangers were becoming more real to Newfoundland men of the sea.

Schooners continued to take goods to and from mainland and European ports, but not without shipping losses by enemy submarines—the *Robert Max* and *Angelus*; the *Helen Forsey* sunk by enemy shells in August 1942, with the death of two men. Sainthill's business of Sydney had a schooner, the *Mildred Pauline* commanded by Captain Abe Thornhill of Fortune, disappear without explanation in August of 1942.

The *Catalina* was a well-known Portuguese motor trawler of 632 tons, owned in Portugal and had frequented Newfoundland ports for several years. During January of 1942 the *Catalina* came to Grand Bank from St. John's. While at St. John's she had landed her sick captain. The first mate took the ship from St. John's to Grand Bank and Fortune to discharge her salt and to load salt fish. After her cargo assignments were finished the *Catalina* would head for Portugal, but would first stop at St. John's to pick up the captain.

In order to get the *Catalina* safely to St. John's, ships' agents advised the mate to hire a navigator. Harry Thornhill of Grand Bank was available and signed on. Thornhill, a well-experienced captain and navigator, had for many years taken banking schooners like the *Christie and Eleanor* to the Grand Banks.

According to enemy records released later, on January 15 the Portuguese vessel steamed along the Grand Banks when Commander Rof Mutzelburg in the *U-203* upped periscope and sighted the *Catalina*. Although the country of Portugal was considered neutral, this ship was in enemy waters transporting food or goods supposedly to an enemy nation. The enemy sub asked no questions, but fired a salvo of torpedoes and in no time the *Catalina* was on the bottom with no survivors.

In August 1943, another South Coast ship disappeared under mysterious circumstances. *Margaret K. Smith* was built in 1922 at Lunenberg's Smith and Rhuland yards—the same business that had constructed the *Bluenose* the previous year. In 1935 the *Margaret K.* had outlived her usefulness as a Nova Scotian banking schooner and was sold to Kearley Brothers at Belleoram.

During the war years Kearleys operated the *Margaret K. Smith* as a coaster under the command of Horatio Kearley, age 26, of Belleoram. He chose his crew from the hard working South Coast seamen he knew well: the Belleoram men—mate Eric Bond, age 27; Charles Dominaux, 24; Silas Savoury, 65 and his eighteen year old son, Charles on his first trip as a seaman; cook Herbert Sheppard, 35 of Rencontre East and Charles Blagdon, age 47, belonged to Coomb's Cove. Captain Kearley had survived a terrible ordeal by frost in 1935 in the abandonment of the *Elsie*.

On August 14, 1943, the *Margaret K. Smith* finished loading general goods in her holds and gasoline in drums on her deck and left for Belleoram. Twelve days after, oil tanker *Imperial Halifax* bound for Canso, Nova

Courtesy Nova Scotia Public Archives

The Lunenberg built *Margaret K. Smith* in her glory years. In her heyday the *Smith* competed against the famed *Bluenose* in the annual International Fishermen's Races—in August 1943 the *Margaret K. Smith* disappeared off Nova Scotia.

Scotia, ploughed through wreckage and wooden splinters scattered over the sea off Cape Breton.

When the tanker docked, authorities were alerted. Naval Control from Halifax sent vessels to investigate and alerted all shipping in the area to keep a general lookout. Telegrams confirmed the *Margaret K.* had not reached Belleoram. Ships in the vicinity were located and questioned, but they had seen no sign of the missing schooner.

In the meantime, an investigation of the wreckage brought to Canso seemed to indicate it belonged to the *Margaret K. Smith.* Crewmen aboard the tanker identified the wreckage as that of a small schooner. Joseph Kearley, cousin of the missing captain, looked at the remains of a deckhouse cabin and its furnishings and identified it as the *Margaret K. Smith's.*

The wreckage showed signs of an explosion which left the possibility that the cargo of gasoline had somehow blown up. Other seamen believed the *Margaret K. Smith* had been run into by another ship or had foundered in heavy seas. No definite answer was ever found to determine the schooner's fate and no bodies of the seven crewmen were ever found.

Stan Savoury, the son and brother of two of the missing men, was at sea on another schooner when the wreckage was brought into Canso, and knew nothing of the calamity until he reached Gloucester. By that time positive identification of the wreck had been made. Savoury remembers the anxious moments when news first came through of the *Margaret K. Smith*:

> We were in Gloucester then on the *Golden Stream* when I received a message from my wife in Belleoram. The skipper had the message all one day before he gave it to me. Never thought about me, he said. So supper time he said, 'I got a message for you, Stan. It might concern some of your family.' When I opened the envelope, it said, 'Give up hope. Father and brother are gone.'
>
> I didn't know what to do, so I wired a message home, but it got hung up. They called down from Western Union asking why did I want to know so much information about the *Margaret K Smith*. It was war time. I told them I had a father and brother on her and their schooner was missing. And that was good enough. The message went through. I went home the first chance I got.

Wreck of the ANTOINE C. SANTOS—Losses from enemy submarines on the high seas continued throughout the war; yet the rocks along Newfoundland's South Coast also victimized unlucky vessels.

On April 15, 1942, the Essex-built banker *Antoine C. Santos*, in company with the *Pauline C. Winters*, left

Harbour Breton laden with frozen herring bait for her spring fishing voyage. Late that evening in thick fog, the *Antoine C. Santos* ran aground near Miquelon Head on Miquelon Island. The *Winters* kept two miles farther north and sailed on to the banks, not knowing the other ship had met with disaster.

Despite all attempts to put her off, the *Santos* could not be moved from the field of underwater rocks she had struck about 200 feet from shore. Captain Jacob Thornhill had the anchor carried out on two dories, dropped overboard and the cable attached to the windlass up forward.

But each time strain was put on, the cable slipped and the *Santos* never moved an inch from her position. She was well-weighed down with tons of salt and frozen herring. Within a few hours water seeped into her holds gradually filling the *Santos* and this further complicated any attempts at freeing her.

In 1942 France was still occupied by German forces and, since St. Pierre was a French territory, the *Santos'* crew, except Thornhill and engineer Russell Walters, was detained in St. Pierre and lodged in a St. Pierre hotel until their release on April 23. William J. Hillier, Albert Hillier, Abe George Hillier, Ike Douglas, Simeon Miller, George Tom Hillier, Walter Hillier, Charlie Hillier, George Barnes of Brunette Island; Raymond Hynes, Leo Stewart and his brother, Harbour Breton; cook Charlie Thomas Strowbridge, Grand Bank; Tom Thornhill, Anderson's Cove and the other eight crew returned to Fortune on the coastal vessel, *Reo II.*

Within a day of the wreck, Thornhill and Walters had wired the Western Marine Insurance Company at Grand Bank to send the local wreck commissioner, John Matthews, to Miquelon to begin salvage on the abandoned hulk.

Dories, gear, food, sails, trawl tubs and all moveable equipment were stacked on the land near the wreck site. Then the three men removed the masts. A large saw was borrowed from a business at Miquelon and they rowed out on several successive days to take down the masts.

This was accomplished by sawing through the *Santos* on the side toward the land; that side was by now partly submerged in water. Two parallel cuts were made; a mast width apart. This section of the schooner timbers were removed and the mast lowered by slacking the rigging on the opposite side.

When the wreck commissioner had determined that all material deemed salvageable had been taken from the *Santos* the three men returned home. To send a costal schooner for them was not profitable, and besides, she could not travel to Miquelon and return in one day. If an easterly wind came up overnight while a vessel waited in Miquelon Bight to return to Grand Bank, there was nowhere to anchor and the danger of stranding was imminent.

The three men opted to row home in one of the *Santos'* dories. They left Miquelon Bight at 8 a.m. and rowed the thirty miles to Grand Bank in twelve hours, pulling in Grand Bank harbour a little after eight that night. There was not a draft of wind to help them, for if so, two small sails could have been raised.

While off Fortune during the long row, one of the men wished the wind would come up south east which in effect would have forced them to go into Fortune harbour. Then a taxi could have been hired, making the trip a little easier. But the wreck commissioner would have none of that idea; costs had to be cut and the row to Grand Bank continued.

J.B. Patten's business later removed the *Santos'* engine. This engine, installed in 1940 on the St. John's Dry Dock, was considered to be in good shape and a diver using tackles pulled it from the wreck. It was later placed in Patten's coasting schooner *A and R Martin*.

Some time after, an offshore wind and a heavy current pushed the derelict *Antoine C. Santos* off the ledge. She slipped into deeper water and sank.

Salvage from the MAGNAHELD—The loss of the freighter *Magnaheld* is best told by a female resident of the Cape Shore:

> In April of 1943, a thick fog hovered over all Placentia Bay. It was 11 p.m. when I heard the first distress signals of a ship which at first I thought was the fog horn at Point Verde.
>
> Next morning my father called us and told us a large ship was part way up on the Virgin Rocks, just off Big Barrisway (Placentia Bay). That same day insurance men came by car to Big Barrisway and went out to the ship.
>
> When they came back to land, they declared the boat a total wreck and it couldn't be salvaged, so everyone around could go aboard it. The name of this ship was the *Magnaheld*, a transport ship headed for Argentia with a full load of supplies for the Naval Base.
>
> Its cargo consisted of different kinds of machinery. There were linens of different assortments such as: sheets, pillow cases, mattress covers, navy suits, coats, jackets, pants and leather gloves. Men from various parts of Newfoundland had 2 or 3 of these suits.
>
> There were dishes which are still being used and heavy woollen blankets. I recall washing the salt water out of 500 blankets in one evening. Other

articles found were: Coleman lanterns, medicine cabinets, ball bearings, brake linings and different parts of cars. Different kinds of waxes, paint removers, varnishes, soaps, mops and brooms were also found. There was quite a lot of food aboard such as sacks of coffee, beans, carcasses of steers, cases of fruits and cigarettes.

This was a Klondike for the people of the Cape Shore area. That summer fishermen made more money selling stuff they took off the *Magnaheld* as the price of fish was very low.

I remember a year after this wreck, we were cleaning up and mother told one my brothers to roll away a drum that was behind out house. He opened the drum and found it was full of some kind of powder which he showed to mother. She found it was custard powders.

Years after several different methods were used to remove the *Magnaheld* from the Virgin Rocks. Scows were hooked up to her but failed. They tried blasting her. Later the Air Force at Argentia used her as target practice.

Yet, by a small storm in the month of November, the stranded freighter slipped off and went to the bottom.

BEATRICE BECK and DIXIE Missing—*Beatrice Beck* arrived in Burgeo in the early fall of 1943 en route to St. John's with a cargo of molasses and alcoholic beverages. Her crew consisted of Captain Arch Matthews, Elias Anderson of Burgeo; Leonard Anderson, Otter's Point, near Burgeo and three men from Barbados.

After a few days in Burgeo, she left for St. John's, discharged her cargo, loaded drums of dry cod for the West Indies and departed around mid-October. From

Courtesy Walter Simms

Beatrice Beck anchored off Cuttails, Burgeo. This schooner was built in Smith and Rhuland yards, Lunenberg, Nova Scotia, in 1923. *Beatrice Beck* passed through a succession of owners ending with Henry Clement of Burgeo who later sold her to a business in Bridgetown, Barbados.

Her loss was attributed to the fact that the schooner was not designed for the foreign trade and her aged timbers may not have withstood mid-ocean storms. Other seamen speculated the *Beatrice Beck* was rammed or torpedoed by an enemy sub.

that point on, *Beatrice Beck* disappeared; finally, on January 21, 1944, she was declared lost with crew.*

Captain Arch Matthews, born in Burgeo in 1903, went to sea at an early age. For several years he sailed with Captain Max Vatcher on the tern *Enid E. Legge* learning seamanship and navigation. With his deep sea ticket he took command of Clement's schooner *Bastian*, but lost her at White Point near Canso, Cape Breton. Then he captained the *Beatrice Beck* until he disappeared three years later with his Burgeo shipmates—Elias Anderson, who had fought in France in the Great War, and Leonard Anderson, no relation to Elias.

Less than a year later another South Coast schooner disappeared under mysterious circumstances—the 27-ton *Dixie*, built in Lockeport, United States, in 1894.

* Appendix E lists all Burgeo vessels lost with crew.

Courtesy of Walter Simms

The *Bastian*, a 110-net ton tern built in Denmark in 1920, came to Burgeo when Henry Clement bought her 1925, who put her under command of George Yarn of English Harbour West and later Captain Samuel Cluett, Belleoram. Typical of the European schooners, *Bastian* has a round stern and her lifeboat hangs over the side on davits. She was lost on January 23, 1941. Captain Arch Matthews, George Skinner, William Crant (sp?) Elias Anderson, Charles Porter and Ronald Hiscock escaped the wreck without injury.

Previously owned by Clement's firm at Channel, Joseph Bullen of Harbour Breton brought her to Bay de L'Eau Island in 1912 and had her rebuilt.

Like most schooner owners, Bullen used his vessel to carry supplies after the fishing season closed; in October 1944 he went to obtain lumber at Bay D'Espoir, a community renowned for its reserves of timber.

On the fifth of November he left Bay D'Espoir en route to English Harbour West. With lumber below, stacked on deck and with a dory in tow containing several sheep, the *Dixie* was last sighted by Pass Island residents going through the Pass Island Tickle. This was the last that was known of the schooner and her crew—Joseph Bullen, aged 68; his son Joseph, 25, both married, and Willie G. Jensen, a youth of fourteen. All belonged to Bay de L'Eau Island.

A prolonged northeasterly gale blew up during the voyage which probably pushed the *Dixie* onto the rocks near Seal Cove, Fortune Bay; however, no debris was ever found. Two weeks later, when no news came nor wreckage found, the families were notified by Reverend Herbert Mackay, the resident Church of England clergyman.

Chapter Eleven

Schooners Large and Small Go Down

GARNISH appears in the first official *Census* of New-foundland in 1836 with a population of seventy-six. The date of first settlement in unknown, although it is thought the Grandys moved to the area from St. Pierre in 1763. The town appears on Captain Cook's 1775 map as Little Garnish and is referred to in his report as one of the coast's 'bar harbours.' The population grew steadily till it reached its highest point of 797 in 1935 after which numbers declined. In the past decade, census shows population is again increasing.

As with the majority of Newfoundland communities, the fishery as been the economic mainstay of Garnish since the days of first settlement. The salmon fishery in earlier years was enhanced by the fact that the Garnish River was a natural spawning ground and the lobster and herring fishery thrived at the turn of the century.

Over the years the inshore fishermen prospered and many men found work on the offshore bankers up to the 1950s. Employment on sailing schooners was not without danger and loss of life: on September 18, 1930,

Around 1900 Samuel Harris set of Grand Bank up his general merchandise store at Garnish. From this central location Harris collected fish and supplied the fishermen of the eastern side of Fortune Bay.

the *Carranza* sank taking several of Garnish's young men with her; ten fishermen disappeared when the *Partanna* was wrecked in 1936.

Garnish, like many communities around the South Coast, had its small shipbuilding yards and some schooners built there include: *Carrie and Evelyn* launched in 1911; and the *Jean and Mona* built with a Commission Government bounty in 1935.

HERBERT L. RAWDING   A Giant Goes to the Bottom—Captain Alex Rodway had three times abandoned sinking schooners in the northwest Atlantic—the *Excellence* in 1933; the *Stina*, 1934; and the *Mabel Frye*, 1936. Experienced skippers with foreign trade knowledge, well versed in navigational skills, were in demand in Placentia Bay and now he was given

Above, the *Daphne and Phyllis*, launched in 1946, lies in the Garnish barrisway as workmen put the finishing touches to her. Due to shallow water, she was launched side on at the highest tide. This schooner was destroyed by fire off St. Pierre on December 11, 1959.

charge of the *Herbert L. Rawding*. In 1945, several years after the loss of the *Frye*, Wareham's of Harbour Buffett sent Rodway to South Carolina where the *Rawding*, a four-masted vessel of 1,109 net tons, was for sale.

From Charleston, South Carolina, Rodway took the *Herbert L. Rawding* to Turk's Island for salt and then to Harbour Buffett. When she sailed in ports along Newfoundland's South Coast, the *Rawding* was the largest schooner ever seen by most inhabitants.

For two years she plied her trade to American and Canadian ports, then her owners outfitted her with an engine. The throbbing vibrations of the engine put too much strain on her old timbers and on her final salt laden voyage in June 1947, from Cadiz, Spain, to New-foundland, she sank.

To man a ship of this size Captain Rodway carried eleven crew: mate Thomas Ashford of Harbour Breton; second mate George Upshall and cook Wallace Dicks, Harbour Buffett; engineer George Pomeroy, Bay

Roberts, brothers Freeman and Calvin Gilbert, Lewis Pauls, Haystack; cook's helper Ted Porter, Nova Scotia; deckhands William Follett, John Flynn, Presque; and Isaac Peach, Spencer's Cove, all Placentia Bay men except three. Several days out, a gale opened seams already weakened by the engine's throbbing and the schooner leaked badly. Salt-clogged pumps could not keep against the water rising in the holds.

About six hundred miles off Lisbon, Portugal, things were looking very grim for the *Rawding* and her crew. Rodway thought first he might turn back to Lisbon, but to haul the schooner broadside to the wind when turning would finish her quickly. It would be best to go before the wind into shipping lanes in what was termed the Grand Circle, a shipping track between North America and Europe. The evening before rescue, the crew prepared the lifeboat in case another ship could not be sighted.

Courtesy Jack Keeping and Captain Alex Rodway

The *Herbert L. Rawding*. On the day she sailed into her new home port, Harbour Buffett, quite a crowd gathered on the hill overlooking Buffett to see the large four-masted schooner.

Herbert L. Rawding, the largest schooner owned on the South Coast, was going down when in the early hours of June 10, the American ship *Robert J. Hart* came by. Captain Quigley asked if the *Rawding*'s boats were usable and Rodway replied that they were. It was almost daylight when the Newfoundland crew rowed over to their rescue ship in the *Rawding*'s small boat. From there they watched as the schooner went under.

Rawding's rescue ship, bound from Philadelphia to Naples, continued her journey, but before she did Captain Quigley called Gibraltar to inform port authorities there what had happened. Since Quigley did not want to delay his voyage, he asked if a small boat from Gibraltar would pick up the shipwrecked men. A message came back confirming the time and place of transfer.

Once in Gibraltar, with its heavy volume of ships from all parts of the world, most of the *Rawding*'s crew quickly found transportation to Newfoundland. But a convenient voyage home was not always the case when shipwrecked sailors were rescued by vessels from foreign lands and carried to countries like Spain, Portugal or France.

Being stranded in these countries often meant delays in finding a suitable westbound ship or making the arrangements to get back to Newfoundland. However for Rodway, during his stay in the British protectorate Gibraltar, everything went smoothly. Here the crew was supplied with clothing at the British facilities. Captain Rodway recalls:

> We went on into Gibraltar. Most of the crew left for England since there was a boat coming through the Straits from the Suez bound for England. I stayed in Gibraltar, me and mate Tommy Ashford be-

cause we had to file a letter of protest so that insurance would be advised of the loss.

After that was done a ship from Montreal came in; the mate and I boarded her for Canada. All told it took a month from the time we lost the *Rawding* to the time we arrived back home.

After that incident Rodway returned to Harbour Buffett to run the S.S. *Ilex*, a 233-ton steel steamer purchased from the United States War Commission in 1947. Built in 1919 at Fort George, Ontario, and classed as a sail/steam vessel, she was owned by Alberto Wareham. Wareham used her in the foreign trade, in particular to carry lobster to the United States—the *Ilex*, at the time of her loss, collected fish for Jamaica.

While harboured in Fermeuse during storm conditions on October 27, 1948, a fire originated in her engine

Courtesy of Vibert Shave

The 133-ton *Thomas & Edith* was built in Burin 1935-36 for the foreign-going trade. Master builder John Doody supervised her construction. On August 5, 1948, she sailed for Bonavista laden with coal, struck a ledge in fog in St. Mary's Bay. Her crew, all residents of Burin: Captain Raymond Shave; engineer Thomas Brenton; cook Charles Francis; sailors Alton Brenton, Clarence Francis and Isaac Moulton, left the wreck without incident.

apparently ignited by a back draft. Fire from one of her oil fired boilers blew into the engine room igniting fumes. There was much draft below ship as all ventilators were opened and in a matter of seconds the entire engine room was ablaze.

Engineer Arch Sutherland, a Scotsman, narrowly escaped being trapped below as he worked on the engines at the time. The fire spread so rapidly Captain Rodway and his crew abandoned ship without saving any belongings. By the next day the entire upper structure was ablaze as the steamship *Ilex* completely burned out on the inside. She finally drifted in and grounded near Port Kerwin.

The Loss of JAMES U. THOMAS, RUBY AND NELLIE, ALBERTO WAREHAM—On October 17, 1947, the *James U. Thomas*, owned in Grand Bank by Sam Forsey, was destroyed by fire five miles west of McCallum, Hermitage Bay. Built in Shelburne in 1906, this schooner was first named *Defender*. In 1937 when Forsey bought her at Bay Bulls she had been renamed and registered as *James U. Thomas*.

On April 23, 1948, Captain Sam Pardy of Bay L'-Argent, a veteran sea captain, was badly burned in the face and hands while fighting a fire—he bore the scars until his death in 1987. Fire broke out in the engine room of his schooner, *Ruby and Nellie*, and could not be contained. After the schooner burned and sank Pardy and his crew were picked up by Captain Gordon Evans in the *Rex Perry*.

On November 13, 1956, after returning with a load of general cargo from Sydney, Nova Scotia, the *Alberto Wareham* burned at Port Royal near Harbour Buffett, when an explosion in the engine room set her afire.

In 1949 the last of the large banking schooners built in Newfoundland was launched at Creston. The 134-foot long *Alberto Wareham*, carried twelve dories and a crew of 28 men. On her maiden voyage William Gosling of Burin was captain and Frank Witherall of Fortune, cook. *Alberto Wareham* was later engaged in the coastal trade in command of Captain Lawrence Welsh.

Alberto Wareham drifted and finally sank at Mussel Harbour near Port Royal with the tops of her masts showing at low tide. A diver went down, opened her hatches and some flour was taken up. This flour was salvaged and used. When bags of flour come into contact with water, a layer, about one inch thick, forms around the inside of the bag leaving the inside flour in good condition.

ALICE M. PIKE, GOLDEN STREAM Two More Casualties—One of the first accidents of the 1950s was the fishing schooner *Alice M. Pike*, an eighty-five ton schooner built in 1911 in McGill's shipyard at Shelburne. Owned by St. John's business Harvey and Company, for many years this schooner operated out of Belleoram under Captain Benjamin Keeping. In the

With white caps breaking over her, the *Marshall Frank* lies near the shore at Framboise Cove, Nova Scotia, on February 19, 1949. Surviving the wreck were: engineer Walter Keeping, Russell Thornhill, Leo Pope, Harold Keeping of Grand Bank; cook Frank Witherall, Fortune; John Strowbridge, Joseph Sheppard, George Sheppard, Jim Cox, John Snook, Wreck Cove; Captain Myles, Jim Blagdon, Cecil Blagdon, Charles Sheppard, Richard Price, Tib Blagdon, Jim Burt, mate Charles Myles, Wyn Myles, Boxey; and Herb Baker, Mose Ambrose.

Five lost their lives—Leo and Conrad Blagdon of Boxey, Garfield Greene and Norman Ball of Rencontre West and John Blagdon of Coomb's Cove.

1940s she was sold to the Barbours of Newtown, Bonavista Bay, and then to Walter Collins of Carmanville.

On October 31, 1950, Collins asked Captain Arch Blundon to take the *Pike* and a load of salt fish from Lumsden to St. John's. That night Captain Blundon and mate Stewart Abbott anchored the schooner in Lumsden harbour to prepare for loading the next day, but the wind came up a gale from the north northeast. Although the *Alice M. Pike* had both anchors down, one of the chains broke and she began to drift.

Blundon decided to hoist the jumbo, jib and foresail and head for the smoothest place on the beach ahead, in the same place where the S.S. *Thackeray* went ashore in

The *Irene Corkum* under sail. On October 16, 1951, the *Irene Corkum* was lost on Flint Island, Nova Scotia.

1947. After the schooner grounded, the crew, with the help of fishermen on the shore, rigged up a bosun's chair. All the crew were dragged ashore by the sagging ship-to-shore ropes through the surf and heavy seas. In a matter of hours the *Alice M. Pike,* a workhorse schooner around Newfoundland's coast for nearly forty years, went to pieces in the heavy seas.

On October 15, 1951, the *Golden Stream* was abandoned off the South Coast, about ten miles from Pass Island. Netting ninety tons, she was built in Summerville, Bonavista Bay, in 1935. Her rudder case developed a leak which could not be checked. Her Belleoram crew, all safely rescued: Captain John Brinton, Lorne Barnes, Onslow Savoury, Joe Drake, William Foote and Nauss Piercey.

Chapter Twelve

Wake of the Schooners— Gone Forever

B𝖸 THE 1950s modern steel-hulled ships, faster, equipped with recent technology and powered by efficient engines, replaced the slower schooner. Only a few schooners participated in the dory and hook and line fishery; most businesses had converted bankers for what was known as the coasting trade between mainland Canada and the island.

Harbours, which a decade before could boast of dozens of banking schooners, lay empty. The forest of masts and spars had disappeared.

Courtesy Harold Simms, Mass

Archie F. MacKenzie on the stocks at Shelburne, Nova Scotia. This 80-ton two masted schooner was later bought by Chesley Forsey of Grand Bank. In 1947 he sold her to Michael Croke of St. Brendan's, Bonavista Bay. Today she's still afloat in Quebec but called the *Marie Clarisse*.

As seen here bringing a load of fish into St. John's harbour, the *Archie F. MacKenzie* is under power and had been rebuilt in St. Brendan's.

KEITH V. COLIN Abandoned off Nova Scotia—On
February 9, 1954, the South Coast fleet of Grand Banks schooners had another condemned to Davey Jones' Locker: a schooner that had recorded some fast times in the days of schooner races off Nova Scotia and America.

The *Leah Beryl*, a 159-ton Lunenberg built schooner, bought by Hollett and Sons of Burin and renamed the *Keith V. Colin*, carried a load of fish to Halifax when a 70 mile per hour wind storm sent her to the bottom on February 9, 1954.

According to Captain Edward Fitzpatrick of Marystown, it was one of the worst storms he had seen in twenty years on the sea, saying that, "We manned pumps for five hours to keep the old ship afloat but she began to sink beneath our feet—and fast." Mountainous seas opened her aged seams, and water filled her engine room and forecastle.

Twenty miles out from Halifax, south of the Liscomb buoy, Fitzpatrick radioed for help. By that time seas were so high it would have been impossible for a

The *Keith V. Colin* was crewed on her final voyage by hardy South Coast seamen: Captain Edward Fitzpatrick, mate Norman Hodder both of Marystown; engineer John Lundrigan, Louis Myles, James Hollett, Burin; and Daniel Farrell, Fox Cove.

dory, if the men had been able to get it over the side, to last in the rough seas. The six men were trapped on a sinking schooner.

Responding to the call, the rescue trawler *Cape Smokey*, captain Peter Green, steamed out from Halifax to the rescue. By the time *Cape Smokey* arrived, the *Colin*'s deck was awash. Against great odds, Green manoeuvred the rescue vessel near the sinking schooner and plucked off her weary crew within minutes of her rolling over and plunging to the bottom. Captain Fitzpatrick summed it up by telling reporters, "If the *Smokey* hadn't come along when she did, my five men and I wouldn't be here now."

In the treacherous Cabot Strait, the same storm claimed another vessel. The 47-foot *Liberator* out of Glace Bay, Nova Scotia, went down taking her three Glace Bay fishermen with her.

A Fortune Schooner DOROTHY P. SARTY Sinks— When the *Dorothy P. Sarty* sank late in the evening of June 12, 1954, her crew took to the lifeboat, refused a

Courtesy PANL

Owned by Bonavista Cold Storage of Grand Bank, the *Blue Comet* ran aground on Miquelon to total loss on February 9, 1954. Her crew—Captain Jake Thornhill, mate Gordon Skinner, bosun Leo Pope, cook Richard Rose, engineer George Snook, Allister Stone, George Keeping, Samuel Bungay, all of Grand Bank; Joseph Hackett, Terrenceville; William Strickland, Leo Smith, Freeman Rose, Gordon Rose, Sidney Hillier, of Fortune; and Claude Johnson, Jacques Fontaine—were safe.

pickup and rowed to Nova Scotia's coast. Owned by Lake and Lake of Fortune, the 85-ton coaster sprang a leak twenty-four hours after leaving North Sydney.

When Captain Frank Poole saw there was no way to stop the inflow of water he ordered his men over the side. Her crew, engineer Nauss Piercey, age 37; cook Vince Savoury, 40; William Poole, 60; Philip Keating, 28; and Clyde Poole, 31, all residents of Belleoram, rowed twenty-five miles back to Nova Scotia.

En route they were hailed by the captain of the coal carrier *Arthur Cross* who offered to take them aboard. Cheerfully they waved the vessel on and rowed into shore near the town of Lingan, Nova Scotia, but by that time each man had blisters on his hands the size of half dollars. *Dorothy P. Sarty* sank carrying 150 tons of coal destined for Badger's Quay, Newfoundland.

FINANCE End of a Fish Collector—Businesses like G. & A. Buffett of Grand Bank, which by the 1950s had only two or three banking schooners going to the off-shore grounds, would send their smaller schooners like the thirty-one ton *Finance* to ports along the South Coast to load and bring back salt bulk fish to Grand Bank. At Grand Bank the fish would be 'washed out,' that is, excess salt was washed off and then the fish would be spread on the cobblestone beaches to dry.

The rapidly disappearing schooner fleet meant fewer jobs for seamen were available. Those that wanted work generally went to the waterfront hoping to get on with a vessel needing a man. Often sailors would ask an owner or captain the question: Any chance on getting a chance? George Pardy wondered if one of the few schooners in Grand Bank harbour needed a crewman.

When Tom Price, the captain of the *Finance*, came along and asked if he would go cook on the schooner, Pardy readily agreed. He, Price and the other crew-men—Harvey Grandy and Max Price—made several trips along the South Coast collecting fish in the spring of 1955. But disaster met the *Finance*, already well past a

Mounds of salt bulk fish, brought by large bankers or collected from smaller towns by coasting schooners like the *Finance*, are prepared for overseas market.

schooner's average age having been built in Belleoram in 1905.

Pardy recalls: "We were partly loaded and left Rose Blanche to go to Isle Aux Morts. When we were going in through the harbour we went upon a sunker and lost the *Finance* inside the harbour near the plant. We left her that day, we couldn't do anything with her to get off the rock and had to row ashore."

By the next morning she slid off the ledge and all that could be seen was the top of her masts. Owing to her position near the rocks and the fact that she was filled with water, the *Finance* could not be salvaged and broke up in Isle Aux Morts harbour.

BEATRICE AND GRACE, DANTZIC Two Sink off Nova Scotia—Captain Austin Myles; engineer Joseph Myles and Harold Whittle, all of St. Bernard's; Mike McCarthy, Terrenceville and cook Steve Drake of Bay L'Argent were plucked from the sinking *Beatrice and Grace* off Glace Bay, Nova Scotia. For Captain Myles, a veteran of the sea, it was his second shipwreck; he had

The *Ruby Wiscombe* (left) and the *Gladys Wiscombe* (right), coasting schooners owned by Wiscombe's business, tied to a Marystown wharf in 1955. Within a few years both were victims of fire: the *Ruby* burned off St. Pierre in October 1962 and the *Gladys* caught fire and sank July 15, 1970.

been below deck when an ocean liner rammed and sank the *Beatrice Vivian* in 1936.

The 70-ton *Beatrice and Grace*, originally owned by Frank Bond of Bay L'Argent, was once a fishing schooner, but had been employed in the coastal trade. To this end she loaded coal at North Sydney for Lamaline, left Nova Scotia on September 2, 1955, and sank three and a half hours out of port.

Engineer Myles noticed water trickling in around the propeller shaft and notified the captain. When all efforts to stop the severe leaking failed, Myles radioed for help. The Glace Bay vessel *Annie Margaret* hove into sight and the captain gave orders to abandon ship.

A second mishap was recorded in the fall of 1955: the 107-ton *Dantzic*, registered to George T. Dixon of Fortune, went down. From that port to Halifax Captain Robert Smith and his men had an uneventful voyage until they reached within 20 miles southeast of Scaterie Island near the Cape Breton coast.

The *Dantzic* left Fortune on Monday, November 25, with a cargo of dried fish in boxes, but by noon Tuesday, Smith had contacted North Sydney that his vessel was leaking badly; North Sydney then radioed the *Blue Prince*, a freighter in the same vicinity as the sinking schooner. Water had stopped the engine; the *Dantzic* was drifting out of control and sinking.

As the *Blue Prince* steamed to the area the last communication with the *Dantzic* indicated she would have to be abandoned. Radio contact then ceased.

All ships in the area homed in on her last reported position, off Scaterie. But neither the crew nor the *Dantzic* were to be found. Within the next twenty-four hours seven vessels, including dragger *Scaterie*, *Blue Prince* and British ship *San Wenceslao*, raced through the cold fog and choppy seas to rescue the *Dantzic's* crew:

Seen here sailing out of Grand Bank harbour, the *Dantzic*, built at Summerville, Bonavista Bay in 1945, was previously named the *A.J. Humby*.

Smith, cook Charlie Tom Strowbridge, Arch Thorne, Gilbert Thornhill, Gerald Hillier and Harry Stone. RCAF search and rescue aircraft from Argentia, Newfoundland, and Greenwood, Nova Scotia, joined the search although fog hampered visibility.

After communicating his critical situation and his vessel's position, Captain Smith abandoned ship. By Tuesday afternoon *Dantzic's* death throes were over and she slipped gently into a watery grave; Captain Smith had taken his chances in the Atlantic's choppy waters in *Dantzic's* two dories. The six men now faced high seas and thick fog.

All day Wednesday they could hear search planes and ships through the fog. Flares and beacons made of bedding soaked in kerosene did not attract attention and the two dories drifted aimlessly.

Then at 11 p.m. Wednesday night, after twenty-six hours on the seas, the *Arctic Sealer*, a freighter that had joined the search team, practically ran over the dories. By then the men had reached the end of their endurance. One of the crew later described rowing through a picket fence—exhaustion made him delirious and, although miles from land, he could clearly see a fence ahead. According to Captain Smith, "If the *Arctic Sealer* hadn't come along, we'd have never lived to see daylight. We were mighty near hopeless."

Near a Graveyard of Wrecks the BERMUDA CLIPPER—At Bay St. Lawrence, Nova Scotia, a place where the ribs and broken skeletons of other shipwrecked schooners stuck out of the water, the 246-ton *Bermuda Clipper* left her bones. En route from Prince Edward Island to North Sydney to load coal, the coastal schooner ran into a reef near the tiny community near the tip of Cape Breton Island.

By October 10, 1960, fishermen in the area reported that the *Bermuda Clipper* was fast going to pieces. By that time, she had already been stripped of salvageable equipment and her stern and keel posts had been knocked out by heavy wave action. Captain Tom Snook

Courtesy PANL

The *J.T. Murley*. While bound from Halifax to Marystown with general cargo, the *J.T. Murley* went off course and grounded near the Diamond Shoals at Savoyard, St. Pierre on October 18, 1958. In an attempt to get off the wrecked schooner, one dory overturned and Roy Reid, age 30 of Baine Harbour, William Power, 38 and Captain Charles Butler, 67 of Marystown were lost. Charles Hodder and cook John Butler manoeuvred their dory through the breakers to open sea and were eventually rescued.

The same storm claimed another South Coast vessel: deepsea dragger *Pennyson I* grounded near Ramea. Seven men aboard reached safety, but not without great danger to themselves. As the men attempted to launch the first dory, it smashed; the second dory struck out for shore in waves churned by a 35-mile per hour wind. Both vessel and cargo were a total loss.

of Grand Bank and his crew, having unsuccessfully tried to pull the *Clipper* free, had already left for their Newfoundland homes.

PEARY   Seven Safe from the Sea—Owned in Fortune by George. T. Dixon, the motor vessel *Peary*, a converted tug of 159-net tons and built in Ontario in 1918, sank off Newfoundland's South Coast on August 23, 1961. Dixons had only owned this vessel a short time. When she went down the *Peary* was en route to Halifax from St. Lawrence with salt fish. Captain Edward Fitzpatrick, Leo Lambe and John W. Brake of Marystown; Fred Clark, Edwin Piercey and Lloyd Hillier, Fortune; Chief Engineer James Follett and Garfield Rogers, Grand Bank were plucked off their sinking vessel by the *Fergus* bound for Pictou, Nova Scotia.

A controversial schooner, often plagued by financial woes and frequent marine mishaps, the *Norma and Gladys* lies aground in Baccalieu Tickle. On this occasion she was refloated, but on the night of October 28, 1984, she wasn't so lucky. In Placentia while on route to St. John's her bilge pumps gave out. Fortunately *Wallace R*, out in search of the distressed schooner, came by and picked off the crew—Captain Loyola Fitzpatrick of Point May; mate Clayton Grandy, Grand Bank; John Andrews, St. John's; Bill Chaffey, Musgravetown; Frazer Holloway and Bond Keats of Lethbridge.

For Garfield Rogers, shipwrecks were nothing new—he survived the wreck of the *Laverna* on the Labrador coast in 1936; burning of the *M & L Lodge* in 1948; the loss of the *Harriet and Vivian* on June 27, 1953, and the *MacDonald*. Undaunted by the treacherous ocean and several ships sinking beneath him, Rogers continued his life on the sea and in 1957 he was rescued from the stranded *Merilyn Claire*, making a total of six shipwrecks in his lifetime. His father, William, had been lost at sea when the schooner *Tubal Cain* disappeared in January 1907, en route from Halifax to Grand Bank.

ARAWANA Burns—Captain Arch Broydell, in command of the coasting vessel *Arawana*, and his seven man crew escaped to safety after she caught fire and sank one hundred miles east of Sydney, Nova Scotia, on September 30, 1962. Built in Nova Scotia in 1942, the 171-ton *Arawana* was employed as a mine sweeper out of Plymouth, England, in the latter stages of World War Two. When J. B. Patten purchased the vessel he had the oil storage tank removed and converted her into a freight carrier.

Loaded with coal for Newfoundland, the *Arawana* left Sydney early Sunday, September 30. Fire was discovered burning out of control in the engine room. The flames quickly engulfed the 109-foot craft and Captain Broydell, realizing his situation was hopeless, sent distress calls to all vessels in the area.

First to arrive on the scene was the *M.V. Marie Stone* which efficiently rescued the crew. The SOS was picked up by several ships including the CNR ferry *William Carson* but by the time they arrived on the scene, the seven men were safely aboard the *Marie Stone*.

On Boxing Day 1962, the *Mary Wiscombe* left Fortune to go to Sydney, Nova Scotia, but Captain William

Courtesy the Buffett family

Successfully refloated from a previous stranding near Sydney in 1957, the 180-ton *Merilyn Claire* grounded again on September 17, 1962, this time finally. While delivering flour to ports along Newfoundland's western coast, she ran upon a ledge near Port au Choix and filled with water. Captain Ben Snook, mate Am Murphy, engineer Russ Walters, second engineer Charlie Vincent, cook Sammy Butler, Frank Mullins, all of Grand Bank and Arch Caines, Garnish, rowed into land.
Merilyn Claire had been built in Lunenberg in 1940 and owned by Grand Bank firm Buffett Fisheries.

Farrell decided to turn back because of a fast approaching storm. Later in the night, during a blinding blizzard, as the schooner approached the channel between St. Pierre and Langlade, she struck the rocks at Cape Coupe, the southern most point of land on Langlade.

In the snowstorm three of her five member crew died of exposure; *Mary Wiscombe* became a total loss. All crewmen—Captain Farrell, engineer Thomas Welsh, Albert Hillier, all of Little Bay; cook Charles Scott, Burin; George Brushett, Creston South—climbed the rugged cliffs and attempted to make it across the island to the lighthouse at Pointe Platte. Two of the men were injured and too wet and exhausted to complete the walk and remained behind in a wooded area. Scott continued a little farther, but died of exposure in a shack between

Cape Coupe and Pointe Platte. Farrell and Welsh spent the night there and reached the inhabitants of the lighthouse the next morning.

The following day the two bodies of the seamen who had stayed behind were located; both had perished in the freezing temperatures. Wiscombe's business at Marystown sent another schooner the *J.W. Wiscombe* to the scene of the shipwreck, picked up the three bodies and landed the captain and engineer at Burin.

ISABELLE SPINDLER Afire off Channel Head— *Isabelle Spindler* left English Harbour West on Newfoundland's South Coast at 6 a.m. on her way to Halifax. Her cargo consisted of 600 quintals of fish and 1000 boxes of empty Coke bottles destined for Halifax. Built in Lunenberg in 1919, the 125-foot long *Spindler* was at an advanced age for a schooner in the coasting trade.

Captain Vic Fiander with his crew—Arthur Cox of Wreck Cove; mate Stan Savoury, Belleoram; Tom Baker, St. Jacques; John Rose, Mose Ambrose; cook Arthur Evans and engineer Henry Phillips, both of English Harbour West—intended to discharge there and pick up a load of coal at Sydney for English Harbour, but the *Isabelle Spindler* never completed her voyage.

About forty miles off Channel Head, Port aux Basques, on August 24, 1964, fire broke out on the *Spindler*. Seaman Savoury recalls the events leading up to the fire:

> Phillips had just finished oiling the engine and came up to the galley for lunch. Five minutes after, when Captain Fiander went below and opened the engine room door, she was all afire, all a holy light.

J.W. Wiscombe wrecked at Point May, near the tip of the Burin Peninsula. Dories nearby assess the possibility of salvaging coal. On January 7, 1965, she was en route from North Sydney, Nova Scotia. With her bottom torn out, she was a total loss—her crew, Captain Bernard Whiffen, engineer Patrick Whiffen, cook James Melloy, mate Arch Ford and seaman James Norman—escaped uninjured.

No one knows what exactly happened. This was about 4 p.m. and the *Isabelle Spindler* didn't sink until nine hours later, around one in the morning.

The crew's first concern was to save the schooner, if possible, but the fire had already gained too much headway to be extinguished. Before any plans to abandon ship were made, Fiander went to the cabin to radio for help, but was unable stay there because of the heavy smoke. Someone did take the transistorized two-way radio which had a short range. As Savoury remembers, the captain then told his men to abandon ship:

I was asleep aft. When I got to the deck, I could see the flames and smoke and asked Fiander if we should get our clothes bag. 'Yes,' he said, 'save what you can.' But I never got a chance to get below and lost everything—clothes, new pair of shoes, wallet and glasses. I stood on deck in my shirt sleeves ready to leave ship.

The seas were high, twenty to thirty foot swells but by this time the wind had died out. When we hove the first dory out, it turned bottom up and drifted away from her. Second one we put over, struck the fife rail and partly washed on board. The five of us jumped in holding her along the side of the *Spindler*, we went forward and got Vic (the captain), the last man to leave her. He was forward sitting on the windlass cap.

With the captain and the crew aboard the dory and no one hurt, the crew, afraid the gas tanks would explode, kept the dory several feet away and watched until the *Isabelle Spindler* sank. With limited range, the two-way radio picked up two or three vessels, but could not make voice contact. Savoury recalls:

Hours after we abandoned the *Isabelle Spindler*, the fuel tank rumbled and exploded. The stern of the schooner and the cabin burned with the radar still spinning until the scanner twisted and fell over. A search plane out of Nova Scotia, came over, put his search light on the burning schooner and us, but was unable to land because of the high seas. She reported the position and asked nearby ships to come to our assistance.

Spindler went down head first; then turned on her side enough we could see the rudder in the light of the fire. Then she went on down.

Later a fisheries boat, the *Louise Ruth*, which had been sent to the area by search and rescue, came and picked us up and took our dory in tow.

Thirty-six hours after fire was discovered the weary crew was landed in Grand Bruit. The coastal boat *Bar Haven* took them to Burgeo; from there to Ramea and then Pass Island. *Donald Roberts*, a small schooner, came to Pass Island, picked up the shipwrecked crew and carried them to Coomb's Cove, near their homes.

DELROY   Tragedy in Placentia Bay—Throughout the hours of July 31, 1972, Ray Burkshire's schooner *Bertha Joyce*, continued the search for eight victims of the ill-fated *Delroy*. A search of the area of sea between Merasheen Island and Arnold's Cove by the *Bertha Joyce*, six other vessels, two helicopters and two planes had only succeeded in finding one body of the nine presumed drowned when the 82-ton *Delroy* caught fire on July 27, four days before. The *Delroy*, built in Burnside, Bonavista Bay, in 1949, was owned by Gordon Petite's business at English Harbour West.

Fifteen people—men, women and children—were returning from Merasheen Island when a fire in the

Courtesy of Vera Piercy

Tied up in front of Piercy's premises in Grand Bank harbour are the *Joan Garland*, lost May 4, 1955, off Nova Scotia; and the *Harold Guy*, lost at St. Pierre June 29, 1957.

engine room prevented the crew from shutting down the two diesel engines. The dory capsized when they attempted to abandon the burning ship, still under power and moving ahead.

Six survivors were found clinging to the overturned dory by Burkshire on the *Bertha Joyce*. The rescued included the captain, Reuben Evans of English Harbour West; his brother Clarence; Mrs. Carmen Pitcher; Marjorie Ennis; Loyola Pomeroy and Judy Snow. Unaccounted for were: *Delroy*'s three crew members, William Garrett, English Harbour West; John Yarn and Leo Bullen, Mose Ambrose; passengers Mrs. Nellie Pomeroy; Ernest Pitcher; and William, Sheila and Linda, three children of Mrs. Leo Pomeroy whose body had been recovered. Two crewmen were said to have left the overturned dory to attempt to swim to White Island, some distance away.

CAPE ROYAL Missing Since August 1977—On August 9, 1977, the deep sea trawler *Cape Royal* owned by National Sea and chartered by Burgeo Fish Industries Ltd. of Burgeo, left her home port for Marystown with eight men under the command of Captain William Vardy.

Two and a half days later the 132-foot long trawler had not reported from her 160-mile journey. It left Burgeo at 6 p.m. on Tuesday and was due to arrive at the Marystown shipyard by 10:30 a.m. Wednesday. A routine call for the captain from Burgeo alerted the owners the *Cape Royal* was overdue. Captain Vardy, age 51, with his crew—James Simms, 34; Fred Green, 27; Harold Simms, 23; John Coombs, 29; Victor Kelly, 45; Wilfred Rose, 43; and Peter Harris age 20—was taking the 13 year old vessel to the shipyard for annual refit. All were residents of Burgeo.

By 1956, most schooners had disappeared from South Coast ports. Here land is being prepared for the building of the fresh fish plant in Grand Bank harbour. The stern of an obsolete schooner is visible at bottom right. Modern draggers and fresh frozen fish put companies relying on the curing of salt cod out of business. (Author's collection)

Strong winds developed Tuesday night from the southeast, shifted to the south and then southwest, a typical South Coast weather pattern which would not

Lady Lynn wrecked on the Grand Bank breakwater. Owned by Gordon Petite, English Harbour West and skippered by Albert Scott of Mose Ambrose with crewman Earl Mullins of English Harbour West, the 54-foot long passenger boat went ashore October 20, 1969. Such was her position on the rocks, crew and passengers stepped ashore without getting wet.

Throughout the years over 70 wooden vessels ranging in size from 30 tons to 180 tons were launched from small one-owner shipyards in Grand Bank harbour. One of the first to be launched was George Buffett's *Kitty Clyde* in 1872. In 1955, the 31-ton *Fortune Bay* slipped down the ways. On the right onlookers stand on the deck of the *Pauline C. Winters*, one of the last schooners in Grand Bank.

Fortune Bay was later destroyed by fire in Hatcher's Cove, Brunette Island, on August 16, 1961, while under the charge of Skipper Reg Buffett.

Dragger *Newfoundland Falcon* burns near St. Anthony on August 9, 1990. Too costly to repair, she was sunk in Placentia Bay on August 9, 1991. This dragger, when built in Halifax in 1967 for Northeastern Fisheries of Harbour Grace, was valued at $1,400,000.

have put any undue stress on the dragger or crew. During the time in question no distress call had been received by the coast guard. Having passed her last inspection, the *Cape Royal* was seaworthy and had a Canadian Inspection Certificate valid until July 1978. Families and relatives in Burgeo could not account for the vessel's disappearance.

By August 12 a flotilla of ships, including Canadian Coast Guard vessel *Bartlett*, Fisheries patrol boat *Nonia*, eight Canadian trawlers, a Soviet tug and eleven Soviet trawlers, combed possible disaster areas without finding a trace.

Several days later, on August 17 an empty lifeboat from the missing *Cape Royal* was discovered drifting about 15 miles offshore in Placentia Bay, but no sign of life rafts was seen. Search efforts intensified. Several tracker aircraft from Gander, St. John's and Halifax, plus helicopters concentrated their search off Placentia Bay. An oil slick twelve miles from Lamaline and a hundred miles from the drifting lifeboat seemed to indicate the *Cape Royal* had gone down off the Burin Peninsula.

For over two weeks when weather permitted, searchers scoured the ocean near the coastline, then extended the search area outside Cape Race and investigated several pieces of debris, but no definite conclusion could be reached as to the fate of the dragger or her eight man crew—the *Cape Royal* had vanished.

Appendix A

The Fleet of Tern Schooners Owned by Moulton's Interests of Burgeo.

Ena A. Moulton

Ena A. Moulton. In December 1927, Captain Max Vatcher and crew were forced to abandon this tern, leaking and dismasted, in midatlantic— the crew picked up by the steamer *Darford*. Built in Isaac's Harbour, Nova Scotia, in 1919, she netted 202 tons with an overall length of 116 feet. Picture courtesy Marine Archives, Memorial University.

A. Moulton, built in 1920 in Nova Scotia, later sold to other Newfoundland firms, was abandoned at sea in 1946.

Alice Moulton, built in Lunenberg, Nova Scotia, in 1918, Captain Charles Dicks and crew rescued by a passing ship in October 1919.

Burleigh's crew was rescued by the Grand Bank schooner *Frank R. Forsey* in December 1921.

Catherine M. Moulton, abandoned at sea, Captain George Douglas of Grand Bank and his crew were rescued by the *S.S. Aztec* in October 1925. Two years previously, in December 1923, the *Catherine Moulton* rescued the crew of the tern schooner *Winnifred*, waterlogged and sinking, 90 miles northwest of St. Pierre.

Built in Burgeo in 1908 by J. Davidge, the 123-ton *Chrissie C. Thomey* was later sold to the Canadian Government and lost up north.

Corona of 179 tons net was built in P.E.I. in 1904. On March 31, 1912, she was abandoned in the Atlantic.

Enid E. Legge, in March 1929 abandoned at sea, Captain James Buckland, William Anderson, John Spencer and Sim Strickland rescued.

Francis E. Moulton with Captain Dan MacDonald in command, was lost in 1925, crew safe.

Gladys Street, an old vessel rebuilt in Sheet Harbour and captained for a while by Burgeo's Tom Gunnery, was abandoned at sea in March 1920.

Gordon E. Moulton was abandoned in March 1924. See chapter 4.

J.N. Rafuse abandoned at sea in February, 1922, but Captain Harvey and two crewmen drowned during rescue operations.

Lila E.D. Young, Captain Stanley Collier and crew were taken off this sinking tern by the *S.S. Frieval* on April 8, 1930.

The 366-ton *Milnorine* built in 1918 had a short career for she had to be abandoned at sea by Captain Joseph Vatcher in December 1919.

Ronald B. Moulton, 138 tons and built in 1918, sank in March 1921 en route from Oporto to Burgeo. Her crew and Captain James Guy were taken off by a passing ship.

Four of Moulton's terns met more violent ends: two were sunk by German submarines in World War I—the *Duchess of Cornwall* sent to the bottom in 1916, Captain Tom Gunnery and his crew of Alfred and Isaac Anderson, Arthur Barter, Peter Hollett, and George Grant were imprisoned in Germany until the war ended.

McClure blown up by the enemy in 1917 with no loss of life. Her crew was Conception Bay men: Captain Augustus Taylor, Allen Barrett, Bert Noseworthy, Charles Stevens, William Bailey and Bert Wills.

Ivanhoe left Burgeo for the Bahamas November 5, 1904, and was never seen again. See Chapter 2

County of Richmond, found capsized off Burgeo on February 14, 1921; her crew of six was lost. See Chapter 4.

In April 1920, the 248-ton *Clarence A. Moulton* caught fire while laden with coal for France and burned to the water's edge.

Reginald R. Moulton, built in Dayspring, Nova Scotia; Moulton later sold her to a business in Notre Dame Bay and she was totally wrecked at Burnt Point, near Seldom on September 21, 1931.

Margaret Moulton drove ashore in Portugal, her wreck sold to the Portuguese and renamed the *Maria Carlota*. Her fate remains obscure.

Riseover II, once named *Limelight* and built in 1908 in Prince Edward Island, is offered for sale. Moulton eventually sold this 139-ton tern in the West Indies.

Appendix B

Schooners from Burin Area Lost with Full or Partial Crew

Vessel	Date Lost	Owner and/or Captain	# Lost
Nautilus	January 1865	John Marshall, owner Capt. Burke	All crew - 4
J.M. Martin	1890	Capt. John Martin	Two
Antelope	June 1893	Capt. John Bugden	Two
Hiawatha	September 1915	Hubert Clark owner and captain	3 lost, 3 rescued
Mina Swim	February 1917	LeFeuvre, owner Capt. Jarvis	All crew - 23
Susan Inkpen	Oct/Nov 1917	Len Inkpen, owner	All crew - 5
*Ada D. Bishop**	January 1918	Charles F. Bishop	All crew - 5
Onata	October 1919	Inkpen, owner Capt. James Brushett	2 lost, 4 rescued
Herbert and Ruby	March 1920	E. M. Hollett, owner Capt. Charlie Hollett	All crew - 5
Roy Bruce	January 1924	Robert Hollett, owner and captain	All crew - 6
Vibert G. Shave	Sept. 1930	Chesley Shave, owner and captain	5 lost, 1 rescued
Wilson T	Nov. 1931	P. McFadden of N.B., owner Capt. Fred Myles	All crew - 5

*Ada D. Bishop** had been sold to William Achbonner (residence unknown). She left Twillingate Jan. 10, 1918, and never heard of again.

Orion, owned in Grand Bank, but operated out of Mortier Bay, disappeared with all hands in November 1907 and had 12 crew from Mortier Bay.

**Joyce M. Smith*, owned and operated in Lunenberg and lost with crew in the August Gales of 1928, had seventeen Newfoundland crew including 14 from Burin area.

Appendix C

South Coast Schooners Sunk by German Submarines during World War One

Schooner	Owned at	Date of sinking
Dutchess of Cornwall	Burgeo	December 1916
Harry W. Adams	?	January 1917
Spinaway	Burin	February 1917
Douglas Haig	Ramea	February 1917
Percy Roy	Grand Bank/St. John's	February 1917
Lucy House	Harbour Breton	March 1917
Thomas	Belleoram	April 1917
Cecil L. Shave	Burin/Trinity Bay	February 1918
McClure	Burgeo	May 1917
Dictator	English Hr. West	June 1918
Francis P. Mesquita	Burin	Summer 1918
*Gladys J. Hollett**	Burin	August 1918

*later refloated

In addition several other South Coast schooners disappeared between 1916 and 1918; probably sent to the bottom by subs although this could not be proven:

Susan Inkpen	Burin	October 1916
Jennie Duff	Grand Bank	November 1916
Mina Swim	Burin	February 1917
Lizzie M. Stanley	Burgeo	December 1917
John McRea	Grand Bank	December 1917
Ada D. Bishop	Burin/Twillingate	January 1918
Elsie Burdette	Burgeo	April 1918
*P.F.**	Fortune	November 1918

* Word first came of her disappearance one week after Armistice.

Appendix D

Loss of the *Partanna*

Many and sad are the stories related,
Of wrecks and lost lives
Round the shores of our land,
Many hearts saddened when vessels, ill-fated,
Never return to our rock-bound strand.

Sad is the story that I will now tell you,
As sad as the saddest
That's ever been known,
Concerning the fate of the banker *"Partanna"*
Which now the great ocean has claimed for its own.

When she set sail, to pursue her great calling,
With brave Captain Anstey
On guard at the helm,
Her dories on deck and her sails all filling,
It seem'd that no storm could the ship overwhelm.

The weeks passed away and a month soon rolled
   onward,
But still no report
Of vessel or crew,
The weather was bad on the Banks—some were
   anxious
Well knowing what high waves and tempest can
   do.

The loved ones and friends of the brave men who
   venture
Out on the rough waters
Toil for their bread,
Are never at ease when the stormy winds gather;
The tempest bequeaths them a feeling of dread.

The time had expired when the vessel, returning,
Would sail into port
With her triumphant crew
Whilst some gave up hope there were some who
      were hopeful
But at last, in despair, they gave up hope too.

Then came the day when the sad news was broad-
      cast
There were many sad hearts
That all faint hope forsook.
The wireless station flashed stories of wreckage
Picked up near Trepassey, St. Vincent and Drook.

Some dories and part of the Banker's sail-canvas
And part of the main-boom
Had drifted ashore.
This is all that remains of the splendid *Partanna*
Whilst Captain and crew sail the wild waves no
      more.

The country is saddened from Westward to
      Eastward
From South Coast to North
All are filled with dismay.
All join in expressing their sympathy—heartfelt
To the grief stricken families in Fortune Bay.

Many and sad are the stories related
Of wrecks and lost lives
Round the shores of our land.
The splendid *Partanna* with crew five and twenty,
Shall never return to our rock-bound strand.

Author Unknown

259

Appendix E

Burgeo Vessels Lost With Crew

Vessel	Owner/Captain	Date Lost	Number of Crew
Grace Hall	Clement and Co.		
	Capt. John Anderson	August 1887	12
Annie May	Capt. Louis Colley	April 1890	7 lost
			2 survived
Ivanhoe	Robert Moulton, owner		
	Capt. Cupp Hare	Nov/Dec. 1904	5?
Dannie Goodwin	Robert Moulton, owner		
	Capt. Lafosse	March/April 1911	5?
Heroine	Capt. John Rose, owner	Nov. 1911	5
Lizzie M. Stanley	B & L Export, owner		
	Capt. John Collier	Dec. 1917	6
Elsie Burdette	Robert Moulton, owner		
	Capt. Albert Hann	April 1918	6
Belle of Burgeo	Robert Moulton, owner*	Sept. 1918	5
County of Richmond	B & L Export, owner		
	Capt. Leonard Hare	Feb. 1921	5
Beatrice Beck	Capt. Arch Matthews	Jan. 1944	5
Cape Royal	National Sea, owner		
	Capt. William Vardy	August 1977	8

*At the time of her loss the *Belle of Burgeo* was registered to James Dunne of North Sydney and carried no Burgeo crew.

Sources, by Chapter:

Chapter 1

MASSACHUSETTS/MARY RUTH
- Personal conversation with Jack Keeping, Fortune.
- Information documented at Seamen's Museum, Grand Bank.

MONASCO
- *History of Burin.* Burin Senior Citizens, 1977.
- *Public Ledger,* August 7 and 14, 1857.

SPENCER NORTHCOTT/ALPHA
- "Wreck of the *Spencer Northcott*". In Robert Carr, ed. *U.C. Record Book.* Grand Bank, 1941.
- Written correspondence with Christie Oakley, Montreal.

NAUGHTLESS
- Sherwood, Roland H. *Atlantic Harbours.* Hantsport, Nova Scotia: Lancelot Press, 1972.

ESTHER TIBBO
- Information supplied by William Welsh, Clarenville.

IDOL
- Personal conversation with Christie Bradley and William Buffett, Grand Bank.
- Notes made on margin of list of Grand Bank schooners available at Seamen's Museum, Grand Bank.

SARAH JANE
- Personal conversation with Robert Evans, Grand Bank.
- Written correspondence with Christie Thomasen, Toronto.
- *Evening Telegram* September 16, 1886.

CLYDE VALLEY
- *Evening Telegram* February 22, 1967.

Chapter 2

ROSIE
- Written correspondence with Eric Hillier, Kitchener, Ontario.
- "Offbeat History". By Michael Harrington. *Evening Telegram,* November 23, 1981.

J.D. ROBERTS
- *Evening Telegram* September 30, 1901.

GRACE HALL/ANNIE MAY
- *Evening Telegram,* April 17, 1890. In Public Archives Shipwreck Files.

– Cunningham, Canon H.W. In *Newfoundland Quarterly*, Spring 1941.

IVANHOE/DANNIE GOODWIN
– Information for Moulton's terns taken from John P. Parker's *Sails of the Maritimes*. Toronto: McGraw Hill, 1960.
– Public Archives Shipwreck Files.
– Simms, Walter. *A Souvenir of Burgeo Today and Yesterday*. 1970.

COLUMBINE
– *Daily News*, November 25 and 30, 1905.
– *Evening Telegram*, November 29, 1905.
– Personal conversation with Annie Buffett and Leo Pope, Grand Bank.

RIGEL
– *Daily News*, November 28, 1905.

BRILLIANT STAR
– *Halifax Evening Mail*, November 29, 1905.

ORPHEUS
– *Island Magazine*. P.E.I. Spring 1978 and Fall 1988.
– *Daily Patriot*, P.E.I. November 6, 1906.
– *Examiner*, P.E.I. November 6 and 7, 1906.

T.A. MAHONE
– "Offbeat History" in *Evening Telegram*, April 28, 1962.
– MacDermott, Hugh. *MacDermott of Fortune Bay*. London: Hodder and Stoughton, 1938.

RUBY/JOHN McREA
– *Evening Telegram*, May 26, 1910.
– Personal conversation with Alice Forsey, Grand Bank.

MARY SMITH
– Personal conversation with Sam Smith, Mount Pearl.
– *Evening Telegram*, January 13, 1913.

ANNIE ROBERTS
– Lehr, G. and A. Best eds. *Come and I Will Sing You*. St. John's: Breakwater Books, 1987.
– Unidentified newspaper clipping dated Sydney, October 23 (year not available).

GRAND FALLS/TOBEATIC/ELINOR
– Shipwreck file, Provincial Archives of Newfoundland and Labrador.

MARION
– "A Fortune Bay Christmas". From *Land and Sea*, CBC Television. December 1986.
– Personal conversation with Stephen John Blagdon, Boxey.

HIAWATHA
- Personal conversation with Gordon LeFeuvre, Burin.
- "Story of *Hiawatha* as Told by One of the Survivors". In *Evening Herald* St. John's, September 14, 1915.

ALBATROSS
- Fitz-gerald, Conrad Trelawney, Junior. *The Albatross*. Bristol, England: Arrowsmith, 1935.

S.S. HUMP
- *Daily News*, August 25, 1916.

P.K. JACOBS/CONTEST/CREUSA G
- *Evening Telegram*, October 2, 1900.
- Edwards, Ena Farrell. *Notes Toward a History of St. Lawrence*. St. John's: Breakwater, 1983.

HASPERIA
- *Daily News*, December 29, 1916 and January 23, 1917.
- "*White Mist* Cruises to Wreck Haunted St. Pierre and Miquelon". In *National Geographic*. Volume 132, No. 3, September 1967. A map of St. Pierre shipwrecks is included in this article.

Chapter 3

THOMAS
- Written correspondence with William Baker, Belleoram.
- "Year End Summary". In *Daily News*, December 31, 1914 - 1918. Many references to enemy attacks were from this source.
- *Decks Awash*. Vol. 13, No. 6, 1984.

WILLIAM MORTON
- Undated article in shipwreck file, PANL.
- *New York Times*, February 19, 1919.

GEORGE EWART
- *Valour Remembered — Canada and the First World War*. Directorate of Public Affairs: Ottawa, Ontario.
- Personal conversation with George Ewart Lake, Fortune.
- *New York Times*, October 9, 1917.
- *Evening Telegram*, October 16, 1917.

LIZZIE M. STANLEY
- Cunningham, Canon H.W. In *Newfoundland Quarterly*, Spring 1941.

HILDA R
- *Daily News*, December 12, 1917.

ERIC
- Clipping from Shipwreck File, NSA. (Newfoundland Historical Association)

HELEN MURLEY
– Reports of submarine atrocities were taken from several issues of the *New York Times* including August 12, 1918.

MARION SILVER
– *Evening Telegram*, February 1918. Note: According to Captain Harry Thomasen, the ship referred to in this article is not the *Lottie Silver*, since Thomasen was on *Lottie Silver* when it sank; however according to other sources it must be the *Marion Silver*.

VANESSA
– *Evening Telegram*, January 31, 1919.

BELLE OF BURGEO
– *Daily News*, September 12, 1919.
– Unidentified newspaper clipping.

MARY D. YOUNG
– Personal conversation with Charles Parsons and George Green, Grand Bank.
– *Daily News*, November 18, 1918.

HAWANEE
– *Evening Telegram*, November 27, 1918.

P.F.
– *Evening Telegram*, November 23, 1918.

Chapter 4

FAUSTINA
– *Evening Telegram*, November 12 and 19, 1919.
– *Western Star*, May 5, 1950.

FALCON
– Personal conversation with Gordon Noseworthy and Jack Keeping, Fortune.
– *Daily News*, "Events of the Year" December 31, 1919.

EILEEN LAKE
- *Fisherman's Advocate*, December 7, 1932.
- *Daily News*, January 14, 1922.
– Personal conversation with Gordon Noseworthy, Fortune.

GERTRUDE
– *Evening Telegram*, December 23, 1919.

LOUIS H.
– *Daily News*, December 23, 1919.
– Personal conversation with Annie Buffett and Eugene West, Grand Bank.

ELIZABETH FEARN
– *Daily News*, February 12 and 14, 1921.

JOHN HARVEY
– Dominaux, Arthur H. *Belleoram*. Unpublished book at Newfoundland Centre, Memorial University.

SPARKLING GLANCE
– Undated newspaper clipping in shipwreck file, NSA.

ELSIE
– *Evening Telegram*, January 22, 1935.
– Thomas, Gordon W. *Fast and Able—Life Stories of Great Gloucester Fishing Vessels*. Gloucester, Mass: Gloucester 350th Anniversary Celebrations, Inc., 1973.

COUNTY OF RICHMOND
– *Evening Telegram*, February 21 and 22, 1921.
– Parker, John P. *Sails of the Maritimes*. Toronto: McGraw Hill, 1960.

NINA LEE/QUEENIE B
– "Disappearance of Our Sailing Fleet of Foreign Going Vessels". In *Fishermen's Advocate*, December 7, 1932.
– *Evening Telegram*, May 4, 1921.

MARTHA E
– Personal conversation with William Chapman, Grand Bank.

MARION BELLE WOLFE/VERA P. THORNHILL
– Personal conversation with William Baker and another anonymous source.
– Fizzard, Garfield. *Story of the Thorndyke*. Unpublished brochure.

Chapter 5

CLINTONIA
– *New York Times*, January 9, 1923.

BOHEMIA
– *Daily News*, March 22, 1923.

GLADYS M. HOLLETT
– *Daily News*, April 2, 1923.

RITA CLUETT
– *Evening Telegram*, April 7, 1923.
– *Daily News*, April 4, 1923.

NORMAN W. STRONG/ALICE ROBERTS
– *Evening Telegram*, October 7, 1923.

VERA B
- "Offbeat History" ed. by Mike Harrington. In June 12 edition of *Evening Telegram* (year unavailable).
- Currey, Rev. John Ellis. "The Good Word: Heroism". In *Evening Telegram*, April 8, 1989.

ARGOS/ANNIE M. PARKER
- *History of Burin*. By Burin Senior Citizens, 1977.
- *Daily News*, June 29, 1925.

MAXWELL HORTON
- Logbook of *DAKARIAN* found in Seamen's Museum, Grand Bank.

BIENVILLE
- *Daily News*, December 14, 1926.
- *Decks Awash*, Volume 13, No. 6, 1984.
- Written correspondence from Madeline Stacey, Point May and Otto Kelland, Torbay.

HUBERT MACK
- Personal conversation with Gordon Noseworthy, Fortune.
- "End of the Year Review" in *Daily News*, December 31, 1925.

ELLA M. RUDOLPH
- *Daily News*, December 8, 1926.
- Personal conversation with Eric Tibbo, Grand Bank.
- "Wreck of the *Ella M Rudolph*". In Greta Hussey *Our Life on Lear's Room Labrador*. St. John's: Robinson Blackmore Printing, 1987.
- *Fisherman's Advocate* December 7, 1926.

COLUMBIA
- Written correspondence from George H. Mayo, Mission, B.C.
- Thomas, Gordon W. *Fast and Able — Life Stories of Great Gloucester Fishing Vessels*. Gloucester, Mass: Gloucester 350th Anniversary Celebrations, Inc., 1973.

SUNNER
- Personal conversation with Capt. Harry Thomasen, Grand Bank.

HIRAM D. McLEAN
- Personal conversation with William Snook, Fortune.
- *Daily News*, February 28, 1929.

CATHERINE B
- Written information from Mrs. Gertrude Pelley and Freeman Francis, Hant's Harbour.

Chapter 6

CHAPEL POINT
- Personal conversation with William Snook, Fortune.
- Thomas, Gordon W. *Fast and Able—Life Stories of Great Gloucester Fishing Vessels*. Gloucester, Mass: Gloucester 350th Anniversary Celebrations, Inc., 1973.

GYPSY QUEEN
- *Daily News*, December 17, 1930.

LUCY CORKUM
- Written correspondence with Roy Banfield, Halifax.

PARTANNA
- Personal conversation with Waterfield Green, a kedgie on the *Partanna* in 1931.
- *Daily News*, April 28, 30 and May 1, 1936.

WILSON T
- Personal conversation with James Cluett, Frenchman's Cove and Fred Hickman, Burin.
- *Fisherman's Advocate*, November 6, 1931.

FLORENCE E
- *Evening Telegram*, September 1 and 5, 1932.
- Information on *Bessie Williams* taken from Shipwreck File, NSA.

ARGINIA
- Personal conversation with Robert L. Hillier, Grand Bank and William Snook, Fortune.
- *Evening Telegram*, December 30, 1933.
- Written correspondence with Harold Simms, Mass.

FRANK BAXTER
- *Daily News*, December 13, 1932.
- Shipwreck File, NSA.

HOWARD YOUNG
- Shipwreck File, NSA.

Chapter 7

EXOTIC
- Parker, John P. *Sails of the Maritimes*. Toronto: McGraw Hill, 1960.
- *Evening Telegram*, December 8, 1933.
- Unidentified clipping from *Decks Awash*, Shipwreck File, NSA.

DEMOCRACY/IRON HEAD
- Newfoundland shipwreck file, PANL.

CHARLIE AND ERIC
- Personal conversation with John Barnes, formerly of Femme.
- Shipwreck file, PANL.

EXCELLENCE
- Woodsworth, Charles. "Last Voyage of the *Excellence*". Recorded information and newspaper clipping, supplied Capt. Alexander Rodway. Date of clipping, unknown.

MILDRED ADAMS
- *Evening Telegram*, March 28 and 31, 1932.

STINA
- Unidentified newspaper clipping supplied by Capt. Rodway.
- Recorded information with Captain Alexander Rodway, Toronto.
- *Daily News*, October 27, 1934.

MONICA HARTERY
- *Evening Telegram* December 26, 1933.
- *Daily News*, December 26, 1933.

Chapter 8

VIBERT G. SHAVE
- *Daily News*, December 23, 1930.
- Personal correspondence with Vibert Shave, Burin.
- Many of the references to schooner collisions were taken from the shipwreck files of PANL, St. John's and John Hackett, Terrenceville.

ETHEL COLLETT
- *Evening Telegram*, June 11, 1934.
- Shipwreck file, PANL.

BEATRICE VIVIAN/BRUCE AND WINONA
- *New York Times*, June 14, 1936.
- Personal conversation with Clyde Hollett, Halifax.

MARJORIE J. BACKMAN
- Written correspondence from Fred Hollett, Burin.
- *Fisherman's Advocate*, September 28, 1932.
- Earle, Canon George. "Dories at Change Islands". In *Newfoundland Quarterly*, Vol. LXXXVIII, No. 3, Summer/Fall 1992.

D.J. THORNHILL
- Personal conversation with Am Thornhill, Grand Bank.
- Crew list supplied by Jack Keeping, Fortune.

MABEL A. FRYE
- *Observer's Weekly*, October 20, 1936.
- Recorded information and unidentified clipping from Capt. Alexander Rodway.

ALICANTE/J.B. BADCOCK
- Written correspondence with John Hackett, Terrenceville.

MARIE SPINDLER
- *Book of Newfoundland*. Ed. by Joseph R. Smallwood.

MILLIE LOUISE
- Personal conversation with Gord Noseworthy and Jack Keeping, Fortune.
- *Sydney Post-Record*, July 4, 1938.

MARY SABINA/S.S. CAPE PINE
- Personal conversation with Gordon Noseworthy, Fortune.
- *Evening Telegram*, June 16 and August 20, 1938.

TYEE
- Robinson, Geoff and Dorothy. *It Came by the Boat Load*. Canada: 1984.
- *Daily News*, October 29, 1938.

ALLEN F. ROSE
- *Daily News*, December 2, 1938.

ANNIE YOUNG
- *Come and I will Sing You*. Ed. by G. Lehr and A. Best. St. John's: Breakwater, 1985.

Chapter 9

MARY CARMEL/MARY F. HYDE
- MacDermott, Hugh. *McDermott of Fortune Bay*. London: Hodder and Stoughton, 1938.
- Personal conversation with Curtis Forsey, St. John's and William Chapman, Grand Bank.
- *History of Burin*. Burin Senior Citizens, 1977.
- Unidentified newspaper clipping.

CHARLES L/PALITANA
- Various sources.

IRIS VERNA
- *Daily News*, February 26, 1940.

FLORENCE
- Personal conversation with William T. Thornhill, Grand Bank.
- *Evening Telegram*, September 30, 1940.

ELLEN AND MARY
- Personal conversation with Capt. Harvey Banfield and Clarence Griffin, Grand Bank.

JEAN H. ELFORD
- Personal conversation with Frank Elford and Clarence Pierce, Fortune.
- Forsey, William. "Loss of the *Jean H. Elford*".

MARIANA
- Personal conversation with Stanley Savoury, Grand Bank.
- Written correspondence with Trevor Bebb, Lockeport, Nova Scotia.
- *The Late Capt. J.M. Fudge: His Life Story as a Fisherman and Businessman.* Located in Newfoundland Centre, Memorial University. Author, date and place of publication unknown.

Chapter 10

ROBERT MAX
- Taped conversation with Ted Pardy and John Douglas, Grand Bank.
- "Vet's Column" by Herb Wells. In *Evening Telegram*. March 21, 1981.
- Written correspondence from Joanne Wilson, Halifax.

CARIBOU
- Personal conversation with Mac Piercey, Fortune.

WALTER L. SWEENEY
- *Daily News*, November 1, 1961.

ANGELUS
- *Evening Telegram*, June 4, 1943.
- *Sydney Post Record*, June 2, 1943.
- Kyte, Jean. "Louisbourg Fishermen Rescue U.S. Seamen, 1943". In *Cape Breton Magazine*. January 1986.

MARGARET K. SMITH
- *Daily News*, August 27, 1943.
- Personal conversation with Stanley Savoury, Grand Bank.

CATALINA
- *Evening Telegram* February 26, 1972.

ARCHIE F. MACKENZIE
- Croke, Michael. *Schooners, Skippers and Sharemen of St. Brendan's*. St. John's, 1991.

ANTOINE C. SANTOS
- Personal conversation with William J. Hillier and Russ Walters, Grand Bank.

MAGNAHELD
- Clipping in Shipwreck Files, Newfoundland Historical Association (NHA).

BEATRICE BECK/DIXIE
- Written correspondence with Walter Simms, Corner Brook and Lucy Stoodley, Harbour Breton.

Chapter 11

DAPHNE AND PHYLLIS
- *Evening Telegram,* December 14, 1958.

HERBERT L. RAWDING
- Taped information with Captain Alex Rodway.
- Boaker, Frances. *Atlantic Four Master: The Story of the Herbert L. Rawding.* Mystic Seaport Museum, Connecticut, 1986.

S.S.ILEX
- *Daily News,* October 28, 1944.
- Personal conversation with Capt. Alex Rodway.

THOMAS & EDITH
- Personal interview with Vibert Shave, Burin.

JAMES U. THOMAS
- Ship's registry, St. John's, NF.
- Written correspondence with Harold Simms, Norwell, Mass.

RUBY AND NELLIE
- Unidentified news clipping. Shipwreck files, NHA.

ALBERTO WAREHAM
- "Chronicles of a Bayman". In *Decks Awash.* Vol. 4, No. 6 December 1975.
- Taped information from Art Rodway and Capt. Alexander Rodway, Toronto.

MARSHALL FRANK
- *Daily News,* February 17, 1949.
- Personal conversation with Leo and Randell Pope, Grand Bank.
- Currey, Rev. John Ellis. "The Good Word: Hard Lines". In *Southern Gazette,* February 15 and 22, 1989.

ALICE M. PIKE
- Written correspondence from Harold Simms, Norwell, Mass.
- *Daily News,* November 2, 1950.

GOLDEN STREAM
- Personal conversation with Stan Savoury, Grand Bank.

Chapter 12

KEITH V. COLIN
- Two newspaper clippings from Con Fitzpatrick, Marystown, date and newspaper unknown.

BLUE COMET
- "The Good Word" as told to Rev. E. Currey by Leo Pope. In *Southern Gazette* June 6, 1989.

DOROTHY P. SARTY
– *Evening Telegram*, June 12, 1954.

FINANCE
– Personal conversation with George Pardy, Grand Bank.

RUBY WISCOMBE/GLADYS WISCOMBE/MARY WISCOMBE
– Shipwreck file, NHA.

BEATRICE AND GRACE
– *Daily News*, September 3, 1955.

DANTZIC
– *Daily News*, November 25, 26 and 27, 1955.
– Personal conversation with Captain Robert Smith, Grand Bank.
– *Halifax Chronicle Herald*, November 27, 1953.

J.T. MURLEY
– *Daily News*, October 20, 1958.

PENNYSON I
– *Evening Telegram*, October 21, 1958.

BERMUDA CLIPPER
– *Evening Telegram*, October 10, 1960.

NORMA AND GLADYS
– Unidentified newspaper clipping. Shipwreck files, NHA.
– Personal conversation with Bill Chaffey, Musgravetown.

PEARY
– Unidentified newspaper clipping supplied by Con Fitzpatrick, son of
    Edward Fitzpatrick, Marystown.
– Personal conversation with Garfield Rogers, Grand Bank.

MERILYN CLAIRE
– *Western Star*, Sept. 18 and 19, 1962.
– Personal conversation with Russ Walters, Grand Bank.

ARAWANA
– *Evening Telegram*, October 1, 1962.

DELROY
– *Evening Telegram* July 31, 1972.
– Unidentified newspaper clipping. Shipwreck files, NHA.

ISABELLE SPINDLER
– Personal conversation with Stan Savoury, Grand Bank.

CAPE ROYAL
– *Evening Telegram*, August 17 and 22, 1977.